SpringerBriefs in Computer Science

SpringerBriefs present concise summaries of cutting-edge research and practical applications across a wide spectrum of fields. Featuring compact volumes of 50 to 125 pages, the series covers a range of content from professional to academic.

Typical topics might include:

- A timely report of state-of-the art analytical techniques
- A bridge between new research results, as published in journal articles, and a contextual literature review
- A snapshot of a hot or emerging topic
- An in-depth case study or clinical example
- A presentation of core concepts that students must understand in order to make independent contributions.

Briefs allow authors to present their ideas and readers to absorb them with minimal time investment. Briefs will be published as part of Springer's eBook collection, with millions of users worldwide. In addition, Briefs will be available for individual print and electronic purchase. Briefs are characterized by fast, global electronic dissemination, standard publishing contracts, easy-to-use manuscript preparation and formatting guidelines, and expedited production schedules. We aim for publication 8–12 weeks after acceptance. Both solicited and unsolicited manuscripts are considered for publication in this series.

**Indexing: This series is indexed in Scopus, Ei-Compendex, and zbMATH **

Jiao Shi • Yu Lei • Maoguo Gong • Nan Zhang

Computational Intelligence for Remote Sensing Image Change Detection

Jiao Shi
School of Electronics and Information
Northwestern Polytechnical University
Xi'an, Shaanxi, China

Yu Lei
School of Electronics and Information
Northwestern Polytechnical University
Xi'an, Shaanxi, China

Maoguo Gong
College of Mathematics Science
Inner Mongolia Normal University
Hohhot, Nei Mongol, China

Nan Zhang
School of Electronics and Information
Northwestern Polytechnical University
Xi'an, Shaanxi, China

ISSN 2191-5768 ISSN 2191-5776 (electronic)
SpringerBriefs in Computer Science
ISBN 978-981-92-1403-7 ISBN 978-981-92-1404-4 (eBook)
https://doi.org/10.1007/978-981-92-1404-4

This Springer imprint is published by the registered company Springer Nature Singapore Pte Ltd.
The registered company address is: 152 Beach Road, #21-01/04 Gateway East, Singapore 189721, Singapore

Preface

Remote sensing technology enables non-contact, large-scale observation of the Earth's surface by measuring the reflected or emitted electromagnetic radiation across different spectral bands. It overcomes the limitations of traditional manual observation in timeliness, subjectivity, and spatial coverage, and has become indispensable for disaster management, sustainable development, ecological conservation, and national security. As a core task in remote sensing interpretation, remote sensing image change detection analyzes multi-temporal images to automatically identify temporal evolution patterns in land cover. It provides critical support for dynamic environmental monitoring, post-disaster assessment, and strategic surveillance.

Traditional change detection methods rely on manual features and statistical modeling to discriminate changes in multi-temporal remote sensing data. However, under diverse land cover, radiometric inconsistencies, and noise interference, they often suffer from error propagation, limited representational capacity, and poor generalization across complex or heterogeneous scenes. To address these issues, computational intelligence has emerged as a powerful alternative to conventional approaches. Deep learning, a major branch of this field, automatically learns hierarchical feature representations from raw data using neural networks inspired by biological perception, unlocking powerful, data-driven representational capabilities that capture complex spatio-temporal dynamics in remote sensing imagery. More recently, neural architecture search has been adopted to automate the design of efficient and task-adapted network architectures, thereby further pushing the performance boundaries beyond those achievable with manually designed architectures. These paradigms can offer effective solutions to the fundamental shortcomings of traditional change detection methods.

This book presents a detailed delineation of the state-of-the-art remote sensing image change detection methods based on computational intelligence. The exposition progresses from foundational concepts to advanced methodologies. It begins by defining the change detection task, then establishes a unified theoretical and experimental framework, and further introduces methodological innovations for computational intelligence-based change detection, and finally concludes with an outlook on building more robust and intelligent change detection models. This structured journey offers readers a clear pathway from fundamental principles to frontier research.

As a comprehensive text, the book covers most emerging topics in change detection and computational intelligence, including theories, models, algorithm design, and experimental validation. This book summarizes the research achievements of the authors, their postgraduate students, and former students since 2017. Offering a rich blend of theory and practice, it is suitable for students, researchers, and practitioners interested in change detection and computational intelligence, serving as both a textbook and a reference. We gratefully acknowledge the editors at Springer and the anonymous reviewers for their constructive feedback, which greatly improved the quality of this book. The work was made possible by the support of our colleagues and students. We thank Professors Licheng Jiao, Kay Chen Tan, A. K. Qin, and Gwanggil Jeon for their guidance and mentorship, and doctoral students Tiancheng Wu and Chunhui Tan, as well as postgraduate students Xiaodong Liu, Zeping Zhang, Xi Zhang, and Feng Chen for their contributions to algorithm implementation, experimentation, and manuscript preparation. We also thank the authors of all cited works.

This research was supported by the Shenzhen Science and Technology Program under Grant No. JCYJ20230807145601004, the National Natural Science Foundation of China under Grant No. 62472356, the Natural Science Foundation of Chongqing, China under Grant No. CSTB2023NSCQ-MSX1099, the Natural Science Basic Research Program of Shaanxi under Program No. 2024JC-YBMS-461, and the Fundamental Research Funds for the Central Universities.

Despite our best efforts, shortcomings in content selection and structural organization are inevitable. We warmly welcome comments, criticisms, and suggestions from readers and fellow researchers. Your feedback will be invaluable to our continued improvement.

Xi'an, China — Jiao Shi
Xi'an, China — Yu Lei
Inner Mongolia — Maoguo Gong
Xi'an, China — Nan Zhang

Competing Interests The authors have no competing interests to declare that are relevant to the content of this manuscript.

Contents

Chapter 1
Overview of Remote Sensing Image Change Detection

Abstract Remote sensing enables large-scale, non-contact observation of the Earth's surface and plays a vital role in disaster response, environmental monitoring, and national security. As a core task in remote sensing interpretation, change detection identifies temporal changes from multi-temporal images to support dynamic land cover analysis and strategic decision-making. Classical methods based on manual features and statistical modeling often suffer from error propagation, limited representational capacity, poor generalization across complex or heterogeneous scenes. Computational intelligence, particularly deep learning, has proven to be an effective and efficient solution for overcoming these limitations. This chapter provides a systematic review of remote sensing image change detection, covering both the research background and the evolution of methods.

Keywords Change detection · Remote sensing · Deep learning · Computational intelligence

1.1 Background

Remote sensing is an observational methodology that utilizes sensors aboard satellites, aircraft, and other platforms to acquire the electromagnetic radiation reflected or emitted from the Earth's surface, which is subsequently processed and analyzed to detect and characterize surface features [1]. Remote sensing emerged in the 1960s, evolving from aerial photogrammetry and initially applied primarily to aerial reconnaissance and mapping. In 1972, the United States launched Landsat 1, the first dedicated Earth observation satellite, marking the advent of spaceborne remote sensing and ushering in a new era of systematic global Earth observation. Leveraging the orbital motion of satellites, RS systems can repeatedly acquire up-to-date observations over large regions, thereby facilitating the updating of existing geospatial records and supporting dynamic monitoring of land surface changes. These data not only provides a synoptic representation of the spatial patterns and distributions of natural and anthropogenic features across the Earth's surface, but

J. Shi et al., *Computational Intelligence for Remote Sensing Image Change Detection*, SpringerBriefs in Computer Science,
https://doi.org/10.1007/978-981-92-1404-4_1

also reveals the interrelationships among key geographic elements, including geology, landforms, soils, vegetation, hydrology, and human-made structures, thereby delivering valuable information for diverse applications in both scientific research and operational domains.

With the continuous acquisition of massive volumes of multi-temporal, multi-resolution RSI, generating decision-support information from these data through timely and effective interpretation offers significant value for real-world applications. To meet this need, change detection in remote sensing has emerged as a key methodology for the systematic analysis of multi-temporal imagery. By comparing observations of the same geographic area acquired at different times, change detection enables the identification and characterization of changes in the location, extent, attributes, or condition of surface features, while accounting for sensor-specific imaging characteristics and the spectral–temporal behavior of land cover [2]. Change detection provides a powerful means to investigate and understand the patterns and processes of ecosystems across both spatial and temporal dimensions, and has demonstrated broad application prospects in land use/land cover monitoring, disaster assessment, ecological conservation, and military monitoring (Fig. 1.1). For example, Gärtner et al. tracked changes in natural vegetation cover by monitoring the growth dynamics of tree canopies, enabling the identification of riparian forest degradation [3]. Anniballe et al. [4] employed object-based change detection method for building-level damage assessment and demonstrated its effectiveness following the 2009 L'Aquila earthquake. Furthermore, Normand and Heggy [5] regarded coherence-based change detection as a powerful and effective approach for assessing flash flood—induced erosion and successfully applied it to map watershed-scale surface changes in Libya following Storm Daniel. Notably, Song et al. from the University of Maryland conducted a global land surface change

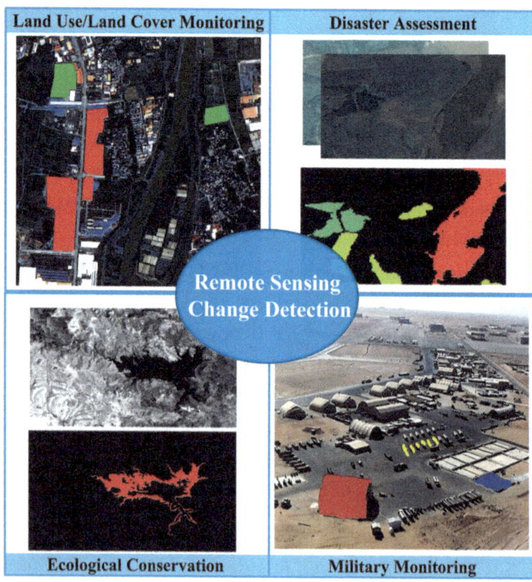

Fig. 1.1 Application examples of remote sensing image change detection technology

analysis from 1982 to 2016 to quantify changes in forests, tree cover, and bare ground, with their findings published in *Nature* [6].

In recent years, the rapid advancement of diverse sensing modalities, including radar, infrared, and electro-optical systems, has driven remote sensing image toward increasingly multi-source, high spatiotemporal resolution and high spectral resolution observations. While this evolution provides an unprecedentedly fine-grained, continuous, and comprehensive observational basis for detecting changes in surface features, it also imposes significant challenges on the design and application of change detection methodologies. In particular, imagery captured by different sensor types exhibits distinct physical characteristics and structural discrepancies. For instance, synthetic aperture radar (SAR) images are inherently affected by speckle noise, while optical images are often degraded by cloud cover and atmospheric interference. These specific characteristics hinder the reliable extraction of consistent and discriminative change signatures from multi-temporal remote sensing data. To address these challenges, deep learning-based computational intelligence techniques have been increasingly leveraged in remote sensing image change detection. By learning robust, adaptive representations directly from the original multi-temporal images and effectively modeling complex relationships across remote sensing observations, these methods are capable of suppressing noise, capturing subtle change patterns, and mitigating radiometric inconsistency. As a result, they have demonstrated remarkable effectiveness in improving the accuracy, robustness, and scalability of change detection systems, and are now widely adopted across a broad range of practical remote sensing applications [7, 8].

1.2 Methodological Evolution of Change Detection Methods

Over the past several decades, the remote sensing image change detection task has undergone a profound transformation. Early methods leveraged manual features and statistical models to achieve stable performance. With the continuous advancement of imaging technologies, remote sensing data has become increasingly complex, featuring large-scale, multi-source, and high-volume, thus making the demand for more adaptive, robust, and intelligent change detection methods increasingly urgent. This shift has driven the adoption of data-driven computational intelligence approaches, particularly deep learning, which not only address the complexities of single-source time series but also enable effective analysis of multi-temporal heterogeneous remote sensing data. In this section, we present a methodological overview of this evolution, beginning with classical change detection methods and progressing to computational intelligence-based paradigms. By tracing key ideas and breakthroughs, this section provides a coherent framework for understanding recent advances and identifying promising directions in modern remote sensing change detection.

1.2.1 Classical Change Detection Methods

Classical change detection methods rely on explicit modeling of spectral or statistical differences between bi-temporal images, which can be broadly categorized into two paradigms: "first-classify-then-compare" and "first-compare-then-classify". The former independently classifies each of the co-registered bi-temporal images and then compares the resulting maps to identify changes [9]. While this paradigm mitigates radiometric inconsistencies between sensors or acquisition times, its performance critically depends on the accuracy of classification results, and error propagation from these results often leads to high false alarm and omission rates in complex remote sensing scenes. Instead, the "first-compare-then-classify" paradigm first derives a difference representation from the bi-temporal images and subsequently analyzes this difference image to produce the final change map, avoiding intermediate classification and its error propagation, thereby yielding more reliable and stable change detection performance. Consequently, this paradigm has received considerable attention in the change detection community.

The most straightforward idea to constructing the difference representation is pixel-wise subtraction of the two original images. However, this method is highly sensitive to multiplicative speckle noise and offers no inherent noise suppression, rendering it rarely used in practice [10]. To address this limitation, reference [11] introduced the log-ratio difference image, which applies a logarithmic transformation to the ratio of the two images. This operation converts multiplicative noise into additive noise, thereby facilitating more effective noise mitigation. Nevertheless, the log-ratio approach does not explicitly account for local image structures or edge information, potentially leading to blurred change boundaries. Subsequently, Inglada et al. [12] proposed the mean-ratio operator, which reduces the impact of isolated noisy pixels by incorporating local averaging. Inspired by neighborhood-based strategies, a growing body of work has focused on fusing multiple difference measures with spatial context. For instance, Zheng et al. [13] developed a composite difference image by combining the arithmetic difference image and the log-ratio image to produce a more robust representation. Additionally, Ma et al. [14] proposed a wavelet-based fusion framework for difference image generation, leveraging multi-scale decomposition to better preserve structural details while suppressing noise.

Following the generation of a difference image, thresholding and clustering are the two most widely adopted methods for analyzing change-related information. The former formulates change detection as a piecewise classification problem, wherein pixels are assigned to either the "changed" or "unchanged" class based on whether their intensity values fall above or below a selected threshold. To enable unsupervised threshold selection, Kittler and Illingworth [15] proposed the well-known Kittler–Illingworth (KL) algorithm, which minimizes classification error under the assumption of Gaussian class distributions. Subsequently, Moser et al. [16] extended the KL framework to accommodate non-Gaussian data. Another prominent unsupervised approach employs the Expectation–Maximization (EM) algorithm, which fits a mixture of Gaussian models to the difference image histogram and derives optimal thresholds through iterative parameter estimation [17]. In contrast, clustering-based methods cast change detection as an image segmentation task, grouping pixels into homogeneous regions according to their similarity in the difference image. These methods are broadly categorized into hard and fuzzy clustering, depending on how pixel memberships are assigned. The K-means algorithm [18] represents a canonical hard clustering technique, in which each pixel is deterministically assigned to a single cluster during iterative optimization. Conversely, the Fuzzy C-Means (FCM) algorithm [19] constructs a membership matrix that allows each pixel to belong to multiple clusters with varying degrees of membership. To enhance robustness against noise, Krinidis and Chatzis [20] incorporated local spatial context into FCM and proposed the Fuzzy Local Information C-Means (FLICM) algorithm, which effectively suppresses isolated noisy pixels. Further improvements were introduced by Gong et al. [21], who developed a refined FLICM variant to better mitigate speckle noise in SAR imagery. Additionally, energy minimization frameworks based on Markov Random Fields have been employed to enforce spatial coherence in the resulting change maps [22]. In recent years, graph-cut optimization [23, 24] and level-set methods [25, 26] have also been applied to remote sensing image change detection. However, these techniques are typically integrated as post- or pre-processing modules within broader pipelines rather than serving as standalone change detection solutions. The aforementioned methods primarily address binary change detection—i.e., distinguishing between changed and unchanged regions. To enable multiclass change characterization, Bovolo and Bruzzone [27] introduced Change Vector Analysis (CVA), which represents multidimensional spectral differences in polar coordinates and establishes a theoretical mapping between phase angles and specific change types. However, conventional CVA operates on only two selected spectral bands at a time, which may lead to loss of discriminative information in multispectral data. To overcome this limitation, the C2VA method [28] was proposed to incorporate all available spectral dimensions into a unified change vector framework, thereby preserving the full spectral signature of change.

More recently, with the diversification of remote sensing platforms and enhanced capabilities for multi-source data acquisition, heterogeneous change detection scenarios have become increasingly common. Due to the inherent differences in imaging mechanisms lead to inconsistent feature representations of the same land cover across modalities, limiting the applicability of homogeneous change detection methods and motivating the development of techniques tailored for heterogeneous scenarios. Early efforts predominantly adopted supervised classification and statistical modeling paradigms to address cross-modal discrepancies. Representative approaches include post-classification comparison [29], direct multi-date classification [30], and object-based change detection [31], as well as kernel canonical correlation analysis [32] and copula-based models [33]. However, most of these methods rely, either explicitly or implicitly, on labeled samples or assumptions about unchanged regions to align heterogeneous observations, limiting their applicability in unsupervised or large-scale scenarios.

1.2.2 Computational Intelligence-Based Change Detection Methods

Classical change detection methods typically rely on manual features and statistical models to identify changes between bi-temporal remote sensing images. However, they are often inadequate for handling a range of challenges in more complex remote sensing data, such as subtle changes, intra-class variability, mixed pixels, and severe noise interference. At the same time, the increasing availability of multi-modal remote sensing data has made heterogeneous change detection increasingly prevalent, where fundamental differences in physical measurement principles and semantic representations prevent direct comparison. These limitations have driven the adoption of data-driven computational intelligence paradigms in remote sensing image change detection.

Effective change detection fundamentally hinges on the discriminative representation of difference information. As a powerful data-driven feature learning framework, deep learning can automatically extract hierarchical and semantic-aware representations from multitemporal images, thereby alleviating the limitations of manual difference features. Early efforts focused on enhancing traditional pipelines with deep generative models. For instance, Zhao et al. [34] pioneered the use of Restricted Boltzmann Machines (RBM) for SAR change detection, demonstrating improved noise suppression and detection accuracy over conventional differencing. Subsequently, Gong et al. [35] proposed a deep belief network (DBN) that bypasses explicit difference image generation by training on pseudo-labels derived from initial coarse change maps, thereby mitigating error propagation from imperfect differencing. To further improve efficiency and robustness, researchers shifted toward region-based or end-to-end paradigms. Gong et al. [36] integrated superpixel-level features with deep representations learned by a DBN, reducing computational cost while preserving spatial coherence. Liu et al. [37] introduced the Bipartite Differential Neural Network, an unsupervised architecture that directly compares bitemporal patches without relying on precise image registration, offering resilience to misalignment. More recently, Fang et al. [38] proposed a general change detection architecture that explicitly models bi-temporal feature interaction through a meta-designed interactive backbone. Dong et al. [39] introduced vision-language model CLIP into change detection tasks, which leverages multimodal representations to capture semantic changes in bitemporal remote sensing images. Zhu et al. [40] proposed a frequency-temporal-aware network that fuses high-frequency and low-frequency features with supervised attention for efficient change detection.

To address the modality gap in heterogeneous change detection, most of the existing methods focus on aligning cross-sensor representations in a shared feature space. Liu et al. [41] proposed the symmetric convolutional coupling network, which leverages Copula theory to couple bitemporal heterogeneous images into a common embedding for direct differencing. However, this method trains only on unchanged samples, leading to weak contrast between changed and unchanged regions and prone to false alarms at boundaries. To mitigate this, Zhao et al.

introduced an approximately symmetric deep network [42] that incorporates reliable labels from both change and no-change classes through a tailored label assignment strategy, improving detection accuracy. An alternative paradigm seeks to translate one modality toward the other, effectively synthesizing pseudo-homogeneous pairs. Niu et al. [43] employed a conditional adversarial network to translate between SAR and optical images, treating the generated output as homogeneous data for subsequent change analysis. Building on this, Luigi et al. [44] proposed the adversarial cyclic encoders network, which uses affinity matrices derived from local neighborhoods as priors and aligns heterogeneous images into a shared latent space via cyclic adversarial autoencoders, followed by simple distance-based differencing. Similarly, Zhan et al. [45] applied a log-transform to SAR imagery to approximate the statistical distribution of optical data, then used stacked autoencoders to jointly learn high-level features for robust sample selection and classification. Some works enhance representation through attention and multi-scale fusion. Lv et al. [46] designed a hierarchical attention feature fusion network that integrates multiscale convolutions with positional attention and multi-perspective filtering to strengthen global semantic representation, achieving strong performance on both homogeneous and heterogeneous scenes. Most recently, Wang et al. [47] combined multi-scale feature extraction with cross-domain structural and semantic alignment, enabling refined change detection without requiring pixel-aligned training pairs.

1.3 Book Structure

The contents of this book cover most emerging topics in remote sensing image change detection, with a particular focus on computational intelligence-based approaches. The organization of the book is as follows:

Chapter 1 provides an overview of remote sensing image change detection, including its research background, practical applications, and methodological evolution from classical statistical approaches to modern computational intelligence—based techniques.

Chapter 2 establishes a unified theoretical foundation for change detection, introducing a formal problem formulation, generalized processing pipeline, standardized evaluation protocols, and benchmark datasets. It also presents key computational intelligence techniques to support subsequent methodologies.

Chapter 3 harnesses the powerful representation learning capability of deep neural networks to overcome the limitations of traditional methods that rely on shallow, handcrafted features. A generative representation learning network with cyclic clustering enables unsupervised multiple change detection, while a superpixel-level deep neural network achieves robust region-level change detection and analysis.

Chapter 4 tackles heterogeneous change detection by learning modality-invariant representations. A self-guided autoencoder iteratively refines pseudo-labels by fusing multiple change maps without explicit transformation or alignment, and a multi-layer composite autoencoder detects changes using minimal labels by fusing predictions from multiple feature hierarchy levels.

Chapter 5 enhances model adaptability via neural architecture search. An evolutionary NAS framework automatically evolves simple, efficient networks for SAR image change detection, while a semi-supervised adaptive ladder network iteratively adjusts the architecture and generates pseudo-labels by fusing semi- and unsupervised outputs,adapting effectively to homogeneous and heterogeneous image pairs.

Besides the above-mentioned change detection issues, Chap. 6 will outline promising and emerging research directions about computational intelligence for remote sensing image change detection.

References

1. Campbell, J.B., Wynne, R.H.: Introduction to Remote Sensing. Guilford Press, New York (2011)
2. Lunetta, R.S., Elvidge, C.D.: Remote Sensing Change Detection: Environmental Monitoring Methods and Applications. Taylor & Francis, London (1999)
3. Gärtner, P., Förster, M., Kurban, A., et al.: Object based change detection of central Asian Tugai vegetation with very high spatial resolution satellite imagery. Int. J. Appl. Earth Obs. Geoinf. **31**, 110–121 (2014)
4. Anniballe, R., Noto, F., Scalia, T., et al.: Earthquake damage mapping: an overall assessment of ground surveys and VHR image change detection after L'Aquila 2009 earthquake. Remote Sens. Environ. **210**, 166–178 (2018)
5. Normand, J.C.L., Heggy, E.: Assessing flash flood erosion following storm Daniel in Libya. Nat. Commun. **15**, 6493 (2024)
6. Song, X.P., Hansen, M.C., Stehman, S.V., et al.: Global land change from 1982 to 2016. Nature **560**(7720), 639–643 (2018)
7. Keller, J.M., Liu, D., Fogel, D.B.: Fundamentals of Computational Intelligence: Neural Networks, Fuzzy Systems, and Evolutionary Computation. Wiley, Hoboken (2016)
8. Cheng, G., Huang, Y., Li, X., et al.: Change detection methods for remote sensing in the last decade: a comprehensive review. Remote Sens. **16**, 2355 (2024)
9. Haboudane, D.: Deforestation detection and monitoring in cedar forests of the Moroccan Middle-Atlas mountains. In: Proceedings of the IEEE International Geoscience and Remote Sensing Symposium (IGARSS), pp. 4327–4330. IEEE (2007)
10. Rignot, E.J.M., Van Zyl, J.J.: Change detection techniques for ERS-1 SAR data. IEEE Trans. Geosci. Remote Sens. **31**(4), 896–906 (1993)
11. Bovolo, F., Bruzzone, L.: A detail-preserving scale-driven approach to change detection in multitemporal SAR images. IEEE Trans. Geosci. Remote Sens. **43**(12), 2963–2972 (2005)
12. Inglada, J., Grégoire, M.: A new statistical similarity measure for change detection in multitemporal SAR images and its extension to multiscale change analysis. IEEE Trans. Geosci. Remote Sens. **45**(5), 1432–1445 (2007)
13. Zheng, Y., Zhang, X., Hou, B., et al.: Using combined difference image and k-means clustering for SAR image change detection. IEEE Geosci. Remote Sens. Lett. **11**(3), 691–695 (2014)
14. Ma, J., Gong, M., Zhou, Z.: Wavelet fusion on ratio images for change detection in SAR images. IEEE Geosci. Remote Sens. Lett. **9**(6), 1122–1126 (2012)
15. Bazi, Y., Bruzzone, L., Melgani, F.: An unsupervised approach based on the generalized Gaussian model to automatic change detection in multitemporal SAR images. IEEE Trans. Geosci. Remote Sens. **43**(4), 874–887 (2005)

16. Moser, G., Serpico, S.B.: Generalized minimum-error thresholding for unsupervised change detection from SAR amplitude imagery. IEEE Trans. Geosci. Remote Sens. **44**(10), 2972–2982 (2006)
17. Dempster, A.P., Laird, N.M., Rubin, D.B.: Maximum likelihood from incomplete data via the EM algorithm. J. R. Stat. Soc. Ser. B (Methodol.) **39**, 1–38 (1977)
18. Yetgin, Z.: Unsupervised change detection of satellite images using local gradual descent. IEEE Trans. Geosci. Remote Sens. **50**(5), 1919–1929 (2012)
19. Ghosh, A., Mishra, N.S., Ghosh, S.: Fuzzy clustering algorithms for unsupervised change detection in remote sensing images. Inf. Sci. **181**(4), 699–715 (2011)
20. Krinidis, S., Chatzis, V.: A robust fuzzy local information C-means clustering algorithm. IEEE Trans. Image Process. **19**(5), 1328–1337 (2010)
21. Gong, M., Zhou, Z., Ma, J.: Change detection in synthetic aperture radar images based on image fusion and fuzzy clustering. IEEE Trans. Image Process. **21**(4), 2141–2151 (2012)
22. Gong, M., Su, L., Jia, M., et al.: Fuzzy clustering with a modified MRF energy function for change detection in synthetic aperture radar images. IEEE Trans. Fuzzy Syst. **22**(1), 98–109 (2014)
23. Gou, S., Yu, T.: Graph based SAR images change detection. In: Proceedings of the IEEE International Geoscience and Remote Sensing Symposium (IGARSS), pp. 2152–2155. IEEE (2012)
24. Gong, M., Jia, M., Su, L., et al.: Detecting changes of the Yellow River Estuary via SAR images based on a local fit-search model and kernel-induced graph cuts. Int. J. Remote Sens. **35**(11–12), 4009–4030 (2014)
25. Li, C., Xu, C., Gui, C., et al.: Level set evolution without re-initialization: a new variational formulation. In: Proceedings of the IEEE Computer Society Conference on Computer Vision and Pattern Recognition (CVPR), vol. 1, pp. 430–436. IEEE (2005)
26. Li, C., Xu, C., Gui, C., et al.: Distance regularized level set evolution and its application to image segmentation. IEEE Trans. Image Process. **19**(12), 3243 (2010)
27. Bovolo, F., Bruzzone, L.: A theoretical framework for unsupervised change detection based on change vector analysis in the polar domain. IEEE Trans. Geosci. Remote Sens. **45**(1), 218–236 (2007)
28. Bovolo, F., Marchesi, S., Bruzzone, L.: A framework for automatic and unsupervised detection of multiple changes in multitemporal images. IEEE Trans. Geosci. Remote Sens. **50**(6), 2196–2212 (2012)
29. Liu, Z., Mercier, G., Dezert, J.: Change detection in heterogeneous remote sensing images based on multidimensional evidential reasoning. IEEE Geosci. Remote Sens. Lett. **11**(1), 168–172 (2014)
30. Volpi, M., Tuia, D., Bovolo, F.: Supervised change detection in VHR images using contextual information and support vector machines. Int. J. Appl. Earth Obs. Geoinf. **20**(2), 77–85 (2013)
31. Qin, Y., Niu, Z., Chen, F.: Object-based land cover change detection for cross-sensor images. Int. J. Remote Sens. **34**(19), 6723–6737 (2013)
32. Volpi, M., Camps-Valls, G., Tuia, D.: Spectral alignment of multi-temporal cross-sensor images with automated kernel canonical correlation analysis. ISPRS J. Photogramm. Remote Sens. **107**(1), 50–63 (2015)
33. Mercier, G., Moser, G., Serpico, S.B.: Conditional copulas for change detection in heterogeneous remote sensing images. IEEE Trans. Geosci. Remote Sens. **46**(5), 1428–1441 (2008)
34. Zhao, J.J., Gong, M.G., Jia, L.: Deep learning to classify difference image for image change detection. In: Proceedings of the IEEE International Joint Conference on Neural Networks (IJCNN), pp. 411–417 (2014)
35. Gong, M.G., Zhao, J.J., Liu, J.: Change detection in synthetic aperture radar images based on deep neural networks. IEEE Trans. Neural Netw. Learn. Syst. **27**(1), 125–138 (2015)
36. Gong, M.G., Zhan, T., Zhang, P.Z.: Superpixel-based difference representation learning for change detection in multispectral remote sensing images. IEEE Trans. Geosci. Remote Sens. **55**(5), 2658–2673 (2017)

37. Liu, J., Gong, M.G., Qin, K.: Bipartite differential neural network for unsupervised image change detection. IEEE Trans. Neural Netw. Learn. Syst. **31**(3), 876–890 (2020)
38. Fang, S., Li, K., Li, Z.: Changer: feature interaction is what you need for change detection. IEEE Trans. Geosci. Remote Sens. **61**, 1–11 (2023)
39. Dong, S., Wang, L., Du, B., Zhang, L., Tao, R., Zhang, X.: ChangeCLIP: remote sensing change detection with multimodal vision-language representation learning. ISPRS J. Photogramm. Remote Sens. **208**, 53–69 (2024)
40. Zhu, T., Zhao, Z., Xia, M., Huang, J., Weng, L., Hu, K., Lin, H., Zhao, W.: FTA-Net: frequency-temporal-aware network for remote sensing change detection. IEEE J. Sel. Top. Appl. Earth Obs. Remote Sens. **18**, 3448–3460 (2025)
41. Liu, J., Gong, M.G., Qin, K.: A deep convolutional coupling network for change detection based on heterogeneous optical and radar images. IEEE Trans. Neural Netw. Learn. Syst. **29**(3), 545–559 (2018)
42. Zhao, W., Wang, Z.R., Gong, M.G.: Discriminative feature learning for unsupervised change detection in heterogeneous images based on a coupled neural network. IEEE Trans. Geosci. Remote Sens. **55**(12), 7066–7080 (2017)
43. Niu, X.D., Gong, M.G., Zhan, T.: A conditional adversarial network for change detection in heterogeneous images. IEEE Geosci. Remote Sens. Lett. **16**(1), 45–49 (2019)
44. Luppi, L.T., Kampfmeyer, M., Bianchi, F.M.: Deep image translation with an affinity-based change prior for unsupervised multimodal change detection. IEEE Trans. Geosci. Remote Sens. **60**(1), 1–22 (2022)
45. Zhan, T., Gong, M.G., Jiang, X.M.: Log-based transformation feature learning for change detection in heterogeneous images. IEEE Geosci. Remote Sens. Lett. **15**(9), 1–5 (2018)
46. Lv, Z., Liu, J., Sun, W.: Hierarchical attention feature fusion-based network for land cover change detection with homogeneous and heterogeneous remote sensing images. IEEE Trans. Geosci. Remote Sens. **61**, 1–15 (2023)
47. Wang, D., Ma, G., Zhang, H.: Refined change detection in heterogeneous low-resolution remote sensing images for disaster emergency response. ISPRS J. Photogramm. Remote Sens. **220**, 139–155 (2025)

Chapter 2
Foundational Theories for Change Detection and Computational Intelligence

Abstract This chapter establishes a unified theoretical foundation for remote sensing change detection, comprising a formal problem formulation, a generalized processing pipeline, standardized evaluation protocols, and benchmark datasets spanning SAR, optical, multispectral, very-high-resolution, and heterogeneous modalities. To support the methodologies developed in later chapters, it further introduces key computational intelligence techniques, including representative deep learning architectures such as deep belief networks, autoencoders, and generative adversarial networks, as well as neural architecture search for automated design of task-specific networks.

Keywords Change detection · Remote sensing · Benchmark datasets · Deep learning · Neural architecture search

2.1 General Framework of Change Detection

Change detection in remote sensing aims to identify meaningful differences on the Earth's surface over time using multi-temporal observations. Despite diverse sensor modalities and application scenarios, most approaches follow a common framework that includes task definition, data preprocessing, change characterization, and performance evaluation, supporting fair method comparison, reproducibility, and practical applicability. This section provides a detailed exposition of this general framework to establish the theoretical foundation for subsequent methodological development and experimental validation.

2.1.1 Problem Statement

As an important application in the field of remote sensing image interpretation, remote sensing image change detection aims to determine the locations of changed

J. Shi et al., *Computational Intelligence for Remote Sensing Image Change Detection*, SpringerBriefs in Computer Science,
https://doi.org/10.1007/978-981-92-1404-4_2

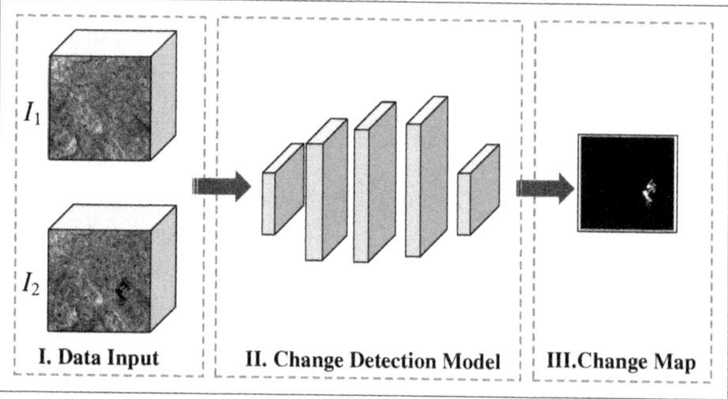

Fig. 2.1 Schematic diagram of change detection

areas by analyzing multi-temporal images. A schematic diagram of change detection is shown in Fig. 2.1, illustrating the process from input images to the resulting change map.

Take a bitemporal change detection problem as an example. Consider two images $\{I_1, I_2\}$ acquired at different times over the same area and having identical dimensions. Let $I_i(x, y)$ denote the pixel value at location (x, y) in the i-th image, where $i = 1, 2$, $1 \leq x \leq h$, $1 \leq y \leq w$, and h and w are the height and width of the image, respectively.

As shown in Eq. (2.1), the objective of change detection is to generate a binary change map I_c by applying a change detection algorithm. Each pixel value $I_c(x, y)$ in this binary map indicates whether the corresponding location in the original images belongs to the changed or unchanged class. Specifically, a value of 0 denotes an unchanged region, while a value of 1 indicates a changed region.

$$I_c(x, y) = \begin{cases} 1, & I_1(x, y) \neq I_2(x, y), \\ 0, & I_1(x, y) = I_2(x, y). \end{cases} \tag{2.1}$$

2.1.2 *Generalized Processing Pipeline*

The general workflow of a change detection task is illustrated in Fig. 2.2. It typically consists of the following stages: image data acquisition, data preprocessing, change information extraction and analysis, change detection result generation, and performance evaluation.

(1) Image Data Acquisition

Satellite remote sensing sensors enable the continuous acquisition of information about the Earth's surface without direct physical contact with ground objects, providing essential data support for monitoring land use and land cover changes across temporal and spatial scales. According to the interaction mode between

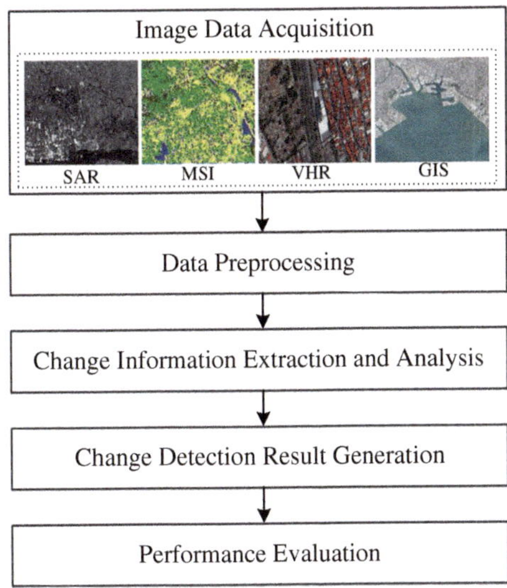

Fig. 2.2 Remote sensing image change detection workflow

sensors and the Earth's surface, satellite remote sensing sensors can be categorized into two types: active and passive. Passive sensors acquire images by receiving solar radiation reflected from ground objects or thermal radiation emitted by the objects themselves. Representative passive optical satellite systems include medium-resolution multispectral platforms such as Landsat and China's Gaofen series (e.g., GF-1, GF-6), which provide regular global coverage with multiple spectral bands at resolutions of several to tens of meters. With the advancement of imaging technology, spatial resolution has been significantly improved, enabling very-high-resolution (VHR) optical satellites to deliver sub-meter to meter-level detail through multispectral imaging, such as SPOT, QuickBird, GeoEye, World-View, EROS, and Gaofen-2. This fine spatial granularity enables clear observation of surface structures and small-scale changes, greatly enhancing the accuracy and practicality of change detection in applications such as urban planning, disaster assessment, and agricultural monitoring. On the other hand, active sensors actively emit electromagnetic waves and receive their echoes. Typical examples include SAR, which enables surface observation under all-weather and day-and-night conditions, significantly enhancing the applicability of remote sensing in complex meteorological environments or nighttime scenarios.

Different types of satellite sensors exhibit significant differences in their operating principles, data characteristics, and observation capabilities. SAR sensors possess all-weather and day-and-night imaging capabilities and are particularly sensitive to surface deformation and vegetation structural changes. However, SAR image is often affected by polarization modes, geometric distortions, and speckle noise. In contrast, optical sensors (including multispectral, hyperspectral, and VHR) rely on solar radiation. They provide intuitive visual representations and rich spectral information with high spatial resolution, but their observation performance is easily constrained by cloud cover, illumination conditions, and atmospheric effects. Hence, before designing change detection algorithms, it is essential to fully account for the characteristics of the data sources, which are determined by the sensor type. Understanding the imaging mechanisms and inherent limitations of the data enables the design of appropriate preprocessing procedures and change detection models, thereby effectively improving the accuracy and robustness.

(2) Data Preprocessing

During the acquisition of remote sensing images, differences in sensors, atmospheric effects, and terrain relief often lead to geometric distortions and spatial misalignment of the same ground objects. Therefore, preprocessing of the raw images is required to improve their usability and ensure consistency. The data preprocessing stage mainly consists of four components: geometric correction [1], filtering [2], radiometric correction [3], and image registration [4].

- **Geometric Correction:** Due to external factors such as sensor altitude, Earth's curvature, and terrain undulation during satellite- or airborne-based remote sensing imaging, geometric distortions are often introduced into the acquired images. Before applying change detection algorithms to identify surface changes, it is generally necessary to perform geometric correction on the input data to eliminate its impact on the detection results. Among the commonly used methods, absolute geometric correction is the most typical approach. Its principle is to register multi-temporal images to a unified geometric reference system by using ground control points, thereby transforming the geometric structure of the distorted images based on reference data and correcting geometric deformation.
- **Filtering:** Filtering is applied to suppress noise present in remote sensing images, thereby improving image quality and enhancing the visibility of difference information. For coherent imaging systems such as SAR, the acquired data are often contaminated by speckle noise, making filtering an essential and indispensable preprocessing step. Commonly used filtering algorithms include median filtering, Lee filtering, and Frost filtering.
- **Radiometric Correction:** Radiometric errors refer to the significant differences in pixel intensity values of the same ground object, caused by factors such as sensor characteristics, atmospheric conditions during acquisition, solar position and illumination angle, terrain-induced illumination effects, and unavoidable noise. These factors lead to radiometric distortions in remote sensing images. The general approach of radiometric correction is to eliminate the discrepancy between the sensor-recorded values and the actual spectral radiance of the targets by performing sensor calibration, radiometric calibration, atmospheric correction, and solar elevation angle correction, thereby reducing radiometric errors introduced by topography.
- **Image Registration:** Image registration refers to the process of matching and aligning two or more remote sensing images of the same scene acquired by different sensors, at different times, or under different conditions (e.g., climate, viewing geometry, or acquisition position). The objective is to ensure that pixels corresponding to the same geographic location are spatially aligned, thereby enabling effective data fusion and subsequent analysis. Common image registration methods can be broadly categorized into three types: transformation-

based registration methods, feature-based registration methods, and grayscale statistical-based registration methods.

(3) Change Information Extraction and Analysis

Change information extraction is the core component of the remote sensing image change detection workflow, aiming to identify and quantify real changes occurring on the Earth's surface from the preprocessed multi-temporal images. This process generally consists of two key steps: change representation and change discrimination with region extraction. In the change representation stage, the original image pair is transformed into an intermediate representation that can effectively highlight changed and unchanged areas, using techniques such as difference image generation, feature fusion, subspace mapping, or deep feature learning. Based on this representation, the change discrimination stage employs methods such as threshold segmentation, clustering, machine learning classifiers, or end-to-end deep neural networks to extract change regions with statistical significance or semantic meaning. To address practical challenges like noise interference, registration errors, and radiometric inconsistencies, designing robust, adaptive, and interpretable change information extraction methods has long been a key research focus in the field of change detection.

(4) Performance Evaluation

In remote sensing image change detection, the performance of algorithms is typically assessed through a combination of subjective visual interpretation and objective quantitative analysis. Visual analysis involves manually examining the change detection result maps, which intuitively reflects the spatial distribution and semantic validity of the detected change regions. Although it is straightforward and easy to implement, this approach is inherently subjective. In contrast, quantitative analysis uses manually annotated change and no-change reference maps as ground truth and evaluates the detection results by computing a series of standardized metrics, thereby providing performance assessment that is repeatable, comparable, and more objective. This section provides a systematic introduction to commonly used quantitative evaluation metrics in remote sensing change detection.

Change detection is essentially a classification problem. Therefore, evaluation metrics used in the field of classification can be employed to assess the performance of different change detection algorithms. Overall Accuracy (OA) and Overall Error (OE) are two commonly used indicators. Among them, OA, also referred to as Percentage of Correct Classification (PCC), is calculated as follows as Eq. (2.2).

$$OA = \frac{TP + TN}{TP + TN + FP + FN} \tag{2.2}$$

where True Positive (TP) represents the number of changed pixels that are correctly detected, False Positive (FP) denotes the number of pixels that are incorrectly detected as changed but are actually unchanged, True Negative (TN) is the number of unchanged pixels that are correctly identified, and False Negative (FN) refers to the number of pixels that have actually changed but are incorrectly classified as unchanged. Correspondingly, OE can be defined as Eq. (2.3).

$$OE = \frac{FP + FN}{TP + TN + FP + FN} \tag{2.3}$$

Relying solely on OA or OE for performance evaluation is often limited, especially when there is a significant class imbalance between changed and unchanged samples. To provide a more comprehensive assessment of change detection results, the Kappa Coefficient κ is widely introduced as another important quantitative evaluation metric. In statistics, κ is employed to evaluate the degree of agreement between predicted and actual classifications. A higher κ value indicates a higher classification accuracy achieved by the model. Specifically, κ can be calculated as Eq. (2.4).

$$\kappa = \frac{OA - PRE}{1 - PRE} \tag{2.4}$$

where PRE denotes the expected agreement by chance, which can be calculated as Eq. (2.5).

$$PRE = \frac{(TP + FP)(TP + FN) + (TN + FN)(TN + FP)}{(TP + TN + FP + FN)^2} \tag{2.5}$$

In addition to detection accuracy, Precision and Recall are also important metrics for evaluating change detection results. Precision indicates the proportion of pixels that are correctly identified as changed among all pixels classified as changed, while Recall represents the proportion of truly changed pixels that are correctly detected as changed. Their definitions are given as Eqs. (2.6) and (2.7).

$$Precision = \frac{TP}{TP + FP} \tag{2.6}$$

$$Recall = \frac{TP}{TP + FN} \tag{2.7}$$

To mitigate the bias that may arise from using a single metric, F_1 score is the harmonic mean of Precision and Recall as defined in Eq. (2.8). A higher F_1 value indicates better model performance, with its value ranging from 0 to 1.

$$F_1 = 2 \times \frac{Precision \times Recall}{Precision + Recall} \tag{2.8}$$

In addition, for binary classification problems, the Receiver Operating Characteristic (ROC) curve is commonly used to evaluate the predictive performance of a model. The ROC curve is a plot with the FP rate on the horizontal axis and the

TP rate on the vertical axis, representing the trade-off between these two metrics. Once the ROC curve is drawn, a further quantitative measure of model performance can be obtained through the Area Under the ROC Curve (AUC), which is computed by integrating the area under the ROC curve. A larger AUC value indicates better model performance and higher practical applicability.

2.1.3 Remote Sensing Image Change Detection Benchmarks

With the rapid development of remote sensing technology, satellite sensors have become increasingly diverse, leading to a wide range of data sources for change detection, including SAR, optical, multispectral, VHR images, and heterogeneous image pairs acquired by sensors with different imaging mechanisms. To address the modeling challenges posed by such multi-source and heterogeneous remote sensing data, this book presents specially designed change detection models and conducts empirical analysis based on a series of publicly available benchmark datasets widely used in the research community. This section provides a brief overview of the key characteristics of these datasets, including sensor types, spatial and temporal resolutions, and other essential attributes, which serve as the foundation for the subsequent experimental design and result analysis.

(1) SAR Benchmarks include three datasets: Bern, Ottawa, and Yellow River. Amone them, Bern dataset consists of two SAR remote sensing images with a spatial size of 301×301. They were acquired over a region around Bern, the capital of Switzerland, in April and May 1999, respectively. During this period, the Aare River's flood inundated large portions of Thun and Bern, and Bern Airport was completely submerged. As shown in Fig. 2.3, the images depict the scene before and after the flood occurred. The corresponding ground truth image is also provided for reference, which is produced with the aid of expert knowledge and prior information.

Ottawa dataset was acquired by the RADARSAT-SAR satellite in May and August 1997, respectively. The spatial resolution of these SAR images is 12 m,

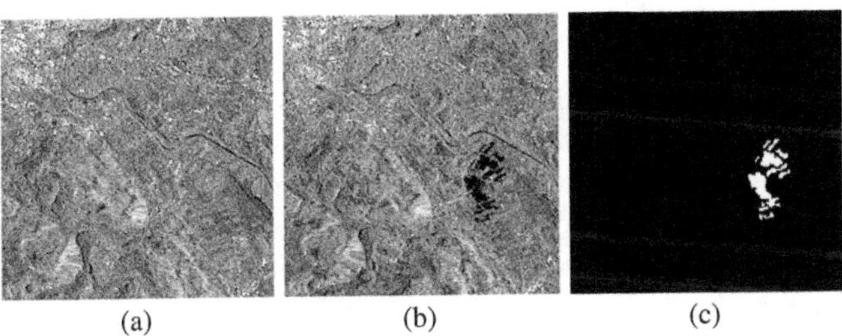

Fig. 2.3 Bern dataset. (**a**) Image acquired in April 1999. (**b**) Image acquired in May 1999. (**c**) Ground truth image

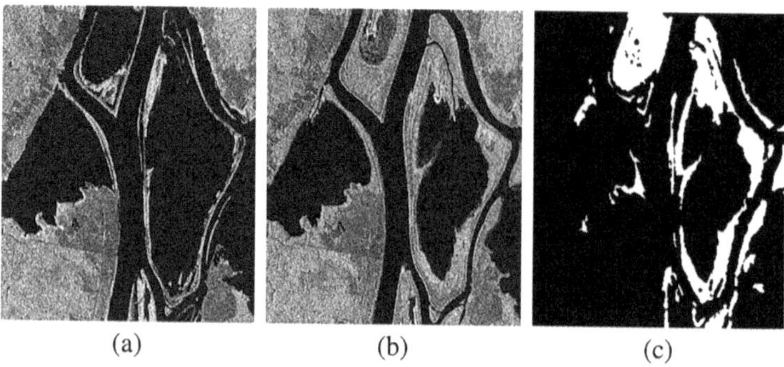
(a) (b) (c)

Fig. 2.4 Ottawa dataset. (**a**) Image acquired in May 1997. (**b**) Image acquired in August 1997. (**c**) Ground truth image

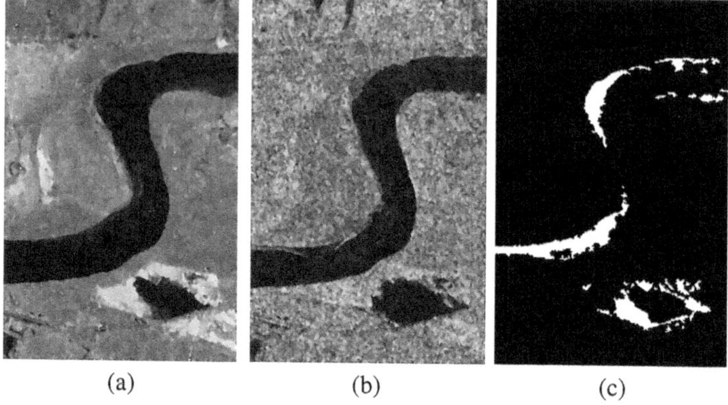
(a) (b) (c)

Fig. 2.5 Yellow River (Inland Water) dataset. (**a**) Inland water in June 2008. (**b**) Inland water in June 2009. (**c**) Ground truth image

and the image size is 290 × 350. This dataset reflects land-surface changes caused by the rainy season in the Ottawa region of Canada. This period coincided with the end of the 1997 rainy season, during which river levels receded and exposed large land areas. As illustrated in Fig. 2.4, significant changes in the river boundaries can be observed between the two acquisition times.

Yellow River dataset consists of two SAR remote sensing images acquired by the RADARSAT-2 satellite over the Yellow River estuary region in China in June 2008 and June 2009, respectively. Because the original Yellow River dataset has a very large spatial size (7666 × 7692), two representative subsets were selected for the experiments and analysis. The selected subsets, referred to as Inland Water and Farmland, each contain two multi-temporal SAR images and a corresponding ground truth image. Figures 2.5 and 2.6 show the selected regions and their respective ground truth images.

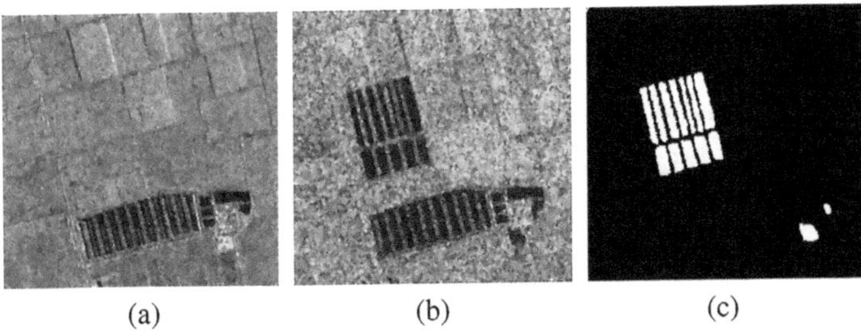

Fig. 2.6 Yellow River (Farmland) dataset. (**a**) Farmland in June 2008. (**b**) Farmland in June 2009. (**c**) Ground truth image

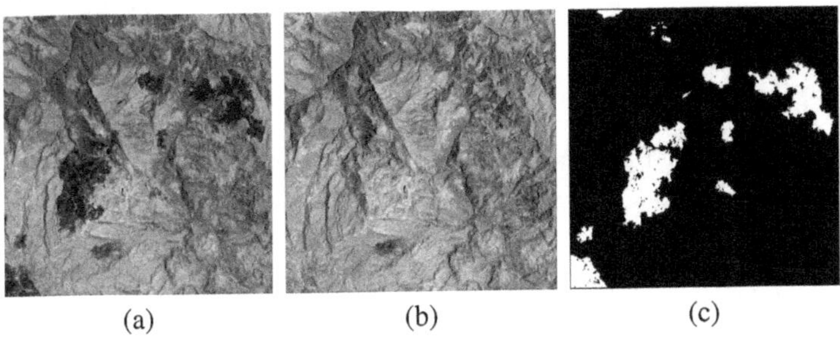

Fig. 2.7 Mexico City dataset. (**a**) Image acquired in April 2000. (**b**) Image acquired in May 2002. (**c**) Ground truth image

(2) Optical Benchmarks comprising the Mexico City and Sardinia datasets, are utilized for the evaluation of change detection model in this book. Among them, Mexico City dataset consists of two 8-bit images acquired by the Landsat-7 satellite with the Thematic Mapper (TM) sensor over the Mexico region. A subregion of 512×512 pixels was extracted from the original scene and used as the test site. As shown in Fig. 2.7a, b, the bi-temporal images were acquired in April 2000 and May 2002, respectively. A comparison of these images reveals that fire events destroyed a large portion of vegetation in the affected area. The corresponding reference change map used for quantitative evaluation is presented in Fig. 2.7c.

Sardinia dataset consists of two 8-bit images acquired by the Landsat-5 satellite with the TM sensor in September 1995 and July 1996. The selected test site has a spatial size of 412×300 pixels and covers Lake Mulargia on Sardinia Island, Italy. As shown in Fig. 2.8a, b, the water level in the lake varied significantly between the two acquisition periods due to seasonal and hydrological changes. The corresponding reference change map is presented in Fig. 2.8c.

(3) Multispectral Benchmarks introduced in this book include three binary and four multi-class change detection datasets, covering diverse land cover changes and acquisition conditions. The first binary dataset is the Yandu dataset, which was acquired by the WorldView-2 satellite over the southern area of Xi'an, China. The two images were captured on September 19, 2012, and February 10, 2015,

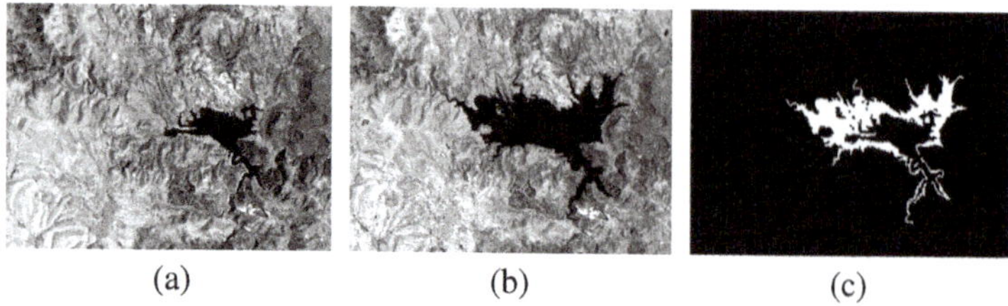
(a) (b) (c)

Fig. 2.8 Sardinia dataset. (**a**) Image acquired in September 1995. (**b**) Image acquired in July 1996. (**c**) Ground truth image

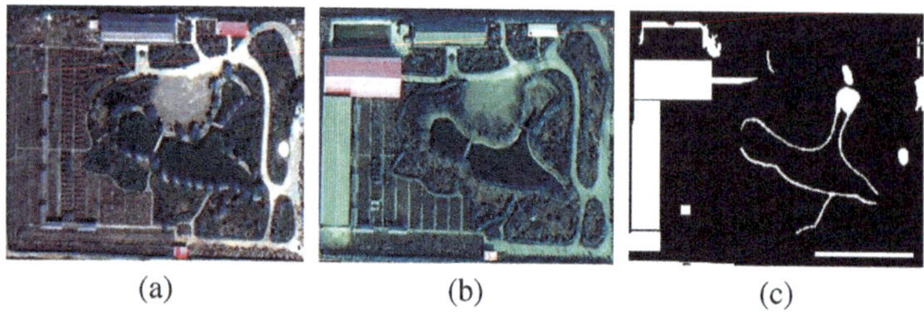
(a) (b) (c)

Fig. 2.9 Yandu dataset. (**a**) Image acquired on September 19, 2012. (**b**) Image acquired on February 10, 2015. (**c**) Ground truth image

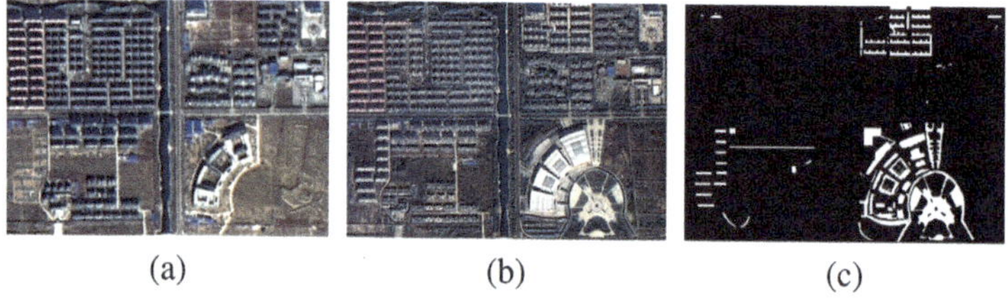
(a) (b) (c)

Fig. 2.10 Minfeng dataset. (**a**) Image acquired on December 9, 2013. (**b**) Image acquired on October 16, 2015. (**c**) Ground truth image

respectively. Both images have a spatial size of 322×266 and a spatial resolution of 0.5 m. As shown in Fig. 2.9, (a) and (b) are the bi-temporal images depicting the same region at different times, while (c) is the reference image annotated based on prior information and expert interpretation.

The second binary dataset is the Minfeng dataset, which consists of multispectral remote sensing images acquired by the GF-1 satellite over the Minfeng area in China. Both images have a spatial size of 651×461 and a spatial resolution of 2 m. They were captured on December 9, 2013, and October 16, 2015, respectively, and record changes related to urban construction and building development. As illustrated in Fig. 2.10, (a) and (b) show the images captured at two different times, and (c) represents the reference map derived from expert interpretation.

The third binary dataset is the Hongqi dataset, which records hydrological changes in the Hongqi area of China. These multispectral images were also acquired

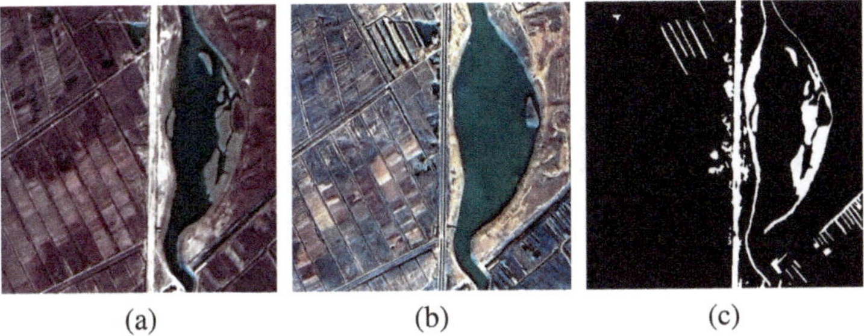

Fig. 2.11 Hongqi dataset. (a) Image acquired on December 9, 2013. (b) Image acquired on October 16, 2015. (c) Ground truth image

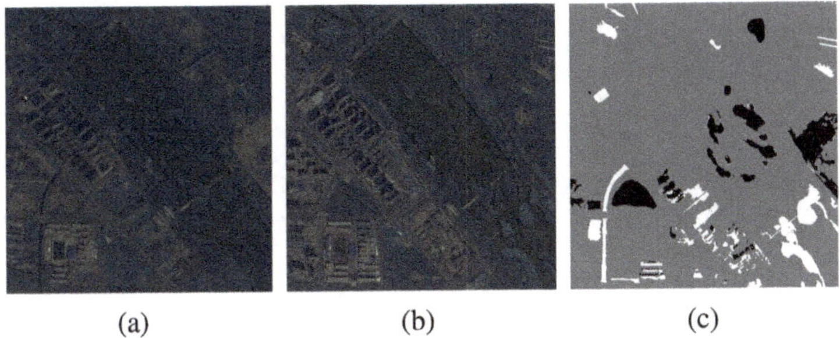

Fig. 2.12 Weihe River dataset. (a) Image acquired on August 19, 2013. (b) Image acquired on August 29, 2015. (c) Ground truth image

by the GF-1 satellite on December 9, 2013, and October 16, 2015, respectively. Each image has a spatial size of 539 × 543 with a spatial resolution of 2 m. As shown in Fig. 2.11, (a) and (b) are the bi-temporal images of the same region, and (c) is the reference image manually annotated with expert knowledge.

The other four datasets are multi-class multispectral remote sensing change detection datasets, namely Weihe River, Bahe River, Xi'an-2 and Xi'an-5. Among them, Weihe River and Bahe River consists of two images acquired by the GF-1 satellite. Each image contains four spectral bands (R, G, B, and near-infrared). The Weihe River dataset consists of images captured over the same region of Xi'an at different times, with a spatial size of 718 × 592. As shown in Fig. 2.12, (a) and (b) are the bi-temporal MSIs, while (c) is the corresponding ground truth map indicating three types of changes.

The Bahe River dataset has a spatial size of 662 × 686. The images were acquired on August 19, 2013, and August 29, 2015, respectively. As illustrated in Fig. 2.13, (a) and (b) represent the same area observed at two different times, and (c) shows the corresponding ground truth, where different gray levels indicate different change types.

The other two multispectral remote sensing datasets are derived from large-format GF-1 satellite images acquired on August 19 and August 29, 2013, respectively, with a spatial resolution of 2 m per pixel. The two subsets, referred to as

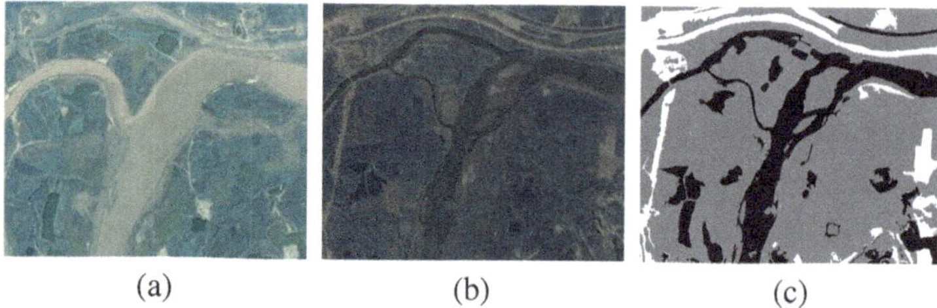

(a) (b) (c)

Fig. 2.13 Bahe River dataset. (**a**) Image acquired on August 19, 2013. (**b**) Image acquired on August 29, 2015. (**c**) Ground truth image

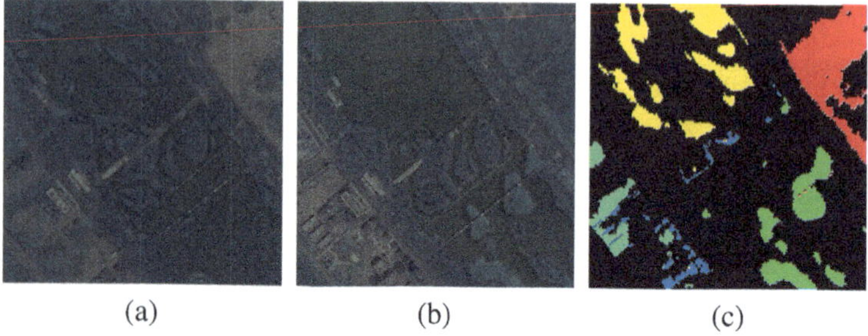

(a) (b) (c)

Fig. 2.14 Xi'an-2 dataset. (**a**) Image acquired on August 19, 2013. (**b**) Image acquired on August 29, 2013. (**c**) Ground truth image

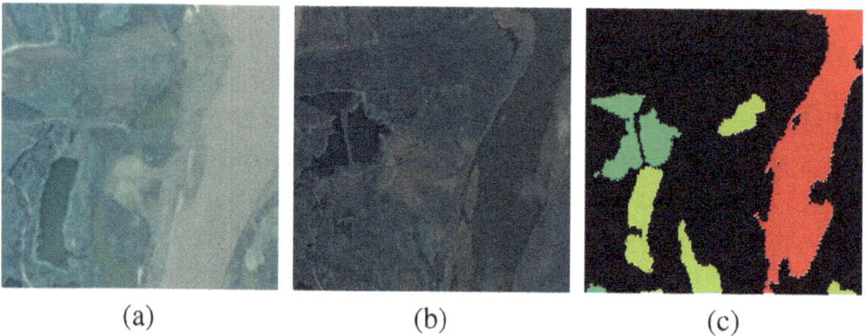

(a) (b) (c)

Fig. 2.15 Xi'an-5 dataset. (**a**) Image acquired on August 19, 2013. (**b**) Image acquired on August 29, 2013. (**c**) Ground truth image

Xi'an-2 and Xi'an-5, were cropped from the original GF-1 scenes and include multiple categories of land-cover changes, such as vegetation variation, urban expansion, and water body alteration. Their spatial sizes are 350 × 350 and 300 × 300, respectively. For visualization purposes, the datasets are displayed in RGB color format, as illustrated in Figs. 2.14 and 2.15.

(4) VHR Benchmarks employed in this book include three datasets: Montpellier, Guangzhou, and Shanghai. Among them, Montpellier dataset is selected from the publicly available Onera Satellite Change Detection (OSCD) dataset [5]. It consists of two images captured by the Sentinel-2 satellite over the city of

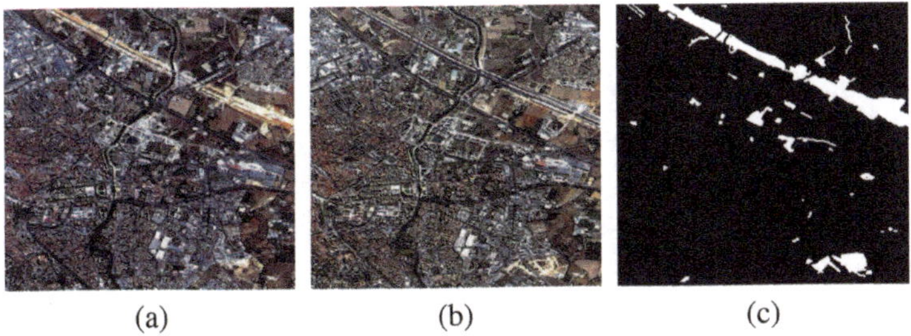

Fig. 2.16 Montpellier dataset. (a) Image acquired on August 12, 2015. (b) Image acquired on October 30, 2017. (c) Ground truth image

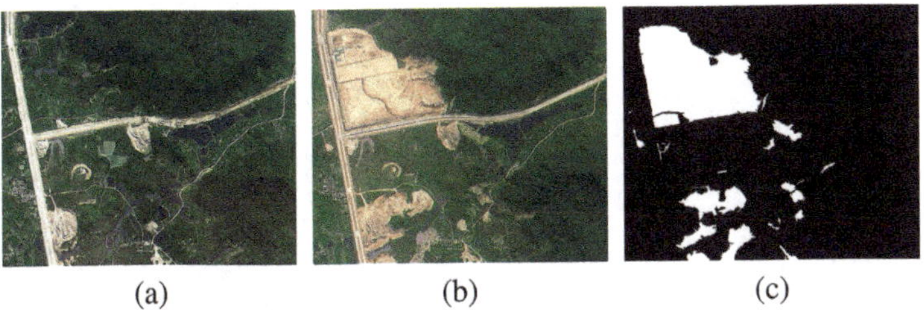

Fig. 2.17 Guangzhou dataset. (a) Image acquired in October 2006. (b) Image acquired in October 2007. (c) Ground truth image

Montpellier, France, on August 12, 2015, and October 30, 2017, respectively. Each image has a spatial resolution of 10 m and a size of 451 × 426 pixels. This dataset mainly records the process of urban expansion and infrastructure development during this period. The corresponding ground truth image was manually annotated by experts, as shown in Fig. 2.16.

The second dataset is the Guangzhou dataset, which contains two images captured by the SPOT-5 satellite over Guangzhou, China, in October 2006 and October 2007. Each image has a spatial resolution of 2.5 m and a size of 877 × 738 pixels. This dataset reflects land-cover transitions related to vegetation and urban construction. The corresponding ground truth image was obtained through field investigation and manual interpretation, as illustrated in Fig. 2.17.

The third dataset is the Shanghai dataset, which consists of two RGB images extracted from Google Earth, representing suburban regions along the Pudong River in Shanghai, China. The images were acquired on November 15, 2015, and December 8, 2017, respectively, with a spatial resolution of 1 m and an image size of 873 × 782 pixels. The reference image highlights the actual change regions based on detailed manual annotation, as shown in Fig. 2.18.

(5) Heterogeneous Benchmarks comprise five multi-sensor datasets that pair optical, multispectral, or near-infrared images with SAR data to capture diverse land-cover changes across different geographic regions and acquisition times. The first is Flood in California dataset, which represents a challenging case of multi-sensor observations over regions affected by severe flooding in Sacramento County, Yuba County, and Sutter County, California. Figure 2.19a was acquired by the

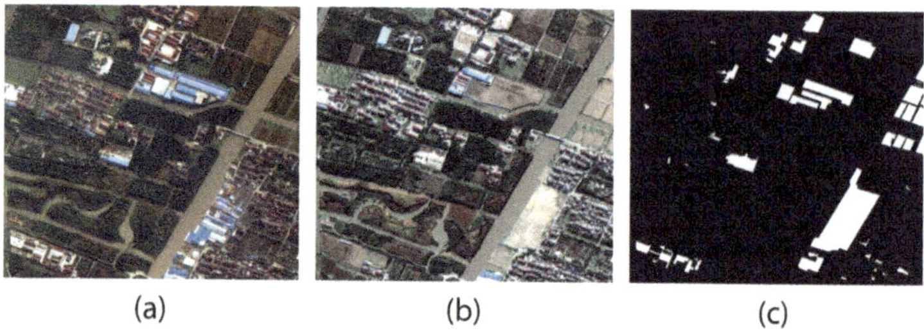

Fig. 2.18 Shanghai dataset. (**a**) Image acquired on November 15, 2015. (**b**) Image acquired on December 8, 2017. (**c**) Ground truth image

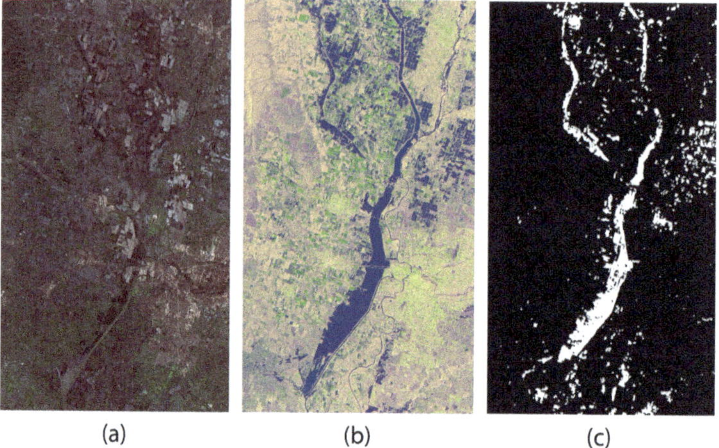

Fig. 2.19 Flood in California dataset. (**a**) Multispectral image acquired by Landsat-8 on January 5, 2017. (**b**) SAR image acquired by Sentinel-1A on February 18, 2017. (**c**) Ground truth image [6]

Landsat-8 satellite on January 5, 2017, containing 11 spectral channels, while the Fig. 2.19b was captured by the Sentinel-1A satellite on February 18, 2017, consisting of 3 channels. Both images have an original spatial size of 3500 × 2000 pixels. This dataset captures the impact of flooding and the corresponding land-cover changes between the two acquisition periods. The ground truth image in Fig. 2.19c was manually annotated based on the reference provided in [6].

The second heterogeneous dataset is the Yellow River Flood dataset, which is designed to analyze seasonal flooding and river course variations along the Yellow River during the high-water period. Figure 2.20a was acquired by the Radarsat-2 satellite in June 2008, while Fig. 2.20b was obtained from Google Earth and originally collected by the Landsat-7 satellite in September 2010. Both images cover the same region and have a spatial size of 291 × 343 pixels. The corresponding ground truth image was manually annotated based on expert interpretation, as shown in Fig. 2.20c.

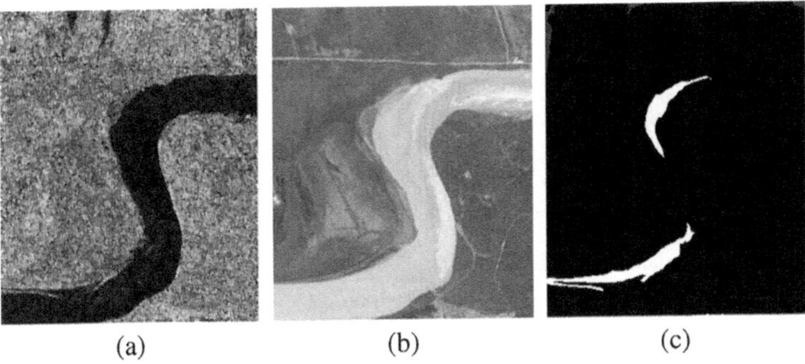

Fig. 2.20 Flood in Yellow River dataset. (a) SAR image acquired by Radarsat-2 in June 2008. (b) Optical image from Landsat-7 (Google Earth) acquired in September 2010. (c) Ground truth image

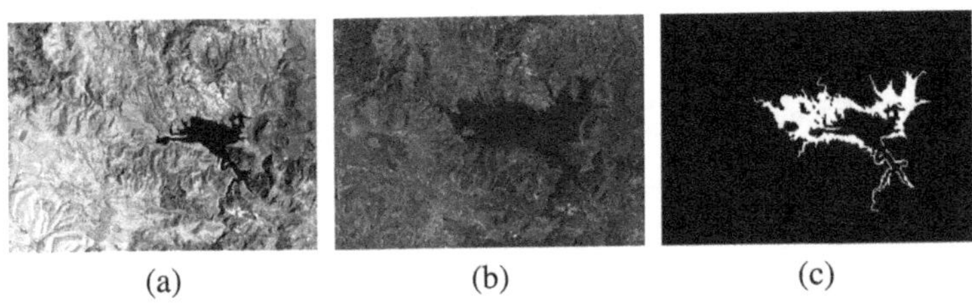

Fig. 2.21 Sardinia dataset. (a) NIR image acquired by Landsat-5 in September 1995. (b) Optical image obtained from Google Earth in July 1996. (c) Ground truth image

The third dataset is the Sardinia dataset, which consists of heterogeneous near-infrared (NIR) and optical images acquired over Lake Mulargia, Italy. This dataset describes the seasonal expansion of Lake Mulargia. As illustrated in Fig. 2.21, the NIR image in Fig. 2.21a, with a spatial size of 412×300, was captured by the Landsat-5 satellite in September 1995, while the optical image in Fig. 2.21b, sized 412×300, was obtained from Google Earth with red, green, and blue bands in July 1996.

The fourth dataset is the Shuguang dataset, which includes a pair of SAR and optical images collected over Shuguang Village in Dongying, China. This dataset reveals farmland land-use transitions and agricultural expansion. As shown in Fig. 2.22, the SAR image in Fig. 2.22a, with a spatial size of 921×593, was acquired by the Radarsat-2 satellite operating in the C-band in June 2008, while the optical image in Fig. 2.22b, sized 921×593, was obtained from Google Earth with red, green, and blue bands in September 2012.

The fifth dataset is the Wuhan dataset, which contains SAR and optical images acquired over the metropolitan area of Wuhan, China. This dataset records urban development changes, such as new constructions and transportation infrastructure. As presented in Fig. 2.23, the SAR image in Fig. 2.23a, with a spatial size of $503 \times 495 \times 1$, was captured by the Radarsat-2 satellite in June 2008, while the optical image Fig. 2.23b, sized $503 \times 495 \times 3$, was obtained from Google Earth in November 2011.

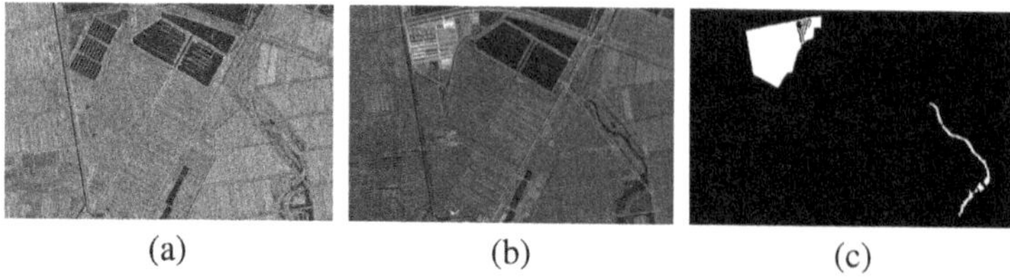

Fig. 2.22 Shuguang dataset. (**a**) SAR image acquired by Radarsat-2 in June 2008. (**b**) Optical image obtained from Google Earth in September 2012. (**c**) Ground truth image

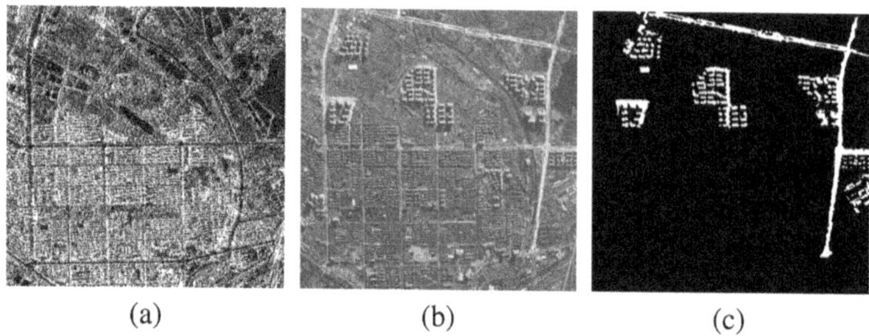

Fig. 2.23 Wuhan dataset. (**a**) SAR image acquired by Radarsat-2 in June 2008. (**b**) Optical image obtained from Google Earth in November 2011. (**c**) Ground truth image

2.2 Foundational Theories for Computational Intelligence

Computational intelligence provides effective solutions for modeling complex and high-dimensional change patterns in remote sensing images. This section introduces key foundational techniques that support the methodologies employed in subsequent chapters, drawing from deep learning and neural architecture search. Representative deep learning architectures include deep belief networks, autoencoders, and generative adversarial networks, which are employed in the unsupervised and semi-supervised change detection frameworks discussed later. Moreover, neural architecture search is introduced as a computational intelligence paradigm for automating the design of such architectures, with the Genetic Algorithm serving as a representative evolutionary search strategy.

2.2.1 Deep Neural Networks

With the rapid advancement of deep neural networks (DNNs) and improvements in computational hardware, remote sensing image change detection is shifting from traditional handcrafted feature methods to data-driven intelligent models. Benefiting from the powerful nonlinear modeling and feature extraction abilities, DNNs can map raw images into high-dimensional semantic spaces to capture discriminative information about land-cover changes, thereby effectively alleviating the accuracy limitations of conventional methods that often suffer from inadequate feature representation.

Existing deep learning-based change detection methods can be categorized into supervised, unsupervised, and semi-supervised paradigms. Supervised methods train end-to-end models using large annotated datasets and achieve high accuracy under ideal conditions. However, acquiring high-quality labels for remote sensing change detection tasks is costly and labor-intensive, limiting their practical applicability. Unsupervised methods learn change patterns directly from multi-temporal images without labeled data, leveraging intrinsic statistical properties or structural discrepancies. Semi-supervised methods exploit a small amount of labeled data together with abundant unlabeled data, striking a balance between supervision and scalability while mitigating the need for extensive labeling and improving detection performance. Given the practical constraints of scarce labeled data, the subsequent chapters of this book focus on unsupervised and semi-supervised deep learning methods for remote sensing change detection. To provide a theoretical foundation for these approaches, this subsection systematically introduces the core principles and implementation procedures of three representative architectures: Deep Belief Networks (DBNs), Autoencoders (AEs), and Generative Adversarial Networks (GANs).

2.2.1.1 Deep Belief Networks

As a simplified variant of the Boltzmann Machine (BM) [7], the Restricted Boltzmann Machine (RBM) [8] is a neural network architecture based on an energy model. It consists of two parts: a visible layer $\mathbf{v} = (v_1, v_2, \ldots, v_{N_v})^T$ and a hidden layer $\mathbf{h} = (h_1, h_2, \ldots, h_{N_h})^T$, as illustrated in Fig. 2.24. Here, N_v denotes the number of neurons in the visible layer, and N_h denotes the number of neurons in the hidden layer.

RBM model performs unsupervised feature learning based on an energy function, which describes the state of the RBM. When the probability distribution tends toward a uniform distribution, it indicates that the energy of the model is high and

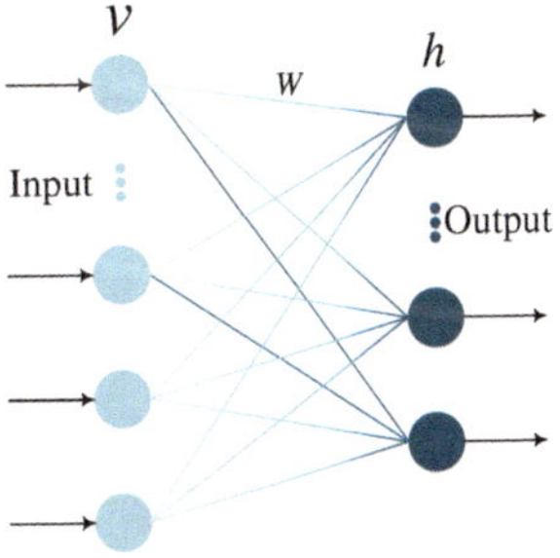

Fig. 2.24 Schematic diagram of RBM structure

the state is unstable. Conversely, when the probability distribution concentrates in certain regions, it implies lower energy and a more stable state. Specifically, for an RBM with network parameters $\boldsymbol{\theta}_{\text{RBM}} = (\mathbf{W}, \mathbf{V}_b, \mathbf{H}_b)$, the energy function between the visible layer $\mathbf{v}$ and hidden layer $\mathbf{h}$ is defined as Eq. (2.9).

$$E_\theta(\mathbf{v}, \mathbf{h}) = -\sum_{i=1}^{N_v} v_{bi} v_i - \sum_{j=1}^{N_h} h_{bj} h_j - \sum_{i,j} v_i h_j w_{i,j} \tag{2.9}$$

where $\mathbf{W} = \{w_{i,j} \mid 1 \leq i \leq n, 1 \leq j \leq m\}$ denotes the weight matrix connecting the visible and hidden layers, $\mathbf{V}_b = (v_{b1}, v_{b2}, \ldots, v_{bN_v})^T$ represents the bias vector of the visible layer, and $\mathbf{H}_b = (h_{b1}, h_{b2}, \ldots, h_{bN_h})^T$ represents the bias vector of the hidden layer,

Based on this energy relationship, the joint probability distribution of the visible layer $\mathbf{v}$ and hidden layer $\mathbf{h}$ can be given by Eq. (2.10).

$$p_\theta(\mathbf{v}, \mathbf{h}) = \frac{1}{Z_\theta} e^{-E_\theta(\mathbf{v},\mathbf{h})} \tag{2.10}$$

where Z_θ is the normalization factor, which is computed as:

$$Z_\theta = \sum_{\mathbf{v},\mathbf{h}} e^{-E_\theta(\mathbf{v},\mathbf{h})} \tag{2.11}$$

Equation (2.10) represents a special form of the Gibbs distribution. When the visible layer vector $\mathbf{v} = (v_1, v_2, \ldots, v_{N_v})^T$ is given, the probability that each neuron in the hidden layer is activated can be derived as Eq. (2.12).

$$p(h_j = 1 \mid \mathbf{v}) = \text{sigm}\left(h_{bj} + \sum_{i=1}^{N_v} v_i w_{ij}\right) \tag{2.12}$$

In RBMs, neurons are modeled as stochastic binary units that take values in {0, 1} [9]. In Eq. (2.12), $h_j = 1$ indicates that the j-th neuron in the hidden layer is activated. sigm(·) denotes the sigmoid activation function, enabling nonlinear mapping of input signals.

Similarly, when the hidden layer vector $\mathbf{h} = (h_1, h_2, \ldots, h_{N_h})^T$ is known, the probability that each neuron in the visible layer is activated is given by Eq. (2.13).

$$p(v_i = 1 \mid \mathbf{h}) = \text{sigm}\left(v_{bi} + \sum_{j=1}^{N_h} h_j w_{ij}\right) \tag{2.13}$$

RBM is a fully unsupervised neural network model that learns a probabilistic representation of the input data through stochastic interactions between its visible and hidden layers. In practical applications, it can map data into various feature

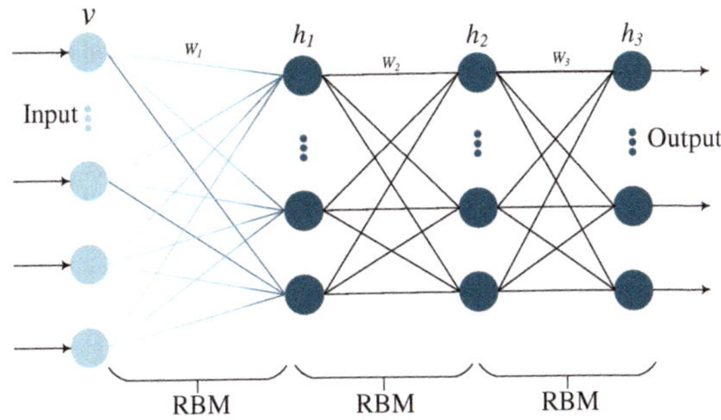

Fig. 2.25 Schematic diagram of DBN structure

spaces for analysis according to the requirements of specific tasks. While connections exist between the visible and hidden layers, neurons within each layer are conditionally independent of one another.When an RBM has N_v visible neurons and N_h hidden neurons, each visible neuron is influenced only by all N_h hidden neurons. Therefore, given the state of the visible layer, the state of the hidden layer can be determined. Conversely, when the hidden layer's state is known, the activation of visible neurons is also conditionally independent. By adjusting the model parameters, the reconstructed visible layer $\hat{\mathbf{v}}$ from the hidden layer can be made approximately equal to the original input $\mathbf{v}$. This means that when data is fed into the visible layer, the representation obtained from the hidden layer serves as an alternative abstraction of the input. Hence, the hidden layer can be regarded as extracting features from the visible layer input, which aligns with the core idea of deep learning.

Due to its simple structure, RBMs are relatively easy to train [10], leading to their widespread application in areas such as feature extraction, image compression, and collaborative filtering. However, since an RBM is a two-layer model, it is limited in handling complex feature extraction tasks. By stacking multiple RBMs, i.e. increasing the number of hidden layers, a Deep Belief Network (DBN) can be construct. The typical architecture of a DBN is illustrated in Fig. 2.25.

It can be observed from Fig. 2.25 that DBN is constructed by stacking multiple RBMs. The hidden layer of the current RBM serves as the visible layer of the next RBM, and the output of the current RBM becomes the input to the subsequent one. During the training process of a DBN, each RBM layer is trained greedily in a layer-by-layer manner until the final layer is reached. After training is complete, unfolding the stacked RBM layers results in a deep network architecture.

2.2.1.2 Autoencoder

Similar to the RBM, the Autoencoder (AE) is an artificial neural network capable of learning high-dimensional feature representations of input data through unsupervised learning. Unlike the RBM, which uses stochastic units to model data

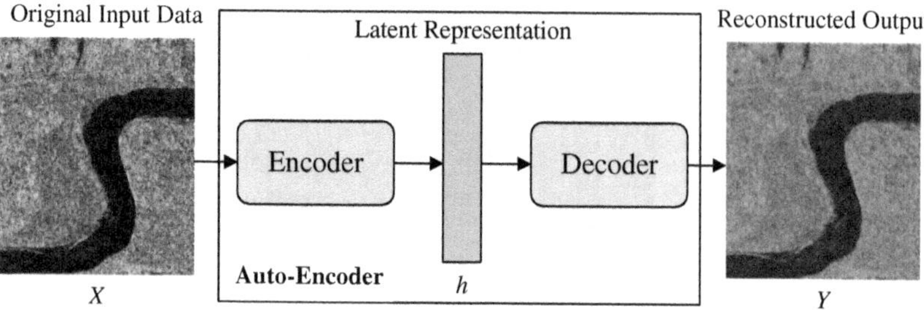

Fig. 2.26 Schematic diagram of AE architecture

probabilistically, the AE employs deterministic transformations for encoding and reconstruction.

As shown in Fig. 2.26, an AE consists of an encoder and a decoder. The encoder compresses the input X into a latent representation $h = f(X)$, and the decoder reconstructs the output as $Y = g(h) = g(f(X))$. Trained via backpropagation, AE minimizes the reconstruction loss $\mathcal{L}(X, Y)$ to ensure $Y \approx X$, thereby learning a meaningful latent representation. A standard AE typically has a single hidden layer with fewer units than the input/output layers, acting as a bottleneck that enforces compression. This architecture enables effective dimensionality reduction while preserving salient features. Consequently, AE are widely used for feature extraction, anomaly detection, classification, and retrieval. Depending on the loss function and training strategy, variants such as Sparse Autoencoders [11], Denoising Autoencoders (DAE) [12], and Convolutional Autoencoders [13] have been developed to address specific tasks.

Compared to shallow networks, deep neural networks (DNNs) can extract more complex and hierarchical features from input data. By stacking multiple AE, a Stacked Autoencoder (SAE) is formed, which enables unsupervised learning of underlying data representations. After pre-training, the encoded features from the deepest hidden layer effectively capture the essential characteristics of the input. The architecture of an SAE is illustrated in Fig. 2.27.

Suppose the input layer of the SAE has N_x units. Since the SAE is trained to reconstruct its input, the output layer also has $N_y = N_x$ units. Let the hidden layer have N_h units, where N_h may be either smaller or larger than N_x. Given a single input sample $\mathbf{x} = (x_1, x_2, \ldots, x_{N_x})^\top$, the encoder produces a hidden representation $\mathbf{h} = (h_1, h_2, \ldots, h_{N_h})^\top$, parameterized by weights $\mathbf{W}^1$ and bias $\mathbf{b}^1$. The encoding mapping can thus be expressed as Eq. (2.14).

$$\mathbf{h} = f_{\theta^1}(\mathbf{x}) = \text{ReLU}(\mathbf{W}^1 \cdot \mathbf{x} + \mathbf{b}^1) \tag{2.14}$$

The output of the decoder is given by Eq. (2.15).

$$\mathbf{y} = f_{\theta^2}(\mathbf{h}) = \text{ReLU}(\mathbf{W}^2 \cdot \mathbf{h} + \mathbf{b}^2) \tag{2.15}$$

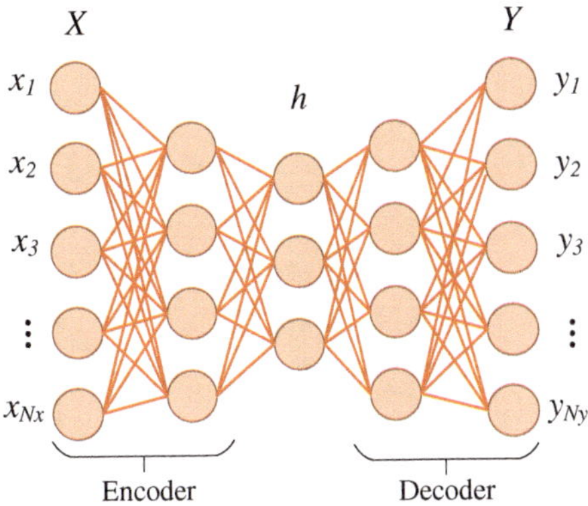

Fig. 2.27 Schematic diagram of SAE structure

where $\theta^2 = [\mathbf{W}^2; \mathbf{b}^2]$ represents the weight parameters and bias of the decoder. ReLU denotes the rectified linear unit function, which is commonly used as an activation function in neural network model optimization processes.

Since the SAE aims to reconstruct its input as accurately as possible, its cost function can be defined as Eq. (2.16).

$$J(\mathbf{W}, \mathbf{b}, \mathbf{x}, \mathbf{y}) = \frac{1}{2}\|\mathbf{y} - \mathbf{x}\|^2 \tag{2.16}$$

Furthermore, to construct training samples for the SAE and optimize the model parameters $\theta = [\theta^1; \theta^2]$, the optimization process refers to Eq. (2.17).

$$\mathcal{J} = \arg\min_{\theta^1,\theta^2} \frac{1}{N_{\text{sample}}} \sum_{k=1}^{N_{\text{sample}}} L(x^{(k)}, y^{(k)}) \tag{2.17}$$

where L represents the loss function of the SAE, N_{sample} denotes the total number of training samples. $x^{(k)}$ and $y^{(k)}$ represent the input and output of the k-th training sample, respectively.

Commonly used loss functions for SAEs include Mean Squared Error (MSE) and cross-entropy. MSE is the most widely adopted for real-valued data, which is defined as the average squared difference between the input and its reconstruction as Eq. (2.18).

$$L_{\text{MSE}}(x^{(k)}, y^{(k)}) = \frac{1}{N_{\text{sample}}} \sum_{k=1}^{N_{\text{sample}}} \|x^{(k)} - y^{(k)}\|^2 \tag{2.18}$$

Cross-entropy is an important concept in information theory [14], primarily used to measure the difference between two probability distributions. The cross-entropy loss is a commonly used loss function in classification tasks. Since change detection can be formulated as a binary classification task with labels 0 (no change) and 1

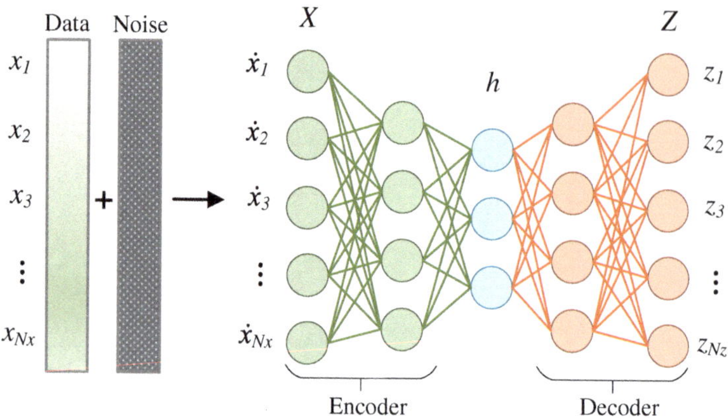

Fig. 2.28 Schematic diagram of DAE architecture

(change), the model outputs a single probability $p \in [0, 1]$ for the change class. The corresponding cross-entropy loss can be given by Eq. (2.19).

$$L_{\text{CE}}(x^{(k)}, y^{(k)}) = -\left[x^{(k)} \log y^{(k)} + \left(1 - x^{(k)}\right) \log\left(1 - y^{(k)}\right)\right] \tag{2.19}$$

DAE is an improved version of the standard AE, which adds random noise drawn from a specific distribution to the input sample $\mathbf{x} = [x_1, x_2, \ldots, x_N]$, resulting in corrupted input data $\mathbf{x}' = [\tilde{x}_1, \tilde{x}_2, \ldots, \tilde{x}_N]$. Then, DAE try to reconstruct the "clean" data $\mathbf{z} = [z_1, z_2, \ldots, z_N]$ from the noisy input, thereby learning more robust data features. The structural schematic of DAE is shown in Fig. 2.28.

Standard AE learns a latent representation by minimizing the reconstruction error between the input and its output. However, this objective alone does not ensure the extraction of meaningful intrinsic features, as the model may simply learn an identity mapping that copies the input to the output. DAE addresses this limitation by training the network to reconstruct the original input from a corrupted version. The hidden layers are forced to capture higher-level, robust features that reflect the underlying data structure rather than memorizing the input. Building on this principle, multiple DAEs can be stacked to form a Stacked Denoising Autoencoder (SDAE), which enhances both generalization and noise robustness, enabling the model to extract increasingly abstract and semantically rich representations. As a result, SDAE can effectively recover the original data from partial or noisy observations.

2.2.1.3 Generative Adversarial Network

The core of Generative Adversarial Network (GAN) lies in a game-theoretic framework between a generator and a discriminator. The generator aims to produce samples that approximate the true data distribution, while the discriminator is

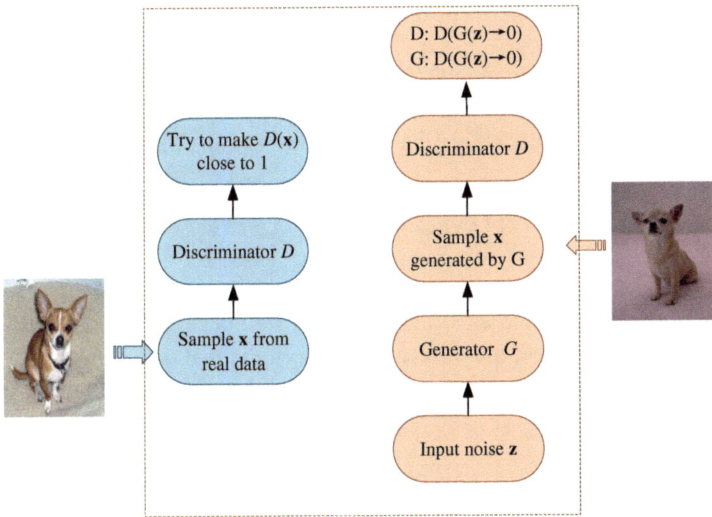

Fig. 2.29 Illustration of the GAN adversarial framework

trained to distinguish real samples from generated (fake) ones. Through this adversarial process, the generator learns to create increasingly realistic samples that the discriminator classifies as real. Ideally, the training converges when the generator fully captures the data distribution, at which point the discriminator can no longer reliably differentiate real from fake samples. This process is illustrated in Fig. 2.29.

Typically, GAN are abstracted as structured probabilistic models involving latent variables $\mathbf{z}$ and observed variables $\mathbf{x}$. The two participating networks are modeled as differentiable functions with corresponding inputs and parameters. Specifically, the discriminator function $D(\cdot)$ takes $\mathbf{x}$ as input and has parameters $\boldsymbol{\theta}^{(D)}$, and the generator function $G(\cdot)$ takes $\mathbf{z}$ as input and has parameters $\boldsymbol{\theta}^{(G)}$. In this way, both adversarial networks can be defined as a parameterized cost function $J\left(\boldsymbol{\theta}^{(D)}, \boldsymbol{\theta}^{(G)}\right)$. The discriminator network attempts to minimize $J^{(D)}\left(\boldsymbol{\theta}^{(D)}, \boldsymbol{\theta}^{(G)}\right)$ while keeping $\boldsymbol{\theta}^{(G)}$ fixed during optimization, and the generator network aims to minimize $J^{(G)}\left(\boldsymbol{\theta}^{(D)}, \boldsymbol{\theta}^{(G)}\right)$ while holding $\boldsymbol{\theta}^{(D)}$ constant. It is important to note that although the cost function of each network depends on the parameters of the other, neither network can update the opposing network's parameters during its own optimization step. Consequently, rather than being a conventional single-objective optimization problem, the learning process of GAN constitutes a two-player game, for which the correct solution concept is a Nash equilibrium [18], as formally defined in Eq. (2.20).

$$
\begin{aligned}
\boldsymbol{\theta}^{(D)*} &= \arg\min_{\boldsymbol{\theta}^{(D)}} J^{(D)}\left(\boldsymbol{\theta}^{(D)}, \boldsymbol{\theta}^{(G)*}\right) \\
\boldsymbol{\theta}^{(G)*} &= \arg\min_{\boldsymbol{\theta}^{(G)}} J^{(G)}\left(\boldsymbol{\theta}^{(D)*}, \boldsymbol{\theta}^{(G)}\right)
\end{aligned}
\tag{2.20}
$$

where $\boldsymbol{\theta}^{(D)*}$ represents the local optimum of $J^{(D)}$, and $\boldsymbol{\theta}^{(G)*}$ corresponds to the local optimum of $J^{(G)}$.

Although the cost function of GAN admits multiple formulations, the discriminator consistently serves the role of distinguishing real samples from generated ones, with its objective typically taking the form shown in Eq. (2.21).

$$J^{(D)}\left(\boldsymbol{\theta}^{(D)}, \boldsymbol{\theta}^{(G)}\right) = -\frac{1}{2}\mathbb{E}_{\mathbf{x}\sim p_{\text{data}}} \log D(\mathbf{x}) - \frac{1}{2}\mathbb{E}_{\mathbf{z}} \log\left(1 - D(G(\mathbf{z}))\right) \tag{2.21}$$

Equation (2.21) corresponds to the standard binary cross-entropy loss, with real samples from p_{data} labeled as 1 and generated samples from p_g labeled as 0. By training the discriminator, the difference between the real data distribution and the generated data distribution can be estimated, and the evaluation method is shown in the Eq. (2.22).

$$\frac{p_{\text{data}}(\mathbf{x})}{p_{\text{model}}(\mathbf{x})} \tag{2.22}$$

To complete the game-theoretic model, it is necessary to define the cost function of the generator network. The simplest form of game model is a zero-sum game, in which the total cost of both players remains constant and always equals zero. For a zero-sum game, the cost function of the generator is defined as Eq. (2.23).

$$J^{(G)} = -J^{(D)} \tag{2.23}$$

Since $J^{(G)}$ is directly related to $J^{(D)}$, the entire adversarial framework can be defined by Eq. (2.24).

$$V\left(\boldsymbol{\theta}^{(D)}, \boldsymbol{\theta}^{(G)}\right) = -J^{(D)}\left(\boldsymbol{\theta}^{(D)}, \boldsymbol{\theta}^{(G)}\right) \tag{2.24}$$

The solution to the zero-sum game can be defined as Eq. (2.25), which is given by the minimax saddle point of the value function in Eq. (2.24).

$$\boldsymbol{\theta}^{(G)*} = \arg\min_{\boldsymbol{\theta}^{(G)}} \max_{\boldsymbol{\theta}^{(D)}} V\left(\boldsymbol{\theta}^{(D)}, \boldsymbol{\theta}^{(G)}\right). \tag{2.25}$$

where the discriminator parameters $\boldsymbol{\theta}^{(D)}$ maximize V for a fixed generator, while the generator parameters $\boldsymbol{\theta}^{(G)}$ minimize the worst-case (i.e., maximized) value of V.

The training of a GAN involves two alternating phases, namely updating the discriminator and updating the generator. Each phase is typically optimized using stochastic gradient-based methods. In every iteration, a batch of real samples $\mathbf{x}$ is drawn from the true data distribution p_{data}, and a batch of latent vectors $\mathbf{z}$ is sampled from the model's prior distribution $p_{\mathbf{z}}$. Then, the parameters $\boldsymbol{\theta}^{(D)}$ and $\boldsymbol{\theta}^{(G)}$

Algorithm 1 GAN training algorithm

Require: Training dataset $\mathbf{X}$, number of discriminator training steps k per epoch (typically $k = 1$)
Ensure: Trained network parameters $\boldsymbol{\theta} = [\boldsymbol{\theta}^{(D)}, \boldsymbol{\theta}^{(G)}]$
for each epoch **do**
  for k steps **do**
    Sample m noise samples $\{\mathbf{z}^1, \mathbf{z}^2, \ldots, \mathbf{z}^m\}$ from the noise distribution $P_g(\mathbf{z})$
    Sample m data samples $\{\mathbf{x}^1, \mathbf{x}^2, \ldots, \mathbf{x}^m\}$ from the data distribution $P_{\text{data}}(\mathbf{x})$
    Update the discriminator:

$$\nabla_{\boldsymbol{\theta}_d} \frac{1}{m} \sum_{i=1}^{m} \left[\log D(\mathbf{x}^{(i)}) + \log\left(1 - D\left(G(\mathbf{z}^{(i)})\right)\right)\right]$$

  end for
  Sample m noise samples $\{\mathbf{z}^1, \mathbf{z}^2, \ldots, \mathbf{z}^m\}$ from the noise distribution $P_g(\mathbf{z})$
  Update the generator:

$$\nabla_{\boldsymbol{\theta}_g} \frac{1}{m} \sum_{i=1}^{m} \left[\log\left(1 - D\left(G(\mathbf{z}^{(i)})\right)\right)\right]$$

end for

are updated sequentially based on their respective gradients. The complete training procedure is summarized in Algorithm 1.

2.2.2 *Neural Architecture Search*

Deep learning-based change detection methods exploit the strong end-to-end representation learning capability of neural networks to automatically extract multi-level, task-specific abstract features directly from raw data. These methods significantly outperform methods based on hand-crafted features and effectively reduce reliance on complex feature engineering. However, existing deep learning models are often tailored to specific datasets or imaging conditions, requiring extensive expert-guided trial-and-error tuning. Such dependence not only increases development costs but also leads to limited generalization ability and poor robustness, making these models difficult to deploy in real-world remote sensing change detection scenarios that exhibit complex and diverse characteristics.

To address these limitations, Neural Architecture Search (NAS) [15] has emerged as a promising technique to automatically design high-performance neural network architectures within a large, structured search space. NAS can construct task- and dataset-specific architectures that often match or surpass handcrafted expert models in performance, thereby significantly reducing the dependence of deep learning on domain knowledge and human expertise. Moreover, NAS demonstrates substantial potential in uncovering novel and highly efficient network architectures

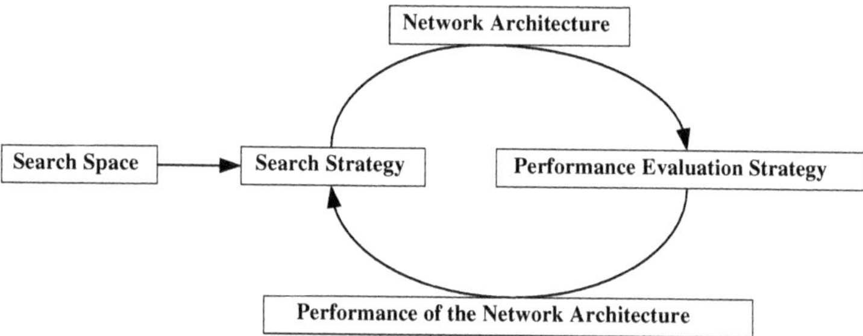

Fig. 2.30 Abstract representation of the neural architecture search process framework

that may surpass human-designed models. It provides an automated paradigm for developing high-precision, robust, and multi-source remote sensing change detection frameworks.

2.2.2.1 Core Components

Generally, a basic workflow of NAS is illustrated in Fig. 2.30, and the core mechanism of NAS can be summarized into three key components: the search space, the search strategy, and the performance evaluation strategy.

- **Search Space**: The search space is primarily utilized to define the scope of network architecture exploration. By integrating prior knowledge regarding typical architectural characteristics associated with a specific task, the search space can be effectively constrained, thereby reducing its complexity and improving the efficiency of the search process. However, this approach may also introduce human bias, which could hinder the NAS method from discovering network architectures that surpass current human-level understanding.
- **Search Strategy**: Researchers define structural search strategies that specify the exact methods for constructing architectures within the designed space. In this process, a balance must be struck between search speed and search quality. On the one hand, the search strategy is expected to efficiently identify high-performing candidate architectures. On the other hand, it must prevent premature convergence to local optima, thereby maintaining sufficient exploration throughout the search process. Currently known search methods include random search, Bayesian optimization, genetic algorithms, reinforcement learning, and gradient-based approaches.
- **Performance Evaluation Strategy**: The goal of neural architecture search is typically to identify a neural network architecture that achieves superior performance on a specified task. The performance evaluation strategy refers to the methodology used to assess and select candidate architectures obtained during the search process, typically by training each candidate on input data and evaluating its performance on a validation set. However, this procedure

Algorithm 2 Genetic algorithm

```
Initialize population P by randomly generating N individuals;
Evaluate the fitness of each individual in population P;
while termination condition is not satisfied do
    Select individuals based on their fitness values to determine which will participate in
    reproduction for the next generation;
    Perform crossover operation on selected individuals to generate offspring;
    Apply mutation operation to the newly generated offspring;
    Evaluate the fitness of the newly generated offspring;
    Combine the old population P and the new offspring population C to form a new combined
    population P';
    Select the top N best individuals from P' to update the population P;
end while
Output the optimal solution.
```

typically incurs substantial computational overhead and extended training time, which significantly constrain the scale and depth of architectural exploration. Consequently, reducing the cost of performance evaluation has become a major focus in recent NAS researches.

2.2.2.2 Genetic Algorithm-Based Search Strategy

As a population-based optimization method, the Genetic Algorithm (GA) [16], first formalized by John Holland in the 1970s, is widely regarded as the pioneering framework that established the canonical evolutionary computation paradigm [17]. GA iteratively improves a population of candidate solutions through selection, crossover, and mutation without requiring gradient information, making it particularly effective for optimizing complex, non-differentiable, and discrete search spaces. These properties align closely with the architecture design problem in NAS, making GA an effective evolutionary search strategy. Specifically, the basic workflow of GA is illustrated in Algorithm 2. When applied to NAS for change detection, the core steps including architecture encoding, fitness evaluation, and genetic operations require additional attention to task-specific constraints such as limited labeled data, discrete network structures, and the need for robust generalization, thus enabling the automatic discovery of high-performing, lightweight neural architectures tailored to real-world remote sensing scenarios.

References

1. Ni, J., Li, Q., Cao, X.: Fundamentals and Practice of Remote Sensing and Geographic Information Systems. Electronics Industry Press (2004)
2. Kuan, D.T., Sawchuk, A.A., Strand, T.C., Hunt, B.R.: Adaptive noise smoothing filter for images with signal-dependent noise. IEEE Trans. Pattern Anal. Mach. Intell. **7**(2), 165–177 (1985)

3. Peng, W., Bai, Z., Liu, X.: Introduction to Remote Sensing. Higher Education Press (2002)
4. Sun, J.: Principles and Applications of Remote Sensing. Wuhan University Press (2003)
5. Daudt, R.C., Le Saux, B., Boulch, A., Gousseau, Y.: Urban change detection for multispectral Earth observation using convolutional neural networks. In: Proceedings of the IEEE International Geoscience and Remote Sensing Symposium (IGARSS), pp. 2115–2118 (2018)
6. Luppino, L.T., Bianchi, F.M., Moser, G., Anfinsen, S.N.: Unsupervised image regression for heterogeneous change detection. IEEE Trans. Geosci. Remote Sens. **57**(12), 9960–9975 (2019)
7. Smolensky, P.: Information processing in dynamical systems: foundations of harmony theory. In: Rumelhart, D.E., McClelland, J.L. (eds.) Parallel Distributed Processing, pp. 194–281. MIT Press (1986)
8. Ackley, D.H., Hinton, G.E., Sejnowski, T.J.: A learning algorithm for Boltzmann machines. Cogn. Sci. **9**(1), 147–169 (1985)
9. Zhang, J., Ding, S.F., Zhang, N., Tang, Y.Y.: A survey on restricted Boltzmann machines. J. Softw. **30**(7), 2073–2090 (2019)
10. Hinton, G.: A practical guide to training restricted Boltzmann machines. Momentum **9**(1), 599–619 (2010)
11. Zhang, F., Du, B., Zhang, L.: Saliency-guided unsupervised feature learning for scene classification. IEEE Trans. Geosci. Remote Sens. **53**(4), 2175–2184 (2014)
12. Vincent, P., Larochelle, H., Bengio, Y., Manzagol, P.-A.: Extracting and composing robust features with denoising autoencoders. In: Proceedings of the International Conference on Machine Learning, pp. 1096–1103 (2008)
13. Masci, J., Meier, U., Cireşan, D., Schmidhuber, J.: Stacked convolutional auto-encoders for hierarchical feature extraction. In: Proceedings of the International Conference on Artificial Neural Networks, pp. 52–59 (2011)
14. Shannon, C.E.: The mathematical theory of communication. Bell Labs Tech. J. **3**(9), 31–32 (1950)
15. Elsken, T., Metzen, J.H., Hutter, F.: Neural architecture search: a survey. J. Mach. Learn. Res. **20**(55), 1–21 (2019)
16. Holland, J.H.: Adaptation in Natural and Artificial Systems: An Introductory Analysis with Applications to Biology, Control, and Artificial Intelligence. MIT Press (1992)
17. Dumitrescu, D., Lazzerini, B., Jain, L.C.: Evolutionary Computation. CRC Press (2000)
18. Ratliff, L.J., Burden, S.A., Sastry, S.S.: Characterization and computation of local Nash equilibria in continuous games. In: 2013 51st Annual Allerton Conference on Communication, Control, and Computing, pp. 917–924 (2013)

Chapter 3
Deep Neural Networks-Based Remote Sensing Image Change Detection

Abstract With its powerful representation learning capability, deep learning effectively alleviates the poor robustness of manual feature extraction in remote sensing change detection. In this chapter, two deep learning—based approaches for remote sensing image change detection are presented. First, a generative representation learning network combined with cyclic clustering is proposed for unsupervised multiple change detection in multispectral images, which extracts spatial-temporal-spectral features via recurrent learning and adaptively infers the number of change categories through cyclic training. Second, a superpixel-level deep change feature analysis network is introduced to suppress noise and outliers in high-resolution remote sensing change detection. It selects training samples unsupervisedly and fine-tunes superpixel representations through supervised learning for robust classification.

Keywords Adversarial learning · Multiple change detection · Multispectral images · Superpixel · Covariance features

3.1 Generative Representation Learning Network for Unsupervised Multispectral Images Change Detection

Multispectral imagery, enriched with abundant temporal, spectral, and spatial information, offers substantial potential for comprehensively characterizing the Earth's surface and its dynamic evolution, thereby facilitating a wide range of change detection applications.[1] Nevertheless, the high dimensionality and intrinsic complexity associated with such data present considerable challenges for multiple change analysis, particularly in the absence of effective and systematic feature

[1] **Acknowledgement:** Reprinted from *IEEE Geoscience and Remote Sensing Letters*, 19, Jiao Shi, Zeping Zhang, Chunhui Tan, Xiaodong Liu, Yu Lei, Unsupervised Multiple Change Detection in Remote Sensing Images via Generative Representation Learning Network, 1–5, Copyright (2022), with permission from IEEE.

J. Shi et al., *Computational Intelligence for Remote Sensing Image Change Detection*, SpringerBriefs in Computer Science,
https://doi.org/10.1007/978-981-92-1404-4_3

extraction strategies. Moreover, conventional multiple change detection methods typically rely heavily on manual intervention, which constrains their efficiency, scalability, and level of automation in practical applications. Here, a generative representation learning network (GRN) and a cyclic clustering technique are combined into a unified model, which is driven to learn spatial-temporal-spectral features for unsupervised multiple change detection. GRN aims to efficiently extract and merge robust difference information with a recurrent learning mechanism for self-adaptive classification refinement, in which different types of changes can be identified and highlighted. Furthermore, a cyclic training strategy is designed to refine the clustering-friendly features, in which similar change types are gradually merged into the same classes. Meanwhile, the number of change types will be optimized through a self-adaptive way and eventually converge to its stable state, which is close to the real distribution. Experimental results on real multispectral data sets demonstrate the effectiveness and superiority of the proposed model on multiple CD.

3.1.1 Introduction

Change detection (CD) is a critical issue in remote sensing domain that attracts an increasingly number of interests, which has been widely used in urban development studies [1], land use/cover monitoring [2], etc. Nevertheless, binary CD only highlighting the changes, i.e., [3–5], while high-resolution data and rich spectral information provided possibilities for further distinguish different types of changes. In contrast with binary CD, multiple CD is a more challenging task, especially when dealing with multispectral/hyperspectral images. The increased dimensionality of the feature space substantially amplifies both representational and computational complexity in multiple CD tasks. This heightened complexity not only imposes greater demands on model design and processing efficiency but also introduces significant challenges in accurately estimating the possible number of changes present in the data.

Researchers have made efforts on multiple CD, change vector analysis (CVA) [6] indicates that the types of changes can be distinguished in a polar domain. Based on CVA, compressed change vector analysis (C^2VA) [7] was subsequently proposed, which allows visualization and detection of multiple changes by considering all available spectral channels within a 2-D representation. However, C^2VA aggregates information from all spectral channels into a unified feature representation, which inevitably results in the loss of underlying latent information and consequently increases the risk of omissions and inaccuracies in CD.

Recently, DNNs gain wide attention as the powerful capacity for feature learning. In [8], a deep learning and mapping (DLM) framework was proposed for ternary CD based on stacked denoising auto-encoders where a non-linear relationship is built between features. To effectively represent different types of changes and estimate the changing degree, a deep representation learning network (DRLnet) [9] was proposed with a recurrent learning mechanism for a better performance of classification. In [10], combining pre-trained network to extract features for change vector analysis has been proven to be effective in avoiding unstable pseudo-labels. However, this approach incorporates an external prior feature extraction model, thereby constraining its reusability, as such models are typically trained on specific datasets and are often difficult to acquire or generalize effectively in practical application scenarios. DNN-based multiple CD methods often rely too much on manual participation, and the estimation of possible change types is still an open issue in these approaches [9, 10]. In contrast to a mere encoder that learns mapping between data, Generative Adversarial Networks (GAN) learns mapping between data distributions. In [11], GAN is used to map multisensory multitemporal data into a common domain to mitigate multisensor difference for subsequent multitemporal deep feature extraction and comparison.

To address the challenges arising from the lack of reliable pseudo-labels in remote sensing CD and to reduce reliance on manual intervention, a GRN is proposed for multiple change detection in multispectral imagery. The main contributions can be summarized as follows:

1. A spatial-temporal-spectral features learning framework is proposed, which is driven by over-clustering and adaptive recurrent learning mechanism to learn discriminative representation and distribution for different types of changes.
2. The discriminative differential features learning is guided by a self-adaptive recurrent learning mechanism where the number of types of changes is adjusted by a self-adaptive way and asymptotically reaches to an optimal one.
3. An adversarial representation learning network is applied to learn the distribution of differential features and generate the final multiple change detection map, which is conducive to accommodate other datasets.

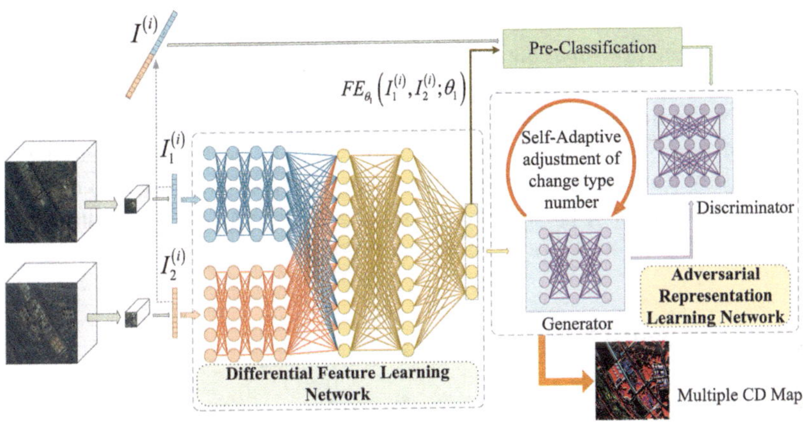

Fig. 3.1 The flowchart of proposed GRN

Algorithm 3 GRN for multiple change detection

Input: Remote sensing images I_1 and I_2, initial number of change types M_0, maximum iterations E.

Output: A final multiple CD map y and trained weights $\boldsymbol{\theta} = [\boldsymbol{\theta}_1, \boldsymbol{\theta}_2, \boldsymbol{\theta}_3]$, where $\boldsymbol{\theta}_1$, $\boldsymbol{\theta}_2$ and $\boldsymbol{\theta}_3$ are weights of Differential Feature Learning Network, generator and discriminator of Adversarial Representation Learning Network, respectively.

Training:

Step 1) Sampling from remote sensing images I_1 and I_2 and identify the label of each sample with pre-classification.

Step 2) Training the Differential Feature Learning Network and update the $\boldsymbol{\theta}_1$.

Step 3) Training the generator and update the $\boldsymbol{\theta}_2$.

Step 4) Training the discriminator and update the $\boldsymbol{\theta}_3$.

Step 5) Adaptively modifying the number of change types M_t according to Eq. (3.6).

Step 6) Pre-classification is applied to the outputs of Differential Feature Learning Network and then update the labels of samples.

Step 7) If stopping criteria E is satisfied, then stop training and output weights θ. Otherwise, go to Step 2.

Testing:

Input I_1 and I_2 to the trained network, to the trained network, the final multiple change detection result can be obtained from the output of generator, where $y = generator(FE_{\theta_1}(I_1, I_2))$

3.1.2 Methodology

As shown in Fig. 3.1, GRN is proposed for unsupervised multiple CD by capturing the difference information to discover the distribution of change areas. First, the initial pseudo-labels were generated by pre-classification with C^2VA on samples extracted from original images [12, 13]. Subsequently, a Differential Feature Learning Network (DFLN) is developed to extract discriminative representations directly from the raw input data. An Adversarial Representation Learning Network (ARLN) is introduced to generate additional pseudo-labels and further optimize the DFLN. As training progresses, GRN is guided by an over-clustering strategy in conjunction with an adaptive recurrent learning mechanism, enabling it to progressively learn more discriminative feature representations and to capture the underlying distribution patterns corresponding to different types of changes. The proposed method can be described as Algorithm 3.

3.1.2.1 Differential Feature Learning

Applying analysis on the original spectral data often cannot achieve satisfactory performance because the existence of noises and redundant information in the available spectral channels. DFLN is designed to learn robust and abstract representations from original images, thereby effectively suppressing noise and reducing feature redundancy. The features learned by the network would capture key discriminative information that friendly for multiple change detection and suppress irrelevant variations, e.g., illumination, parallax, and shadow. To achieve the aforementioned goals, the loss function is designed as follows.

$$L_{FE}(I_1, I_2; \theta_1) = \frac{1}{2N} \sum_{i=1}^{N} \left\| cr^{(i)} - y^{(i)} \right\|_2^2 \tag{3.1}$$

where

$$cr^{(i)} = C^2VA\left(FE_{\theta_1}\left(I_1^{(i)}, I_2^{(i)}; \theta_1\right)\right) \tag{3.2}$$

where the $FE_{\theta_1}(\cdot)$ indicates feature extraction function and $y^{(i)}$ indicates the pseudo label of ith feature which is encoded in one-hot encoding. However, it is evident that $C^2VA(\cdot)$ is non-differentiable, implying that it cannot provide gradient information for backpropagation and therefore cannot be optimized through standard gradient-based learning procedures. Suppose that $C^2VA(\cdot)$ categorizes differential features in linear space, Eq. (3.1) can be rewritten as Eq. (3.3).

$$L_{FE}(I_1, I_2; \boldsymbol{\theta}_1) = \frac{1}{2N} \sum_{i=1}^{N} \left\| FE_{\theta_1}\left(I_1^{(i)}, I_2^{(i)}; \boldsymbol{\theta}_1\right) - \mathbf{P}y^{(i)} \right\|_2^2 \tag{3.3}$$

where $\mathbf{P}$ indicates a feature mapping matrix, which can be calculated by Eq. (3.4). The loss function $L_{FE}(I_1, I_2; \boldsymbol{\theta}_1)$ is differentiable and optimized by back propagation algorithm.

$$\mathbf{P} = FE_{\theta_1}\left(I_1^{(i)}, I_2^{(i)}; \boldsymbol{\theta}_1\right) \cdot \left(y^{(i)}\right)^{+} \tag{3.4}$$

where $\left(y^{(i)}\right)^{+}$ represents the Moore-Penrose generalized inverse matrix of $y^{(i)}$.

Ultimately, once the DFLN has been fine-tuned, discriminative feature representations can be effectively obtained. Later, these features are used as inputs of the generator to generate a classification result. At the same time, the differential features will be categorized by C^{2}VA and the results of them are input to discriminator.

3.1.2.2 Adversarial Representation Learning

Generally, reliable samples are difficult to acquire in the practical application of remote sensing image analysis. If a DNN is constructed to classify change types under conditions of insufficient training samples, overfitting becomes unavoidable, which consequently leads to unreliable and erroneous classification results. In the implementation, an adversarial representation learning is designed for generating discriminative features and learning the distribution of multiple change types, as shown in Fig. 3.2. The input of generator are features learned by DFLN and its

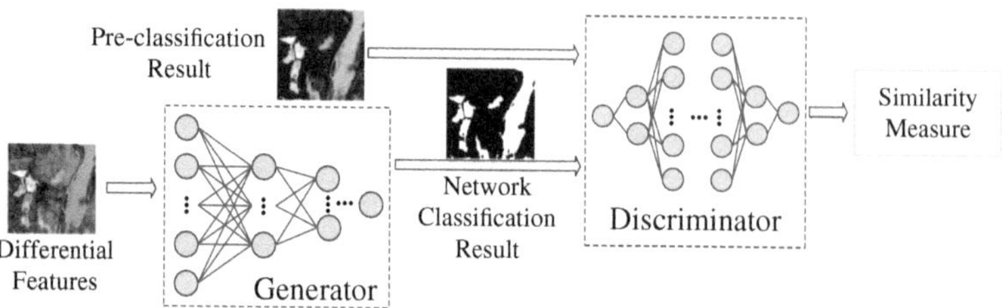

Fig. 3.2 The flowchart of adversarial representation learning

output is classification result. Consequently, two results (obtained by DNN and C^2VA) are sent to the discriminator and identified by it.

3.1.2.3 Adaptive Update of Change Types

Due to the reason that the initial labels acquired by pre-classification are not reliable at first, the proposed network cannot be trained well relying on these initial labels. In this method, an adaptive recurrent learning mechanism is designed to solve this problem by fine-tuning the network gradually. Specifically, the number of change types is typically reduced from an initially relatively large value, enabling the DFLN to progressively fine-tune itself and enhance its capacity to learn discriminative features from the original representations. This process facilitates the identification of an optimal number of change categories m and the generation of reliable labels. Each adjustment in the number of change types can be interpreted as an additional iteration of optimization prior to the final fine-tuning of the network.

Assume that the number of change types has been adjusted t times. The variation of errors in DFLN and ARLN between each iteration is e_1 and e_2, respectively. Consequently, the total variation of errors is defined as Eq. (3.5).

$$e = \frac{|e_1|}{|e_1| + |e_2|} e_1 + \frac{|e_2|}{|e_1| + |e_2|} e_2 \tag{3.5}$$

Suppose there is a positive correlation between the increase of validation errors and the change step length, the number of change types in next time can be acquired by Eq. (3.6).

$$M_{t+1} = \lfloor \lambda e \cdot M_t + M_t \rfloor \tag{3.6}$$

where $\lambda \in [0, 1]$ indicates correlation degree between the increase of error and change step length. In detail, M_{t+1} is rounded down and the least change step length is 1.

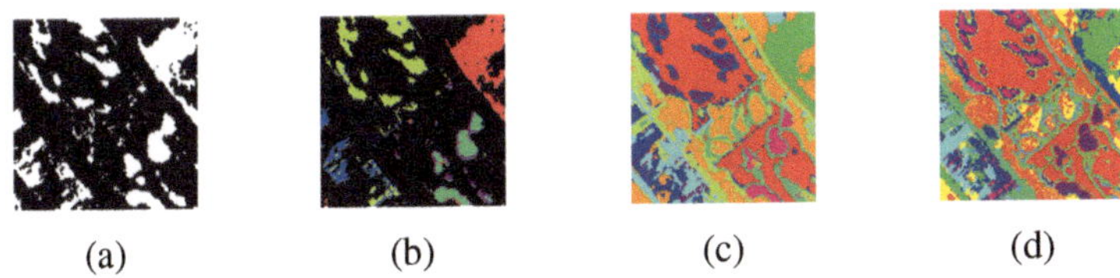

Fig. 3.3 CD results of GRN on Xi'an-2 dataset. (a) Binary. (b) 5 types. (c). 10 types. (d) 20 types

Fig. 3.4 CD results of GRN on Xi'an-5 dataset. (a) Binary. (b) 3 types. (c). 10 types. (d) 20 types

3.1.3 Experimental Study

The experiments are conducted on two real-world multispectral remote sensing datasets, namely Xi'an-2 and Xi'an-5, which were described in detail in Chap. 2. Both datasets comprise four spectral bands (Red, Green, Blue, and Near-Infrared) captured by the GF-1 satellite on August 19 and August 29, 2013, respectively, with a spatial resolution of 2 m/pixel. The Xi'an-2 dataset has a size of $350 \times 350 \times 4$, whereas the Xi'an-5 dataset has a size of $300 \times 300 \times 4$.

3.1.3.1 Experimental Results

To ensure the reliability of the initial labels, the initial number of change types is usually set as four times or more than the ground truth of change type number. In the experiment, the initial number of change types M_0 is 20 and the multiple CD results of Xi'an-2 dataset and Xi'an-5 dataset are shown in Figs. 3.3 and 3.4, respectively, where different colors represent different types of changes.

As Figs. 3.3 and 3.4 depicts, the accuracy of CD increases obviously along with the decrease of change types number. During the optimization process driven by the self-adaptive recurrent learning mechanism, the GRN progressively separates unchanged samples from changed ones. As training proceeds, the delineation of change regions becomes increasingly consistent with the ground truth, as illustrated in Fig. 3.3. Especially, the multiple CD map shown in Fig. 3.3b is very close to the ground truth image though extremely few noises remain. Figure 3.3a shows the binary CD map of GRN, which almost covers all change types compared to ground truth image.

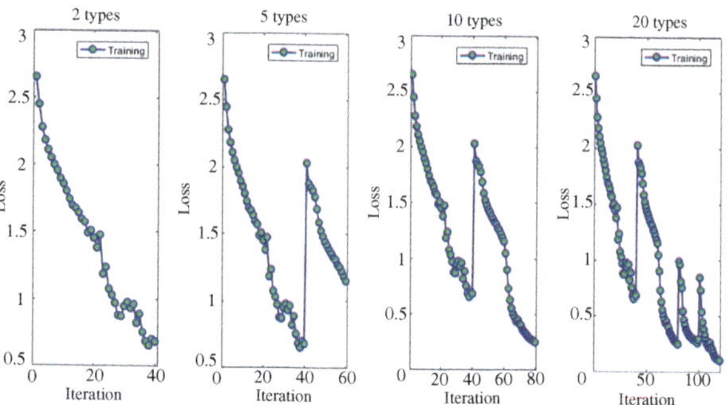

Fig. 3.5 The optimization curves on Xi'an-2 dataset

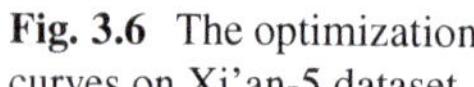

Fig. 3.6 The optimization curves on Xi'an-5 dataset

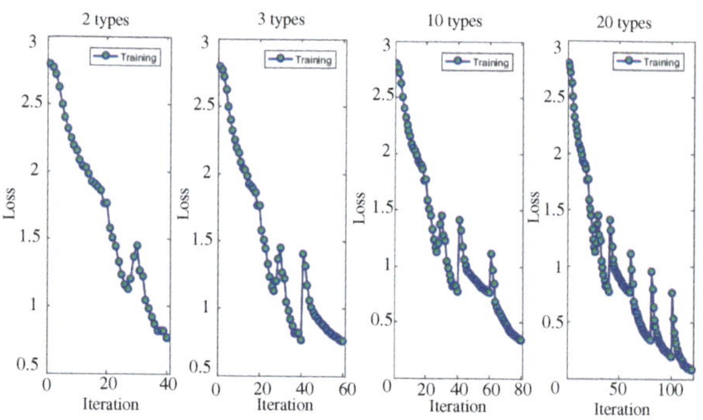

Corresponding optimization curves of adversarial representation learning of Xi'an-2 dataset and Xi'an-5 dataset are shown in Figs. 3.5 and 3.6, respectively, in which the traverse axes represent the number of iteration and the vertical axes represent the values of the loss function. As shown in Figs. 3.5 and 3.6, as the number of iteration increases, the loss decreases gradually, and later stage achieves a lower value. An interesting finding is that there is saltation at the switch point between two successive stages, which can be explained by one certain type of change that may not be assigned with the same class label between two successive stages. Moreover, oscillatory behavior is inherently observed in the loss evolution of adversarial representation learning during iterative training, owing to the minimax game between the generator and the discriminator. Since the network is fine-tuned through an adaptive recurrent optimization mechanism, a new optimization phase is initiated whenever the number of change types is adjusted. As the training process advances, the loss gradually converges and stabilizes.

To evaluate the effect of the proposed method quantitatively, Overall Accuracy (OA), Kappa coefficients κ, First error measure (F_1 score), and the area under the receiver operating characteristics curves (AUC) are calculated. Moreover, as results shown in Table 3.1, C^2VA [7], DCVA [10] and SAE+KM are applied on these datasets for comparison. The SAE+KM method employs a Stacked Autoencoder (SAE) for feature learning, after which the detected change regions are clustered

Table 3.1 The evaluation result of multiple CD

Datasets	Methods	Metrics			
		OA	κ	F_1	AUC
Xi'an-2	C^2VA	0.8117	0.3389	0.4364	0.7557
	DCVA	0.9068	0.6989	0.7541	0.9016
	SAE + KM	0.9044	0.7421	0.8048	0.8388
	GRN	**0.9912**	**0.9723**	**0.9138**	**0.9430**
Xi'an-5	C^2VA	0.8153	0.5561	0.6854	0.8128
	DCVA	0.8701	0.6259	0.7039	0.8673
	SAE + KM	0.9446	0.8647	0.9034	0.9333
	GRN	**0.9876**	**0.9522**	**0.9355**	**0.9646**

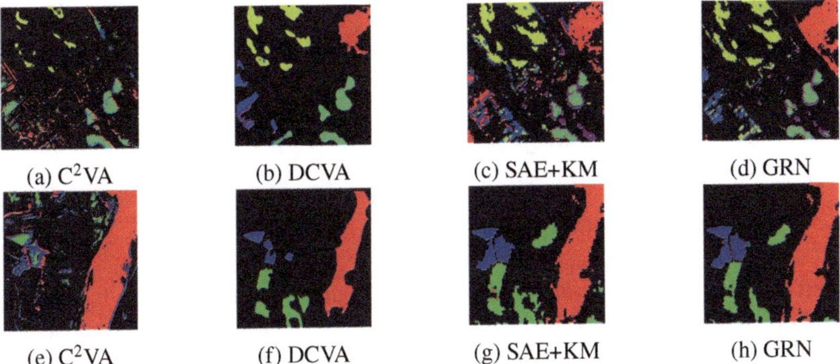

Fig. 3.7 CD results of different methods on Xi'an-2 and Xi'an-5 datasets. (**a**)–(**d**) present the CD results on Xi'an-2 dataset, while (**e**)–(**h**) correspond to the CD results on Xi'an-5 dataset

into different categories using the K-means algorithm. In contrast, DCVA utilizes a pre-trained model for feature extraction and classifies change types based on CVA. However, this reliance on a pre-trained model limits its ability to adapt to the global data distribution across different datasets.

Table 3.1 summarizes the quantitative comparison among different methods over two real multispectral datasets, in which GRN achieves the highest evaluation values. Visual comparison results also demonstrate the effectiveness of GRN in Fig. 3.7. C^2VA produces a noisy change map, and it fails to highlight some clearly changed regions. DCVA and SAE+KM perform much better than C^2VA, while some other false alarms and missed detection caused by shadows and edges of buildings. It is evident from the presented results that GRN produces more accurate boundaries for changed objects and it is less prone to error due to edges and shadows. On the other hand, as illustrated in Fig. 3.7e–h, all three comparative methods fail to effectively highlight certain change categories, whereas GRN successfully captures these variations. The quantitative classification results of different change types on Xi'an-5 dataset are summarized in Table 3.2. It can be observed that GRN achieves the best performance in identifying CT1 and CT3, and attains nearly the highest accuracy in distinguishing CT2 as well.

Table 3.2 The result of classification on Xi'an-5 dataset

Dataset	Change class	Methods			
		C^2VA	DCVA	SAE + KM	GRN
Xi'an-5	CT0 (Unchange)	0.8387	**0.9777**	0.9365	0.9602
	CT1	0.9956	0.6778	0.9866	**0.9985**
	CT2	0.0000	0.4660	**0.9291**	0.9258
	CT3	0.5057	0.3518	0.9091	**0.9333**

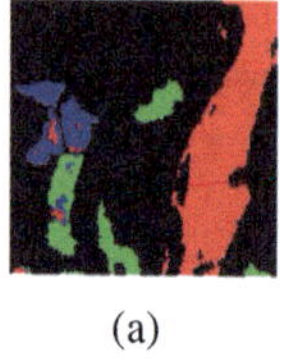
(a)

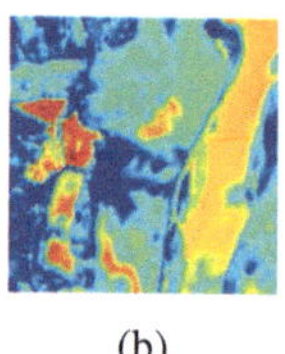
(b)

(c)

Fig. 3.8 Transferability results of multiple CD. (**a**) Multiple CD. (**b**) Intensity map. (**c**) Binary CD

3.1.3.2 Analysis of Transferability

Based on the foregoing analysis, the GRN demonstrates strong capability in capturing the spatial contextual information of the target data and subsequently categorizing samples according to their underlying distribution characteristics. In theory, the proposed method exhibits good scalability and transferability to other similar datasets. That is, GRN can accomplish CD tasks by leveraging a model that has been pre-optimized on related datasets with comparable data distributions. To verify this characteristic, the GRN model of being optimized with Xi'an-2 dataset is applied on Xi'an-5 dataset and the related result is shown in Fig. 3.8.

In the experiment, the multiple CD result and binary result are displayed in Fig. 3.8a, c, respectively. Moreover, the intensity map is shown as Fig. 3.8b, in which the changed area is more likely to exist in the regions of warm colors. The results suggest that the transferable models can detect most of the changed regions on the dataset having similar distribution. As illustrated in Fig. 3.8, GRN exhibits strong generalization capability, thereby demonstrating its effectiveness in transfer learning scenarios. This property significantly reduces the computational cost and resource consumption.

3.1.4 Conclusions

Traditional DNN-based CD methods typically require reliable labeled training samples and often rely heavily on manual intervention. Furthermore, accurately estimating the potential number of multiple change types remains a challenging problem. In this section, GRN is proposed for multiple CD, in which a DFLN and an adversarial representation learning network are integrated to efficiently extract and fuse difference features of raw data with an adaptive recurrent learning mechanism. Through iterative extension, GRN gradually improves the capacity to discriminate different types of changes.

Experimental results validate the effectiveness of GRN in automatically identifying and distinguishing multiple types of changes in multispectral remote sensing imagery. In addition, transfer learning experiments demonstrate that the proposed model exhibits strong scalability and transferability to datasets with similar data distributions, thereby reducing computational resource requirements and further improving its practical extensibility.

3.2 Deep Change Feature Analysis Network for Remote Sensing Images Change Detection

Change detection on surface of earth plays an important role in global-scale pattern of climate and biogeochemistry of the world, which helps to comprehend the connections and associations between human and nature.[2] Remote Sensing and Geographic Information Systems can possibly provide accurate data in regards to land use and land cover changes. However, pixel-based change detection methods are limited in suppressing outliers and noise; they often fail to process remote sensing images with high spatial-/spectral-resolution. To conquer these drawbacks, a superpixel-level change detection and analysis method is proposed in this section. Superpixels are the atomic regions gathering pixels with similar property, which will be more efficient and robust than pixels. Deep neural network is a powerful feature learning and classification tool, it can represent superpixel abstractly and classify them robustly. The learning progress of deep architectures includes unsupervised sample selection and supervised feature learning, unsupervised progress aims at selecting training samples for deep neural network, supervised progress aims at learning the representation of superpixels and fine-tuning the whole network to finish classification. Experimental results on multi-temporal images have demonstrated that the proposed approach can handle the task of change detection and analysis effectively and accurately.

3.2.1 Introduction

Natural variation of land-cover plays most important part in global-scale pattern of climate and biogeochemistry of the world. The surface of the earth has significant power on the planet's hydrologic cycle, biogeochemical cycles, energy balance etc., which in turn considerably manipulate the environment system [14]. Although

[2] **Acknowledgement:** Reprinted from *Sustainable Cities and Society*, 68, Jiao Shi, Xi Zhang, Xiaodong Liu, Yu Lei, Deep change feature analysis network for observing changes of land use or natural environment, 102760, Copyright (2021), with permission from Elsevier.

some land cover changes are caused by natural processes, such as vegetation types transition and geomorphological evolution, or climate change caused by orbital, and human activity also gradually change the earth surface through economic activities such as estrepement, overgrazing, denudation, or, to some extent, human-induced climate change. Mapping, monitoring and surveying the effects of changes in the physical properties of earth surface have been recognized by the scientific community [15].

In recent years, sustainable development between natural environment and city is being taken into consideration as a result of rapid population growth and the plunder of resources of development, etc. Geographic environment changes reflect the influence of human activities and can be affected by many factors including land use change or natural disasters, which can be easily observed by change detection techniques on remote sensing images [16]. Change detection refers to change information analysis between two remote sensing images acquired in the same place at different times [17]. Various change detection methods have been proposed in the past few decades, which can be divided into two categories: pixel-based change detection and object-based change detection. The main difference between them is the basic unit used for comparison.

Pixel-based image change detection means that independent pixels are taken as the basic unit for image analysis. In general, pixel-based image change detection contains three steps: (1) Image preprocessing. (2) Generation of difference map (DM). (3) Analysis of DM. Classical image segmentation methods are often implemented in this step to compute the changed map. Thresholding and clustering methods are the most popular algorithms to analyze DM. Otsu [18], the expectation maximization (EM) algorithm [19] and the Kittler-Illingworth (KI) minimum-error thresholding algorithm [20] are classical thresholding methods. In clustering-based methods, fuzzy clustering methods (FCM) are most widely used due to the fact that fuzzy measurement can retain more information than hard clustering methods. Krinidis et al. improved FCM and proposed a robust algorithm called fuzzy C-means clustering algorithm based on local information (FLICM) [21], which makes the noise insensitive and protects the image detail well. Gong et al. improved the fuzzy factor in FLICM and proposed a clustering algorithm called reformulated FLICM (RFLICM) [22] to classify difference image in an unsupervised way. However, pixel-based change detection methods fail to integrate spatial information and texture information, they are not robust to noise and limited in processing high-spatial-resolution image.

Contrary to the pixel-based methods, object-based change detection methods utilize image segmentation methods to segment multi-temporal images first, and consider each segmentation region as the basic comparison unit to detect changes. These methods have the ability to provide improvements in controlling speckle noise and eliminating misaligned errors, especially in high-spatial-resolution regions. Since objects are the basic processing units in object-based change detection, the most important thing in object-based algorithms is to define changes between two objects [23]. To enhance the segmentation accuracy, the concept of superpixel is proposed by Ren et al. [24]. Superpixel is different from an object, and an object often means a specific instance, while superpixel is an image block composed of some pixels which have similar texture, color, and brightness, several superpixels can make up of an object. Superpixel generating algorithms can roughly be divided into graph-based methods and gradient-descent-based methods. Graph-based methods utilize the idea of minimum spanning tree to segment images, they have the ability to preserve image details well and have fast processing speed, but the size and shape of superpixels are irregular [25, 26]. For gradient-descent-based methods, most algorithms adopt the basic idea of clustering and have the ability to generate regular superpixels, but the speed is very slow and fail to control the amount, size and compactness of superpixel. The existing methods include watersheds method [27], meanshift method [28], quick-shift method [29], turbopixels method [30] and simple linear iterative clustering (SLIC) method [31].

Taking superpixel as a basic processing unit can accelerate pixel-based algorithms and even improve the results to some extent. In [32], SLIC algorithm is used to gather some pixels to superpixels, then taking each superpixel as a basic processing unit to realize segmentation, it can reduce the complexity of an image and make the segmentation easy to handle. In the field of human pose estimation, Mori et al. segment images to superpixels, and detect the contours of the human body and locate the joint and limbs, then combine each part of the human body [33], it enhances the efficiency and accuracy in image pattern search. In [34], Gong et al. utilized superpixel algorithm for extracting changed features and selecting pseudo labels, which proved superpixels have the ability to eliminate the redundant information. This algorithm uses changed features of superpixels for pre-classification, but in the stage of fine classification, it is essentially pixel-based method. In [35], Wu et al. proposed a superpixel-level unsupervised change detection algorithm based on SVM-classifier, which overcomes the limitation of pixel-based algorithms and brought a great efficiency improvement.

In recent years, deep learning [36] has drawn increasing attention to researchers because deep architectures can effectively learn and represent features hidden in the data [37]. Deep learning algorithms imitate human brain by stacking layers into deep architectures to discover higher-level representations, and they have been widely used in the fields of recognition [38], computer vision [39], natural language processing [40], etc. Deep neural network has derived several basic frameworks, such as sparse auto-encoder (SAE) [41], deep belief network (DBN) [42], convolutional neural network (CNN) [39], etc. Deep learning has been also used in the field of classification [43]. In [3], Gong et al. implement stacked restricted Boltzmann machines (RBM) to establish a deep network to recognize the changed areas.

In practical issues, two types of changes may not provide efficient information. Therefore, recent studies draw lots of attention on the change analysis. The progress of change analysis is complex, especially when it comes to multi-spectral images since it needs to consider more information and cope with complex conditions. For handling this issue, Bovolo et al. proposed change vector analysis (CVA) [6] which was then upgraded, called compressed change vector analysis (C^2VA) [7]. Since intensity-based methods are usually easy to be corrupted, Su et al. adopted stacked denoising auto-encoder (SDAE) [44] to learn robust and abstract features of each pixel [45]. However, CVA or C^2VA framework only considers the information of image channel. Besides, they fail to consider the spatial neighborhood information of pixels, which will be sensitive to noise. Therefore, it is essential to develop an accurate and robust algorithm to handle these problems. In order to solve aforementioned problems, three contributions are made and displayed below.

1. A SLIC-based covariance feature extraction method is applied on effectively extracting structural features from original remote sensing images. This method not only solves the problem of pixel-based methods' easily being interfered by speckle noise but also avoids the redundancy information of superpixel-based features.
2. A DBN-based difference representation learning network is designed for precisely acquiring deep features of covariance acquired from superpixels. The dual network aiming to learn difference between two remote sensing images lifts the restriction of difference image based analysis that was used by other change detection methods ever before, which promotes detection performance.
3. A weight optimization of DNN is proposed that is guided by a sparse feature based clustering and recurrently updates the weights of the whole network for learning pivotal representation of features.

3.2.2 *Methodology*

For accomplishing the task of change analysis and enhancing the accuracy of change analysis, a superpixel-level change analysis method called SC^2VA-net is proposed, in which a SLIC-based covariance feature extraction method is applied on extract structural features from original remote sensing images and a DBN-based difference representation learning network is designed to learning deep feature for following classification, and the corresponding description is displayed in Algorithm 4. The flowchart of the method is shown in Fig. 3.9.

Algorithm 4 SC^2VA-net

Input: Two SAR remote sensing images I_1 and I_2.
Output: A final change detection map.
Step 1) Joint simple linear iterative clustering algorithm is first implemented for generating same segmentation map;
Step 2) Sparse auto encoder is used to remove redundant information for representing superpixel in an abstract manner;
Step 3) Change vectors of superpixels are mapped into polar coordinate and clustering algorithm is implemented to generate pseudo labels according to different magnitudes and angles;
Step 4) Constructing deep belief network and fine-tuning with the label generated above, in return, updating the label according to the fine-tuned network;
Step 5) With the training progress of the network, the change map is updated simultaneously, a robust and high-precision change map can be obtained with the end of iteration.

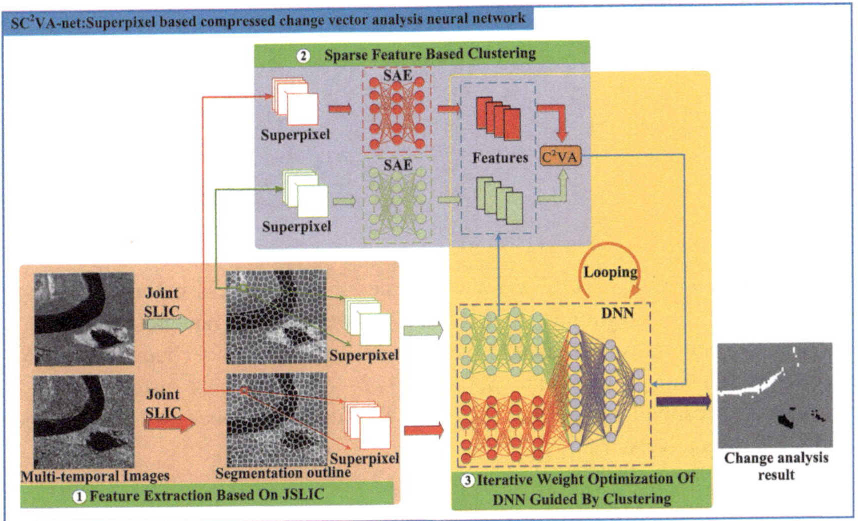

Fig. 3.9 Illustration on the proposed superpixel-based change detection and analysis method

3.2.2.1 Preliminaries

C^2VA is a widely used unsupervised change detection method. Consider two multi-temporal remote sensing images I_1 and I_2 over the same region. At first, a change detection map I_D is produced by subtracting the spectral feature vectors with corresponding spatial positions in I_1 and I_2 as followed Eq. (3.7).

$$I_D = I_2 - I_1 \tag{3.7}$$

Let $I_{b,D}$ represents bth ($b = 1, 2, ..., B$) component of I_D. The magnitude ρ and direction variables α can be derived from Eqs. (3.8) and (3.9), respectively.

$$\rho = \sqrt{\sum_{b=1}^{B} I_{b,D}^2} \tag{3.8}$$

$$\alpha = arccos\left(\frac{\sum_{b=1}^{B}(t_b r_b)}{\sqrt{\sum_{b=1}^{B} t_b^2 \sum_{b=1}^{B} r_b^2}}\right) \tag{3.9}$$

where t_b and r_b are the bth components of BD vectors t and r, respectively.

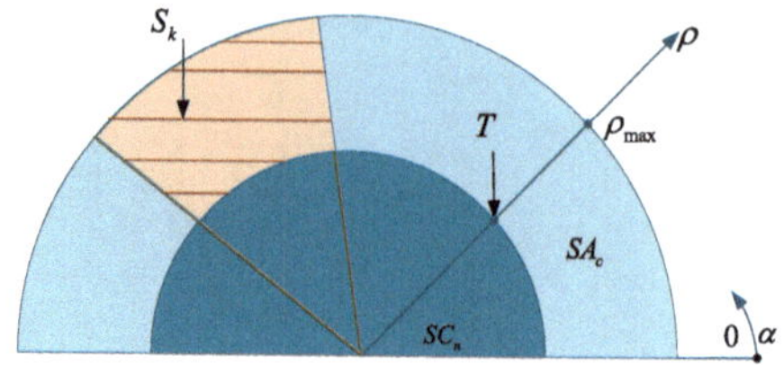

Fig. 3.10 Regions of compressed representation of C^2VA

As depicts in Fig. 3.10, C^2VA set the rules that the pixels belong to changed ones in which the magnitude ρ of them is smaller than T but greater than ρ_{max} and the rest belong to unchanged pixels where SA_c represents changed ones, SC_n represents unchanged ones and $S_k (k = 1, 2, \ldots)$ represents different types of changes. Correspondingly, SA_c , SC_n and S_k can be described as Eqs. 3.10, 3.11 and 3.12, respectively.

$$SA_c = \{\rho, \alpha : T \le \rho \le \rho_{max}, 0 \le \alpha \le \pi\} \tag{3.10}$$

$$SC_n = \{\rho, \alpha : 0 \le \rho \le T, 0 \le \alpha \le \pi\} \tag{3.11}$$

$$S_k = \{\rho, \alpha : \rho \ge T, \alpha_{k_1} \le \alpha \le \alpha_{k_2}, 0 \le \alpha_{k_1} \le \alpha_{k_2} \le \pi\} \tag{3.12}$$

where α_{k_1} and α_{k_2} are angle thresholds which are the boundaries of different types of changes in polar coordinates. Then, the optimal thresholds of T, α_{k_1} and α_{k_2} can be calculated by expectation maximization algorithm.

3.2.2.2 SLIC-Based Covariance Feature Extraction

Simple linear iterative clustering (SLIC) is a simple but efficient superpixel method. It can exert excellent boundary adherence and it has been widely used. Color and distance similarity are two core factors in SLIC to segment images. This method is simpler and faster than other superpixel segmentation methods. Besides, it is easy to use and can be flexible in the compactness and number of superpixels. It converts color images into CIELAB color space and five dimensional feature vectors $C_i = [l_i a_i b_i x_i y_i]^T$ under X–Y coordinates, then construct metrics for five dimensional feature vectors to cluster pixels locally. The main steps are as follows:

(a) *Initialization of seed points.* Supposing there are N pixels in an image, pre-segmentation for K superpixels in the same size, the size of each superpixel is N/K, the distance of every seed point is about $S = \sqrt{N/K}$. For the purpose of avoiding the seed points lying on the edge of an image and reducing the interference for the subsequent clustering process, 3×3 neighborhood of centers is needed to move the position to where has the lowest gradient.
(b) *Distance measures.* Computing the distances of each pixel to all seed points, and labeling each pixel with the closest seed point. The process through constant iteration until convergence. The similarity measures are as follows:

$$d_{lab} = \sqrt{(l_k - l_i)^2 + (a_k - a_i)^2 + (b_k - b_i)^2} \tag{3.13}$$

$$d_{xy} = \sqrt{(x_k - x_i)^2 + (y_k - y_i)^2} \tag{3.14}$$

$$D_i = d_{lab} + \frac{m}{S} d_{xy} \tag{3.15}$$

where d_{lab} stands for the color difference between pixels, d_{xy} is the spatial distance between pixels, D_i is the similarity between pixels, S denotes the space between seed points, m represents balance parameter and it is used to measure the similarity between color value and spatial information.

When there is not a balance between changed regions and unchanged regions in remote sensing images, multiscale superpixel is a good way to overcome this problem for a robust performance. Therefore, a multiscale superpixel feature based change detection is also introduced after in this section. For an efficient process, multiscale SLICs are applied on a difference map (DM) that is generated by log-ratio operator with two original remote sensing images. Then, change detection analysis will be undertaken on these multiscale superpixels respectively for an integrated change detection result.

$$I_{DM} = \log\left(\frac{I_1}{I_2}\right) \tag{3.16}$$

Superpixels contain reliable textural and topological features naturally, which is robust to outliers. However, superpixels also have the phenomenon of information redundancy. For better comparison, abstract features have been extracted and applied to detect different kinds of change information during change analysis progress. In the proposed algorithm, covariance features are extracted to characterize homogeneous superpixels as described in [46]. Covariance features effectively represent superpixels in the aspects of spectral, texture and spatial. Let I to be the segmented image, $\{X_m\}_{m=1\ldots M}$ stands for the d-dimensional features, M is the total number of superpixels, S is a superpixel block, N is the number of pixels in superpixel S. The mean X_μ, variance X_{σ^2}, fill factor X_η and log normalized standard deviation X_{nsd} make up the covariance features of each superpixel.

$$X_\mu(m) = \frac{1}{N} \sum_{(i,j)\in R} I(i, j) \tag{3.17}$$

$$X_{\sigma^2}(m) = \frac{1}{N} \sum_{(i,j)\in R} I^2(i, j) - X_\mu^2(m) \tag{3.18}$$

$$X_\eta(m) = \frac{\max(I(i, j)|_{(i,j)\in R})}{\sum_{(i,j)\in R} I(i, j)} \tag{3.19}$$

$$X_{nsd}(m) = 10 \cdot \log(\frac{X_{\sigma^2}(m)}{X_{\mu}(m)} + 1) \tag{3.20}$$

where m stands for the index of superpixels, $I(i, j)$ is the position of pixel in a region S. Four-dimensional covariance features are extracted to represent each superpixel.

3.2.2.3 C²VA for Superpixels Pre-classification

Compressed change vector analysis (C^{2}VA) [7] is a classical algorithm to deal with change analysis issues, which utilize the information of changed intensity and changed direction to locate changed regions. However, multi-temporal images are usually corrupted seriously by speckle noise, C^{2}VA algorithm fails to remain robust and accurate when dealing with a more complicated scene. In the proposed algorithm, samples are needed to train deep neural network, C^{2}VA algorithm can locate principal changes of multi-temporal images, which can be gathered for training.

When computing the covariance features of superpixels, two groups of features are computed, which are denoted as $\boldsymbol{X}_1$ and $\boldsymbol{X}_2$. C^{2}VA algorithm measure the similarity between two superpixels by computing the magnitude ρ and the direction ϑ according to the difference between two extracted covariance features.

$$\boldsymbol{X} = \boldsymbol{X}_1 - \boldsymbol{X}_2 \tag{3.21}$$

$$\begin{cases} \rho(k) = \sqrt{\sum_{r=1}^{D} X_r^2(k)} \\ \vartheta(k) = \arccos(\frac{\sum_{r=1}^{D} X_r(k)}{\rho(k)\sqrt{D}}) \end{cases} \tag{3.22}$$

Among them, $\boldsymbol{X}$ stands for the difference of two features, k is the index of superpixels, D is the dimensional of features, $X_r(k)$ denotes the magnitude value of kth superpixel in dimension r. Figure 3.11 exhibits the polar coordinate of C^{2}VA.

After mapping all change vectors into the polar coordinate, it's time to locate changed regions and distinguish changed types. Bovolo et al. adopted KI algorithm to divide data into two categories by finding a threshold T, Su et al. proposed clustering method to divide data in polar coordinate [45]. In the proposed method, C^{2}VA

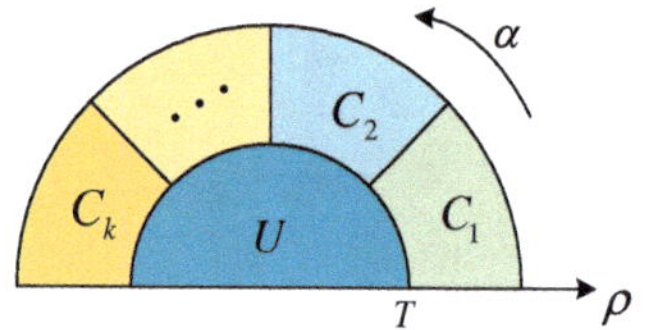

Fig. 3.11 Polar coordinate of C^{2}VA. Divide changed and unchanged class according to ρ, divide changed class into k categories according to α

is just used for selecting training samples, simple clustering method like k-means is implemented for pre-classification. Changed superpixels will be subdivided to detect the changed type by analyzing the direction α of the changed vector. As shown in Fig. 3.11, changed superpixels can be sorted into different categories according to the direction α.

However, superpixel-based covariance features are directly used by C^2VA would lead to a downgrade of performance. Since these features may be interfered by noise, the results of C^2VA would be interfered inevitably and severely. In order to promote the robustness of performance of per-classification, a sparse auto-encoder (SAE) [47, 48] is involved to extract sparse representation of superpixel-based covariance features for a robust pre-classification that provides pseudo labels for samples that are used for the first loop of fine-tuning applied on difference representation learning network. Therefore, SAE can become an indispensable part of the proposed method and by which the performance of classification can be promoted effectively.

3.2.2.4 Sample Selection

The training progress of DNN is related to training dataset, and a sufficient and correct dataset can facilitate to learn powerful deep network. Hence, sample selection is the key to construct robust deep network.

Superpixel is taken as a basic analysis unit in the proposed algorithm, a simple but effective rule called minority subordinating to the majority is used in the proposed algorithm to choose correctly classified superpixels as training dataset. Given a pre-detected change analysis result, whether to choose a superpixel depends on the neighborhood of superpixels are mostly classified as the same category. The specific progress is as follows:

Firstly, compute the center of a superpixel, and take that point as the center to make a neighborhood of $3S \times 3S$ (S denotes the region size of superpixel). Then record the amount of pixels in the region whose label is the same as the central pixel and divide to the whole amount of pixels in the neighborhood to find out whether the superpixel is chosen. The mathematical description is as follows:

$$\frac{N_s[s \in \Omega_k \cap C(k) = l]}{N_s[s \in \Omega_k]} \geq P \tag{3.23}$$

where $N_s[\cdot]$ denotes the number of pixels under specific condition, Ω_k is the neighborhood of the pixel k, $C(k)$ denotes the label of pixel k, P is a parameter which is set to control the selection of the samples. P is set to 0.6, and subsequent experiment section will analysis how the P affect change detection result.

The results of pre-detection can be shown in Fig. 3.12. There are three kinds of superpixels in pre-detection map, which are circled as 1, 2 and 3 in Fig. 3.12. A superpixel has neighborhood in which almost all superpixels have the same labels can be chosen as samples, such as superpixel 1. On the contrary, a superpixel has

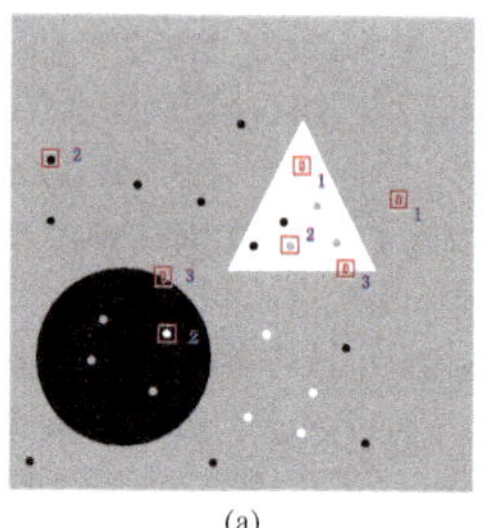

(a)

(b) (c) (d)

Fig. 3.12 Example to illustrate how to choose samples. (**a**) Simulated image. (**b**) Superpixel 1. (**c**) Superpixel 2. (**d**) Superpixel 3

neighborhood in which few or none superpixels have the same labels can be treated as noise blocks, such as superpixel 2. Superpixel 3 is the superpixel of image boundary, which has the neighborhood that more than half superpixels have the same labels, can also be chosen as samples.

3.2.2.5 DBN-Based Unsupervised Representation Learning

Deep belief network (DBN) is a basic deep learning model which is stacked by several restricted Boltzmann machines (RBMs) as depicted in Fig. 3.13. The training of DBN includes pre-training and fine-tuning. DBN is constructed by training layerwisely in the stage of pre-training for obtaining the initial weights of network. When finish the progress of pre-training, back-propagation algorithm is implemented to propagate errors generated by the residual between actual output and expected output to update the weights of deep networks. The training progress of RBM can be regarded as the initialization of the weights in deep neural networks. This progress can solve the drawbacks of long training time and the local optimal solution problem caused by random initialization.

3.2.2.6 Establishment of DBN

Training deep neural network is the most significant part of the proposed algorithm. As shown in Fig. 3.14, superpixels are vectorized firstly since the inputs must be vectors. Next, stacking several RBMs and learning features of each superpixel layerwisely. Finally, unrolling RBMs to establish deep neural network, and BP algorithm is implemented to fine-tune the whole network.

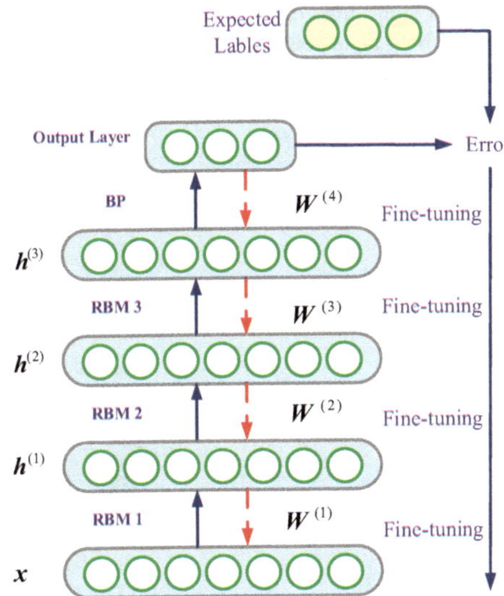

Fig. 3.13 Structure of DBN. Stacking RBMs and training layer by layer to represent each sample abstractly, the parameters of RBMs are initialized in neural network, back propagation algorithm is implemented to fine-tune parameters of the network

As shown in Fig. 3.14a, $S_k^{I_1}$ denotes the kth superpixel in image I_1, $S_k^{I_2}$ denotes the kth superpixel in image I_2. X_k^1 and X_k^2 are unrolled to $S_k^{I_1}$ and $S_k^{I_2}$ respectively. The feature vector of the kth superpixel can be written by $X_k = [X_k^1, X_k^2]$. Figure 3.14b is the pre-training progress, input vector learned by RBMs layer by layer according to the rules described previously. Figure 3.14c is the fine-tuning progress. After pre-training, RBMs are unfolded to construct a deep neural network initialized by the weights and biases of RBMs. Then BP algorithm is used to fine-tune all parameters.

3.2.2.7 Recurrent Difference Representation Learning Framework

In this method, the fine-tuning process of DBN is guided by the result of C^2VA. Although SAE promotes the performance of C^2VA in the beginning of weight optimization, this promotion cannot be last for further optimization of weights due to the lack of capacity to refine these features for a cumulative lifting performance of classification. For a better solution of tackling this problem, a weight optimization method of DBN is proposed in which the improvement of weight parameters refine the features used by C^2VA for a better clustering result which can lead to a further comprehensive optimization process of weight of DBN in turn. In this framework, the training process of deep neural network is guided by the result of C^2VA and the network will be qualified to capture pivotal features from redundant information of superpixels through several iterative adjustments. The details of SC^2VA-net are shown as follows.

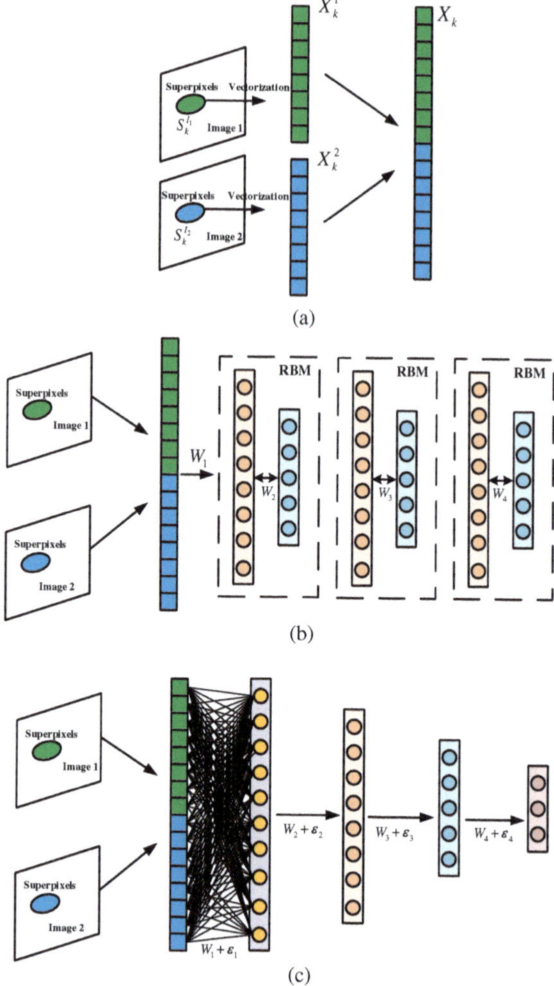

Fig. 3.14 Progress of establishing deep neural network. (**a**) Vectorization of superpixel. (**b**) RBMs are used for pre-training. (**c**) Back-propagation for fine-tuning

Simply, the features extracted from superpixels by stacked SAE will be refined to capture generalized and crucial information in order to generate a perfect classification map in the process of SC^{2}VA-net. At the very first, SLIC-based covariance feature extraction method is applied on two multi-temporal images for acquiring structural features. Then, these features from multi-temporal images are input into deep neural network while the features extracted from superpixels by stacked SAE are distinguished and each input vector is given a label by the result of C^{2}VA. Next, the weights of deep neural network are updated once respect with input vectors and their labels. Later, labels of input vectors will be adjusted by distinguishing the features extracted by deep neural network and the previous operations will be repeated. After several iterations, the network can generate desired features and finally an excellent classification map comes to being.

3.2.2.8 Multi-scale Change Integration

Although superpixels can be more accurate than objects, superpixels still exist mutual constraints between the compactness of pixels and the quality of the segmentation. The two conflicting constraints can affect the change analysis accuracy.

Different scales of superpixels can express different levels of visual content, integrating the information of superpixels in different scale can obtain various visual contents, eliminate the edge of segmentation error and improve the segmentation quality. In the algorithm, a simple but effective multi-scale strategy is utilized for handling with the natural problem of segmentation error in superpixel generating progress. Figure 3.15 shows the proposed multi-scale strategy, the thought of majority voting is implemented in the proposed algorithm. Specifically, different scales of superpixel are segmented by SLIC firstly, and multi-scale features are extracted by covariance features. Next, multi-scale features are fed into deep architecture to compute changed map respectively. Finally, all the scales are combined by voting to form the final changed map. On account of the multi-scale strategy integrates information of different sizes of superpixels, the final classification results will be more persuasive. The effectiveness of multi-scale strategy is verified in experimental part.

Majority voting has been proved to be a simple but effective strategy in classification and change detection tasks [49]. Ensemble learning theory proves that majority voting can usually achieve significantly better performance than single

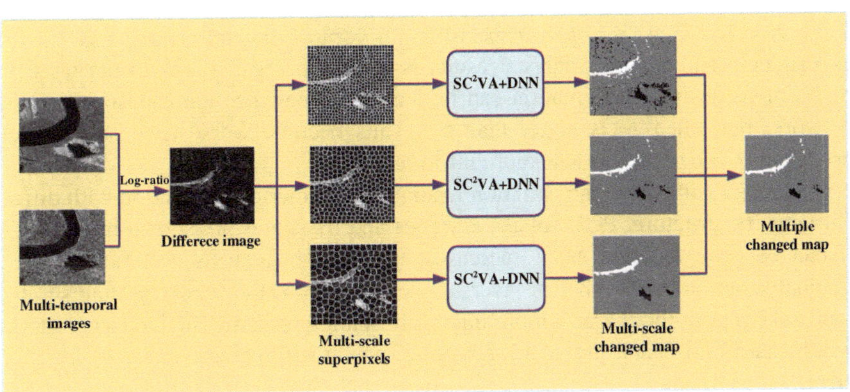

Fig. 3.15 Proposed multi-scale strategy. Two temporal images are computed to DI firstly, then DI is segmented into different sizes of superpixel. Next, the proposed method is used to handle different scales images and obtain various change analysis results. Finally, majority voting strategy is used to get the final result

classifier by integrating multiple weak classifier. In fact, change detection and analysis is essentially a kind of classification problem, it classifies superpixels to three categories (non-change, positive change, negative change). Hence, multi-scale superpixel maps are integrated to achieve higher accuracy than any single-scale ones.

3.2.3 *Experimental Study*

The proposed method is evaluated on five remote sensing change detection benchmarks, including two real SAR image pairs from the Yellow River Estuary, two real multispectral image pairs of Xi'an acquired by the GF-1 satellite, and one synthetic SAR dataset with varying levels of speckle noise. To quantitatively assess performance, standard evaluation metrics, including Overall Error (OE), Percentage of Correct Classification (PCC), Kappa coefficient κ, and F_1-score, are employed. More detailed descriptions of the datasets and evaluation metrics can be found in Chap. 2.

3.2.3.1 Parameter Setting

(1) Effects of Network Structure

In the proposed method, the structure of neural network is a key factor to influence the accuracy of change analysis results. Different structures have different ability to learn abstract features. To analyse the influences of network structure on change analysis results, Yellow River dataset is tested for discussion. In this group of experiment, the parameter P is set to 0.6, the region size of superpixel S = 5, the regularize of segmentation $R = 0.1$, and the depth of hidden layer is set to be $N = 1, 2, 3, 4, 5, 6, 7, 8$ respectively to explore the influence of N on the experiment. The change analysis results is shown in Fig. 3.16. With the increase of N, more abstract information can be learned to enhance the robustness of the network, but when N is larger than 5, results become worse because the back propagation progress will lose more information.

Figure 3.17 illustrate the variation tendency of numerical evaluation with different network structure. PCC values, κ values and F_1-scores are shown in Fig. 3.17. It can be observed that as N increases, the change analysis accuracy increase gradually. When the number of layers comes to $N = 4$, the accuracy attains to the highest. Because there aren't more inner information to learn, the increase of layer will be harmful to back-propagation process, which will increase the reconstruction error.

(2) Effects of Parameter P

P is a parameter set to control the criterion of selecting samples. Different P will generate different dataset, DNN will construct a more robust network when

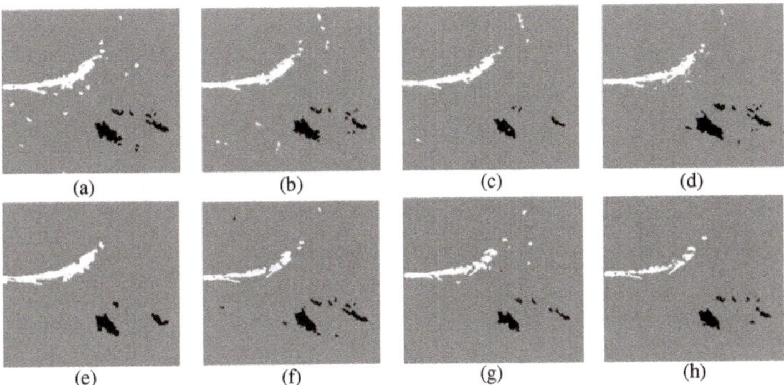

Fig. 3.16 Change analysis results of the proposed method on area of the Yellow River with various numbers of hidden layers. (**a**) The depth of hidden layer $N = 1$. (**b**) The depth of hidden layer $N = 2$. (**c**) The depth of hidden layer $N = 3$. (**d**) The depth of hidden layer $N = 4$. (**e**) The depth of hidden layer $N = 5$. (**f**) The depth of hidden layer $N = 6$. (**g**) The depth of hidden layer $N = 7$. (**h**) The depth of hidden layer $N = 8$

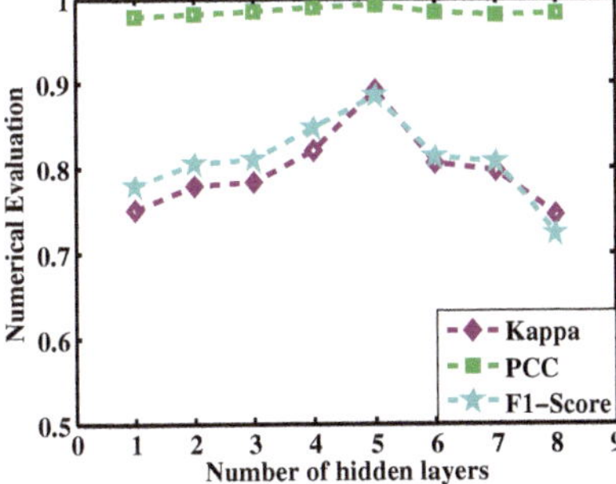

Fig. 3.17 Relationship between the number of hidden layers and κ, PCC, F_1-score on Yellow River dataset

training with a better dataset. To study how the value of P influence change analysis accuracy, Farmland dataset is tested for specific discussion. This group of dataset exhibits the changes of 2008 and 2009 on the coastline of Yellow River. During this year, a piece of farmland was reclaimed and the coastline was moved, because of the tiny changes in coastline and different noise level of the two temporal images, so it is hard to detect and easy to corrupt by noise.

$N = 4$, $S = 5$, $R = 0.1$ and $P = 0.1$ to 0.8 is set to analysis how the P influence the performance. The results are shown in Fig. 3.18. Intuitively, increasing P leads to better noise control and more accurate classification of changed regions. When $P > 0.6$, the boundary become obscure, the accuracy becomes lower. That is because when P increases, the sample selecting progress become more strict, so the selected samples are better. However, when P is larger than 0.6, a significant number of boundary samples are lost, resulting in poor boundary preservation. Figure 3.19 shows the tendency of κ, PCC and F_1-score in different values of P, these numerical evaluation indexes are all attain to the highest when $P = 0.6$.

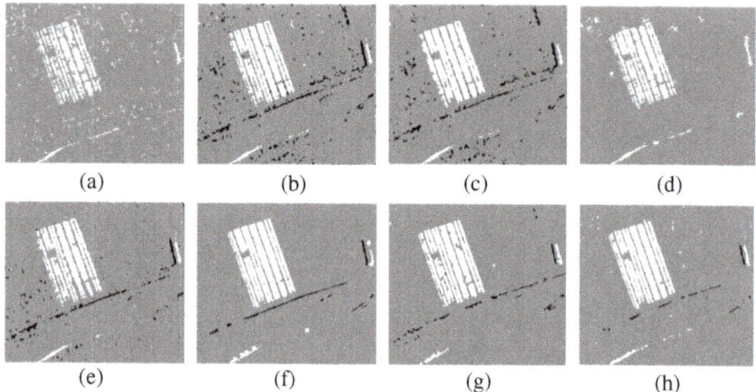

Fig. 3.18 Change analysis results on area of the Farmland dataset obtained by different P. (**a**) $P = 0.1$, (**b**) $P = 0.2$, (**c**) $P = 0.3$, (**d**) $P = 0.4$, (**e**) $P = 0.5$, (**f**) $P = 0.6$, (**g**) $P = 0.7$, (**h**) $P = 0.8$

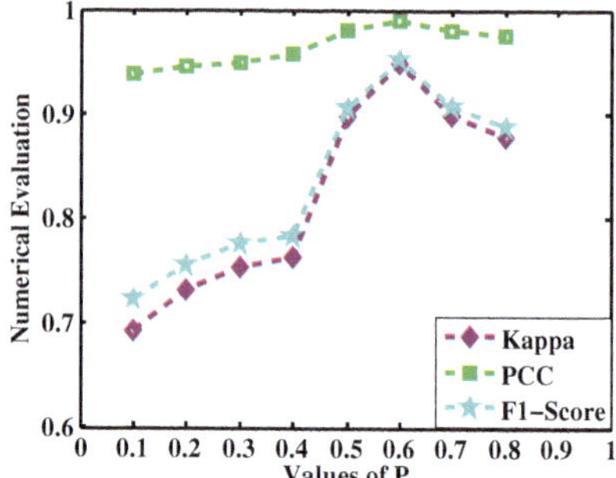

Fig. 3.19 Relationship between the number of hidden layers and κ, PCC, F_1-score on Yellow River dataset

(3) Effects of Parameter S

S is a parameter which controls the region size of superpixels. If the size of superpixel is very small, it will contain less context information. If the size of superpixel is large, it will fail to protect details well. An appropriate value can improve the accuracy of change analysis. To analyze how the region size of superpixels affect change analysis accuracy. In this group of experiment, the number of hidden layers N is set to 4, the parameter $P = 0.6$, the regularization of segmentation $R = 0.1$, and the size of segmentation to be $S = 3, 4, 5, 6, 7, 8, 9, 10$ respectively to discuss how the region size affect final result. As shown in Fig. 3.20, it is obvious that when the size of superpixel is small, the image boundary can preserve well, but it may not quite robust because of lacking context information. With the size of superpixel enlarging, it can contain more context information, but the changed maps may be limited in preserving image boundary well.

Figure 3.21 denotes the evaluation index of the change detection results with different superpixel sizes. As shown in Fig. 3.21a, when the size of superpixel is $S = 5$, the accuracy of change analysis attains highest. Figure 3.21b denotes the running time with different superpixel size. It is obvious that if the size of superpixel is smaller, the generated dataset will be larger, the amount of calculation will be greater, so the running time will be longer.

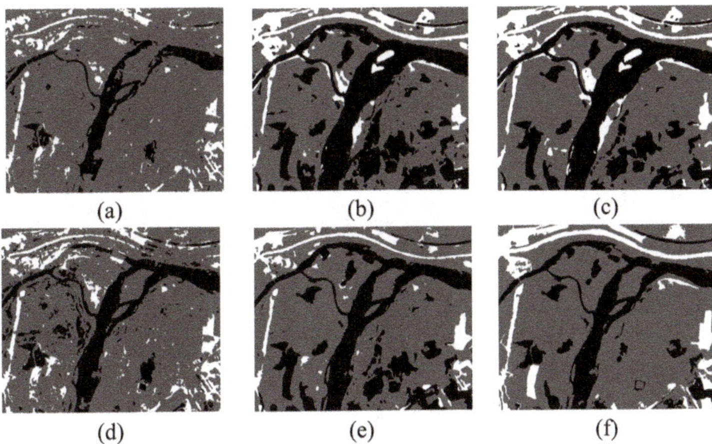

Fig. 3.20 Change analysis results of Weihe river dataset at different superpixel scales. (**a**) $S = 3$, (**b**) $S = 4$, (**c**) $S = 5$, (**d**) $S = 6$, (**e**) $S = 7$, (**f**) $S = 8$, (**g**) $S = 9$, (**h**) $S = 10$

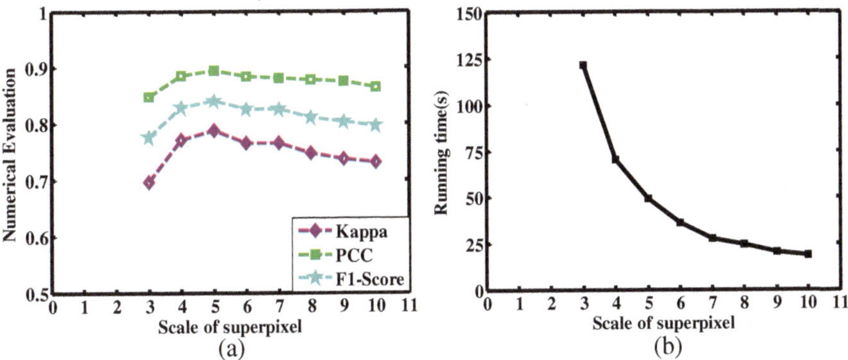

Fig. 3.21 The influence of superpixel scale on change analysis results. (**a**) Relationship between the scales of superpixel and κ, PCC, F_1-score on Weihe River Dataset. (**b**) Running times between different scales of superpixel size

3.2.3.2 Experimental Results

As described above, the proposed algorithm will achieve the best result when the selection criterion P is set to 0.6, the scale of superpixel $S = 5$, the number of hidden layers $N = 4$. In order to demonstrate the performance of the proposed algorithm, several state of art change detection and analysis methods are chosen to compare with the proposed method, which are RFLICM proposed by Gong et al. [22], C^2VA proposed by Bovolo et al. [7], PCA proposed by Deng et al. [50], IR-MAD proposed by Nielsen [16], one object-based change detection method (OBCD for short) proposed by Chen et al. [23] and superpixel-based SVM (S^2VM for short)

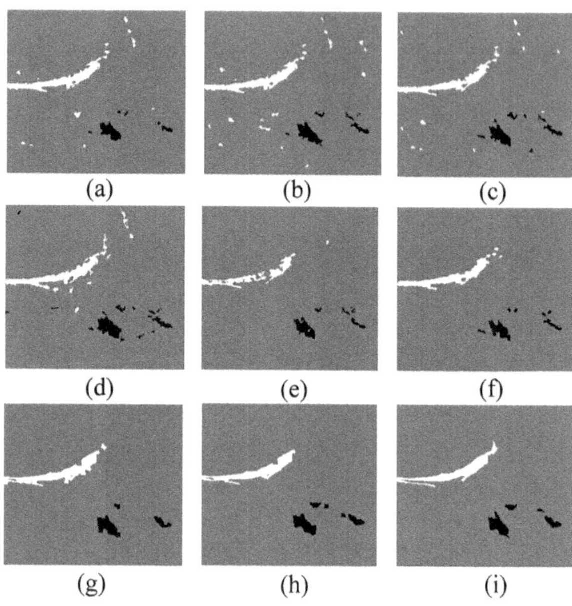

Fig. 3.22 Change analysis results on area of the Yellow River dataset obtained by different methods. (**a**) RFLICM. (**b**) C^2VA. (**c**) PCA. (**d**) IR-MAD. (**e**) OBCD. (**f**) S^2VM. (**g**) $SC^2VA + DBN$. (**h**) Multi-scale $SC^2VA + DBN$. (**i**) The reference image

proposed by Wu et al. [35]. The proposed method will be called to SC^2VA+DBN for short, the multi-scale strategy described above is also used as contrast test.

(1) Results on the Yellow River Dataset

This group of results are shown in Fig. 3.22 and listed in Table 3.3. Figure 3.22a–d are all pixel-based change analysis methods, which are RFLICM, C^2VA, PCA and IR-MAD respectively. Among pixel-based methods, RFLICM can control the effect of noise commendably because it considers neighborhood information, but it fails to preserve the details of changed regions well. C^2VA and IR-MAD methods can preserve image details well but limited in controlling noise. Figure 3.22e is an object-based algorithm. It can be observed that this method can suppress the impact of noise, but the image boundaries are not protected very well. (f) and (g) are all superpixel-based algorithms, they all achieve good performance. Due to the powerful learning ability of DNN, the proposed algorithm achieves better result. (h) is the result of the proposed algorithm incorporating multi-scale information, which can keep more information than the single-scale algorithm. Furthermore, numerical evaluation in Table 3.3 also proves that the proposed algorithm achieves the highest accuracy compared with other methods.

(2) Results on the Farmland Dataset

Figure 3.23 shows the changed maps of different algorithms. Among them, (a)–(d) are all pixel-based algorithms, they can detect main changed regions, but because of the impact of noise, they all look very noisy and have many wrong classified pixels. (e) is an object-based algorithm, it is obvious that OBCD can suppress the impact

Table 3.3 Change analysis results on Yellow River dataset

Method	*OE*	*PCC* (%)	κ (%)	F_1-*score* (%)
RFLICM	1405	98.13	86.55	87.31
C^2VA	1596	97.88	85.24	86.10
PCA	1389	98.16	87.47	88.20
IR-MAD	1692	97.76	84.58	85.46
OBCD	1489	98.02	84.20	84.96
S^2VM	1301	98.07	87.20	87.90
SC^2VA + DNN	664	99.12	89.18	89.53
Multi-scale	**596**	**99.21**	**90.18**	**90.50**

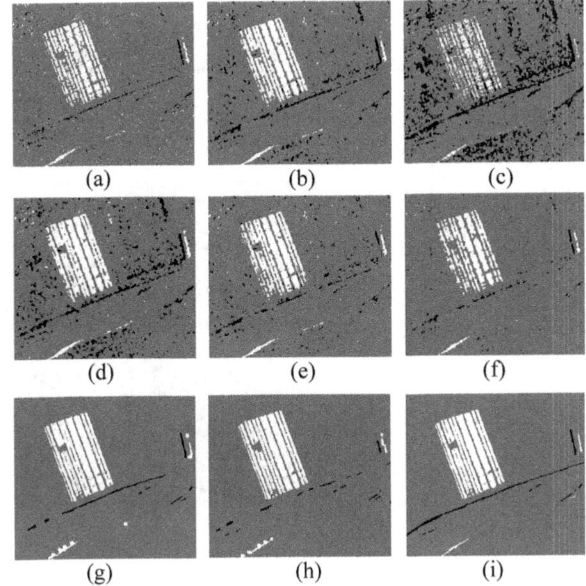

Fig. 3.23 Change analysis results on area of the Farmland dataset obtained by different methods. (**a**) RFLICM. (**b**) C^2VA. (**c**) PCA. (**d**) IR-MAD. (**e**) OBCD. (**f**) S^2VM. (**g**) SC^2VA + DBN. (**h**) Multi-scale SC^2VA + DBN. (**i**) The reference image

of noise but fail to preserve details well. (f) is a superpixel-level algorithm, which uses SVM as a classifier, achieves better result than pixel-based and object-based algorithms. Due to the fact that the proposed superpixel-level algorithm incorporates the powerful feature learning ability of deep neural network, so it outperforms the other approaches. Furthermore, numerical analysis is shown in Table 3.4 proves that the proposed algorithm can achieve the best result in PCC, κ value and F_1-score. Because there are only tiny changes in negative changed regions, the training of negative regions is insufficient. Hence, multi-scale strategy fails to detect all negative changed regions, which cause the consequence that multi-scale strategy fails to improve the performance of the proposed single-scale algorithm.

(3) Results on the Weihe River Dataset

The third group of dataset is a multi-spectral image acquired by GF-1 satellite in Xi'an. Multi-spectral images have more channels, more information and higher

Table 3.4 Change analysis results on Farmland dataset

Method	*OE*	*PCC (%)*	κ (%)	F_1-*score (%)*
RFLICM	8280	94.09	79.48	82.16
C^2VA	7977	94.30	81.97	84.55
PCA	25,134	82.05	51.05	56.98
IR-MAD	12,413	91.13	72.36	76.05
OBCD	7082	94.94	85.30	87.66
S^2VM	6812	95.13	90.73	89.02
SC^2VA + DBN	**1381**	**99.01**	**94.80**	**95.30**
Multi-scale	1586	98.87	93.86	94.43

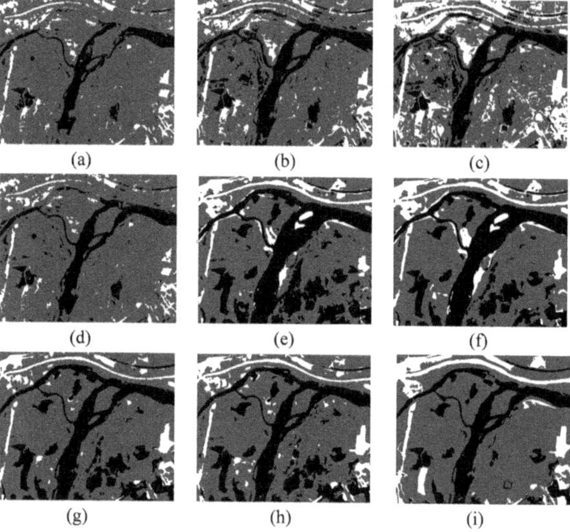

Fig. 3.24 Change analysis results on area of the Weihe River dataset obtained by different methods. (**a**) RFLICM. (**b**) C^2VA. (**c**) PCA. (**d**) IR-MAD. (**e**) OBCD. (**f**) S^2VM. (**g**) SC^2VA + DBN. (**h**) Multi-scale SC^2VA + DBN. (**i**) The reference image

resolution than SAR images, so they are harder to handle. This group of dataset is exhibited to demonstrate the effectiveness of the proposed method on MS images, several algorithms are compared to demonstrate the effectiveness of the proposed method.

The change analysis maps are shown in Fig. 3.24 and the numerical quantitative comparison is listed in Table 3.5. As shown in Fig. 3.24, it is obvious that there exists many noise spots in the change analysis result of PCA. RFLICM can control the effect of noise, but lost many image details. IR-MAD, OBCD and S^2VM can detect the main changed regions, but they all exist wrong classification problems. (g) and (h) are the results of single-scale and multi-scale of the proposed algorithm respectively. Experimental results demonstrate that the proposed algorithm outperforms other algorithms. Table 3.5 also proves this point, the proposed algorithm achieves best OE, PCC, κ and F_1-score. Multi-scale strategy combines different information of different scale, which has the ability to enhance the performance of classification and improve the accuracy of change analysis.

Table 3.5 Change analysis results on Weihe River dataset

Method	*OE*	*PCC (%)*	κ (%)	F_1*-score (%)*
RFLICM	84,204	80.19	61.10	68.85
C^2VA	88,475	79.19	64.83	72.40
PCA	108,519	74.47	57.47	62.78
IR-MAD	79,055	81.40	64.95	72.86
OBCD	88,449	79.19	68.97	77.94
S^2VM	73,360	82.74	72.00	79.95
SC^2VA + DNN	**52,125**	**87.73**	74.65	81.07
Multi-scale	52,234	87.71	**75.08**	**81.50**

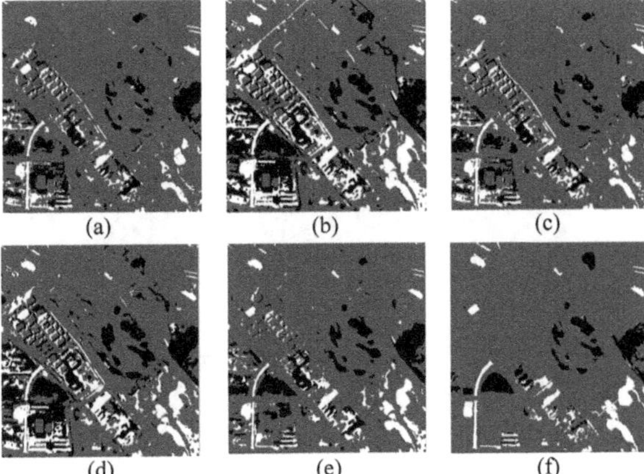

Fig. 3.25 Change analysis results on area of the Bahe River dataset obtained by different methods. (**a**) RFLICM. (**b**) C^2VA. (**c**) PCA. (**d**) IR-MAD. (**e**) OBCD. (**f**) S^2VM. (**g**) SC^2VA + DBN. (**h**) Multi-scale SC^2VA + DBN. (**i**) The reference image

(4) Results on the Bahe River Dataset

The forth group of experiment is carried on the Bahe River dataset, which is also a group of multi-spectral image. Change analysis results are displayed in Fig. 3.25 and the quantitative metrics are shown in Table 3.6. The dataset reflects the changes near Bahe river in Xi'an. From Fig. 3.25, it is obvious that C^2VA, PCA and IR-MAD fail to control noise well, so the results of them have lots of false alarms. RFLICM is robust to noise because it combines the information of neighborhood in the process of classification. Compared with pixel-based algorithms, OBCD can suppress the false changes and identify meaningfully changed regions. (f)–(h) are superpixel-based algorithms. It can be observed that using superpixels as basic processing units yields excellent results by combining the advantages of pixel-based and object-based algorithms. Intuitively, the proposed method achieves the best results. Table 3.6 also proves that the proposed algorithm can obtain much better result than compared methods.

(5) Results on the Simulated Dataset

Simulated dataset is experimented to evaluate the influence of various levels of noise on SAR images. The results of the dataset are exhibited in Fig. 3.26, the proposed method is compared with a pixel-based algorithm (C^2VA) and an object-

Table 3.6 Change analysis results on Bahe River dataset

Method	*OE*	*PCC (%)*	κ (%)	F_1*-score (%)*
RFLICM	54,145	88.07	63.50	68.28
C^2VA	95,523	78.96	61.97	61.15
PCA	98,859	78.23	53.43	55.54
IR-MAD	127,497	71.95	55.30	54.13
OBCD	107,649	76.30	60.78	63.44
S^2VM	56,539	87.55	61.20	64.16
SC^2VA-net	39,823	91.23	67.34	70.68
Multi-scale	**35,894**	**91.74**	**68.23**	**71.44**

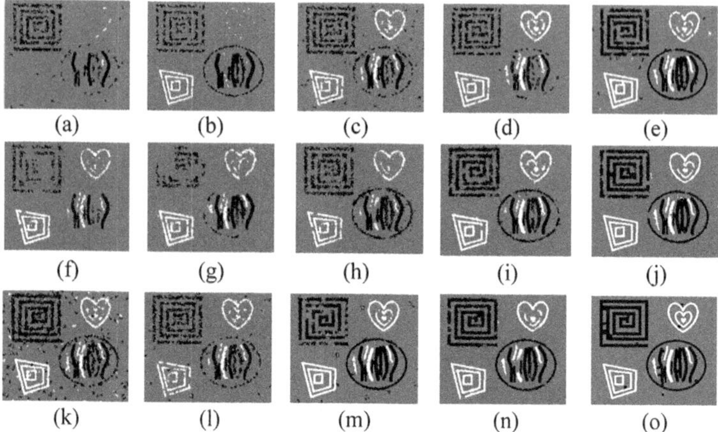

Fig. 3.26 Results on the simulated dataset. (**a**) C^2VA with ENL = 1. (**b**) C^2VA with ENL = 2. (**c**) C^2VA with ENL = 3. (**d**) C^2VA with ENL = 4. (**e**) C^2VA with ENL = 5. (**f**) OBCD with ENL = 1. (**g**) OBCD with ENL = 2. (**h**) OBCD with ENL = 3. (**i**) OBCD with ENL = 4. (**j**) OBCD with ENL = 5. (**k**) SC^2VA + DBN with ENL = 1. (**l**) SC^2VA + DBN with ENL = 2. (**m**) SC^2VA + DBN with ENL = 3. (**n**) SC^2VA + DBN with ENL = 4. (**o**) SC^2VA + DBN with ENL = 5

based change detection method (OBCD). Rosenfield et al. puts forward an efficient way to indicate noise level on SAR images, which is called equal number of looks (ENL) [51], the lower value of ENL represents the higher-level of noise. Five different noise level is chosen to experiment.

As shown in Fig. 3.26, when the noise level is low (like ENL = 5), all algorithms achieve good performance, but the proposed method can be better than C^2VA and OBCD in accuracy and robustness. With the noise level becomes higher (like ENL = 3), C^2VA fails to control speckle noise and the boundary become unsmooth, OBCD can detect the changed regions but the image boundary have been blurred, the proposed superpixel-based algorithm has the ability to control noise and preserve image boundary. When the noise level comes to the highest (like ENL = 1), C^2VA fail to detect changed regions, OBCD can control the speckle noise but fail to detect all changed regions, the proposed algorithm can detect most changed regions, but limited in the effect of noise.

3.2.4 *Conclusions*

Due to the requirements of sustainable development and ecological protection, change detection should place more attention on observing changes of land use or natural environment. The superpixel-level change detection and analysis method proposed here could be used to handle multi-temporal images and analyze the change types in changed regions. The generation of superpixels and establishment of deep neural network are two core parts of the proposed method. Superpixels are taken as the basic analysis unit, which can conquer the drawbacks of lacking spatial information in pixel-based methods and the edge preserving problem in object-based methods. Deep neural network is a powerful tool for data representation, it has the ability to learn from data in higher-level layer by layer and build a robust structure. There are three highlights are described as follows.

1. A SLIC-based covariance feature extraction method is applied on effectively extracting structural features from original remote sensing images. This method not only solves the problem of pixel-based methods' easily being interfered by speckle noise but also avoids the redundancy information of superpixel-based features.
2. A DBN-based difference representation learning network is designed for precisely acquiring deep features of covariance acquired from superpixels. The dual network aiming to learn difference between two remote sensing images lifts the restriction of difference image based analysis that was used by other change detection methods ever before, which promotes detection performance.
3. A weight optimization of DNN is proposed that is guided by a sparse feature based clustering and recurrently updates the weights of the whole network for learning pivotal representation of features.

However, the insufficiency of reliable training samples is still possible to affect the performance of change detection, even though a two-stage training strategy is applied on building a DBN. In addition, the result of superpixel segmentation method plays an important role in the proposed change detection framework and the change detection performance will be debased if SLIC fails to produce a good segmentation result. In the experiment, two SAR images datasets and two multi-spectral images datasets are used for checking the effectiveness of the proposed method, which cannot prove that the proposed method is generalized for any other datasets of any forms. Thus, hyper-spectral images datasets and optical images datasets will be taken into consideration in the future.

References

1. Gong, M., Zhang, P., Su, L., Liu, J.: Coupled dictionary learning for change detection from multisource data. IEEE Trans. Geosci. Remote Sens. **54**(12), 7077–7091 (2016)
2. Wu, K., Zhong, Y., Wang, X., Sun, W.: A novel approach to subpixel land-cover change detection based on a supervised back-propagation neural network for remotely sensed images with different resolutions. IEEE Geosci. Remote Sens. Lett. **14**(10), 1750–1754 (2017)

3. Gong, M., Zhao, J., Liu, J., Miao, Q., Jiao, L.: Change detection in synthetic aperture radar images based on deep neural networks. IEEE Trans. Neural Netw. Learn. Syst. **27**(1), 125–138 (2016)
4. Liu, J., Gong, M., Qin, K., Zhang, P.: A deep convolutional coupling network for change detection based on heterogeneous optical and radar images. IEEE Trans. Neural Netw. Learn. Syst. **29**(3), 545–559 (2018)
5. Gong, M., Yang, H., Zhang, P.: Feature learning and change feature classification based on deep learning for ternary change detection in SAR images. ISPRS J. Photogramm. Remote Sens. **129**, 212–225 (2017)
6. Bovolo, F., Bruzzone, L.: A theoretical framework for unsupervised change detection based on change vector analysis in the polar domain. IEEE Trans. Geosci. Remote Sens. **45**(1), 218–236 (2007)
7. Bovolo, F., Marchesi, S., Bruzzone, L.: A framework for automatic and unsupervised detection of multiple changes in multitemporal images. IEEE Trans. Geosci. Remote Sens. **50**(6), 2196–2212 (2012)
8. Su, L., Gong, M., Zhang, P., Zhang, M., Liu, J., Yang, H.: Deep learning and mapping based ternary change detection for information unbalanced images. Pattern Recognit. **66**, 213–228 (2017)
9. Zhang, P., Gong, M., Zhang, H., Liu, J., Ban, Y.: Unsupervised difference representation learning for detecting multiple types of changes in multitemporal remote sensing images. IEEE Trans. Geosci. Remote Sens. **57**(4), 2277–2289 (2019)
10. Saha, S., Bovolo, F., Bruzzone, L.: Unsupervised deep change vector analysis for multiple-change detection in VHR images. IEEE Trans. Geosci. Remote Sens. **57**(6), 3677–3693 (2019)
11. Saha, S., Bovolo, F., Bruzzone, L.: Unsupervised multiple-change detection in VHR multi-sensor images via deep-learning based adaptation. In: IGARSS 2019–2019 IEEE International Geoscience and Remote Sensing Symposium, pp. 5033–5036 (2019)
12. Du, B., Ru, L., Wu, C., Zhang, L.: Unsupervised deep slow feature analysis for change detection in multi-temporal remote sensing images. IEEE Trans. Geosci. Remote Sens. **57**(12), 9976–9992 (2019)
13. Wang, Q., Yuan, Z., Du, Q., Li, X.: GETNET: a general end-to-end two-dimensional CNN framework for hyperspectral image change detection. CoRR abs/1905.01662 (2019). https://arxiv.org/abs/1905.01662
14. Badmapriyadharisiny, J., Anusudha, K.: Geometric image change detection in urban environment. In: 2017 Fourth International Conference on Signal Processing, Communication and Networking, pp. 1–4 (2017)
15. Wang, R., Murayama, Y.: Geo-simulation of land use/cover scenarios and impacts on land surface temperature in Sapporo, Japan. Sustain. Cities Soc. **62**, 102432 (2020)
16. Nielsen, A.A.: The regularized iteratively reweighted MAD method for change detection in multi- and hyperspectral data. IEEE Trans. Image Process. **16**(2), 463–478 (2007)
17. Jampani, M., Amerasinghe, P., Liedl, R., Locher-Krause, K., Hülsmann, S.: Multi-functionality and land use dynamics in a peri-urban environment influenced by wastewater irrigation. Sustain. Cities Soc. **62**, 102305 (2020)
18. Otsu, N.: A threshold selection method from gray-level histograms. IEEE Trans. Syst. Man Cybern. **9**(1), 62–66 (2007)
19. Dempster, A.P., Laird, N.M., Rubin, D.B.: Maximum likelihood from incomplete data and the EM algorithm. J. R. Stat. Soc. Ser. B **39**(1), 1–38 (1977)
20. Kittler, J., Illingworth, J.: Minimum error thresholding. Pattern Recognit. **19**(1), 41–47 (1986)
21. Krinidis, S., Chatzis, V.: A robust fuzzy local information C-Means clustering algorithm. IEEE Trans. Image Process. **19**(5), 1328–1337 (2010)
22. Gong, M., Zhou, Z., Ma, J.: Change detection in synthetic aperture radar images based on image fusion and fuzzy clustering. IEEE Trans. Image Process. **21**(4), 2141–2151 (2012)
23. Chen, G., Hay, G.J., Carvalho, L.M.T., Wulder, M.A.: Object-based change detection. Int. J. Remote Sens. **33**(14), 4434–4457 (2012)
24. Ren, X., Malik, J.: Learning a classification model for segmentation. In: IEEE International Conference on Computer Vision, p. 10 (2003)

25. Moore, A.P., Prince, S.J., Warrell, J., Mohammed, U., Jones, G.: Superpixel lattices. In: IEEE Conference on Computer Vision and Pattern Recognition, pp. 1–8 (2008)
26. Liu, M., Tuzel, O., Ramalingam, S., Chellappa, R.: Entropy rate superpixel segmentation. In: IEEE Conference on Computer Vision and Pattern Recognition, pp. 2097–2104 (2011)
27. Vincent, L., Soille, P.: Watersheds in digital spaces: an efficient algorithm based on immersion simulations. IEEE Trans. Pattern Anal. Mach. Intell. **13**(6), 583–598 (1991)
28. Comaniciu, D., Meer, P.: Mean shift: a robust approach toward feature space analysis. IEEE Trans. Pattern Anal. Mach. Intell. **24**(5), 603–619 (2002)
29. Vedaldi, A., Soatto, S.: Quick shift and kernel methods for mode seeking. In: European Conference on Computer Vision, pp. 705–718 (2008)
30. Levinshtein, A., Stere, A., Kutulakos, K.N., Fleet, D.J., Dickinson, S.J., Siddiqi, K.: TurboPixels: fast superpixels using geometric flows. IEEE Trans. Pattern Anal. Mach. Intell. **31**(12), 2290–2297 (2009)
31. Achanta, R., Shaji, A., Smith, K., Lucchi, A., Fua, P., Süsstrunk, S.: SLIC superpixels compared to state-of-the-art superpixel methods. IEEE Trans. Pattern Anal. Mach. Intell. **34**(11), 2274–2282 (2012)
32. Mori, G., Ren, X., Efros, A.A., Malik, J.: Recovering human body configurations: combining segmentation and recognition. In: IEEE Computer Society Conference on Computer Vision and Pattern Recognition, pp. 326–333 (2004)
33. Mori, G.: Guiding model search using segmentation. In: Tenth IEEE International Conference on Computer Vision (ICCV), vol. 2, pp. 1417–1423 (2005)
34. Gong, M., Zhan, T., Zhang, P., Miao, Q.: Superpixel-based difference representation learning for change detection in multispectral remote sensing images. IEEE Trans. Geosci. Remote Sens. **55**(5), 2658–2673 (2017)
35. Wu, Z., Hu, Z., Fan, Q.: Superpixel-based unsupervised change detection using multi-dimensional change vector analysis and SVM-based classification. In: ISPRS Annals of Photogrammetry, Remote Sensing and Spatial Information Sciences, pp. 257–262 (2012)
36. Shao, L., Wu, D., Li, X.: Learning deep and wide: a spectral method for learning deep networks. IEEE Trans. Neural Netw. Learn. Syst. **25**(12), 2303–2308 (2014)
37. Bengio, Y., Guyon, G., Dror, V., Lemaire, G., Taylor, D.: Deep learning of representations for unsupervised and transfer learning. In: Workshop on Unsupervised and Transfer Learning, vol. 7, pp. 17–36 (2011)
38. Mahmud, M., Kaiser, M.S., Hussain, A., Vassanelli, S.: Applications of deep learning and reinforcement learning to biological data. IEEE Trans. Neural Netw. Learn. Syst. **29**(6), 2063–2079 (2018)
39. Krizhevsky, A., Sutskever, I., Hinton, G.E.: ImageNet classification with deep convolutional neural networks. In: Advances in Neural Information Processing Systems (NeurIPS), vol. 25, pp. 1097–1105 (2012)
40. Venugopalan, S., Xu, H., Donahue, J., Rohrbach, M., Mooney, R.J., Saenko, K.: Translating videos to natural language using deep recurrent neural networks (2014). arXiv preprint arXiv:1412.4729
41. Zhang, F., Du, B., Zhang, L.: Saliency-guided unsupervised feature learning for scene classification. IEEE Trans. Geosci. Remote Sens. **53**(4), 2175–2184 (2015)
42. Hinton, G.E., Osindero, S., Teh, Y.W.: A fast learning algorithm for deep belief nets. Neural Comput. **18**(7), 1527–1554 (2006)
43. Zhang, H., Gong, M., Zhang, P., Su, L., Shi, J.: Feature-level change detection using deep representation and feature change analysis for multispectral imagery. IEEE Geosci. Remote Sens. Lett. **13**(11), 1666–1670 (2016)
44. Vincent, P., Larochelle, H., Lajoie, I., Bengio, Y., Manzagol, P.: Stacked denoising autoencoders: learning useful representations in a deep network with a local denoising criterion. J. Mach. Learn. Res. **11**, 3371–3408 (2010)
45. Su, L., Shi, J., Zhang, P., Wang, Z., Gong, M.: Detecting multiple changes from multi-temporal images by using stacked denoising autoencoder based change vector analysis. In: International Joint Conference on Neural Networks (IJCNN), pp. 1269–1276 (2016)

46. Huang, X., Yang, W., Xia, G.S., Liao, M.: Superpixel-based change detection in high resolution SAR images using region covariance features. In: International Workshop on the Analysis of Multitemporal Remote Sensing Images, pp. 1–4 (2015)
47. Hu, Y., Fan, J., Wang, J.: Classification of PolSAR images based on adaptive nonlocal stacked sparse autoencoder. IEEE Geosci. Remote Sens. Lett. **15**(7), 1050–1054 (2018)
48. Liu, D., Zhang, N., Jiang, L., Zhao, X., Duan, W.: Nonlinear generalized predictive control of the crystal diameter in CZ-Si crystal growth process based on stacked sparse autoencoder. IEEE Trans. Control Syst. Technol. **28**(3), 1132–1139 (2020)
49. Du, P., Liu, S., Gamba, P., Tan, K., Xia, J.: Fusion of difference images for change detection over urban areas. IEEE J. Sel. Top. Appl. Earth Obs. Remote Sens. **5**(4), 1076–1086 (2012)
50. Deng, J., Wang, K., Deng, Y.H., Qi, G.: PCA-based land-use change detection and analysis using multitemporal and multisensor satellite data. Int. J. Remote Sens. **29**(16), 4823–4838 (2008)
51. Rosenfeld, G.H., Fitzpatricklins, K.: A coefficient of agreement as a measure of thematic classification accuracy. Photogramm. Eng. Remote Sens. **52**(2), 223–227 (1986)

Chapter 4
Deep Neural Networks-Based Heterogeneous Remote Sensing Image Change Detection

Abstract With the diversification of remote sensing observation platforms, change detection has increasingly shifted from homogeneous to heterogeneous multi-source scenarios. The core challenge lies in learning modality-invariant feature representations. In this chapter, two deep learning—based approaches are proposed to address this challenge. First, a self-guided autoencoder is introduced that iteratively refines pseudo-labels through fusion of multiple change maps, enabling robust change detection without requiring transformation or alignment. Second, a multi-layer composite autoencoder leverages minimal labeled data to supervise change detection across multiple feature layers, iteratively refining pseudo-labels through fused prediction confidence to improve performance.

Keywords Heterogeneous change detection · Autoencoder network · Self-guided learning · Semi-supervised learning

4.1 Self-Guided Autoencoders for Unsupervised Heterogeneous Remote Sensing Images Change Detection

When dealing with the large differences in two heterogeneous images, traditional unsupervised frameworks usually convert them into a common domain via auxiliary strategies like transformation and alignment.[1] However, this demands heavy computation and struggles to balance training tasks. To build a concise framework, this section presents self-guided autoencoders (SGAE) for unsupervised change detection in heterogeneous remote sensing images. Unlike traditional methods reducing the differences of heterogeneous images to highlight changes, SGAE guides identification information flow in unlabeled data through self-guided itera-

[1] **Acknowledgement**: Reprinted from *IEEE Transactions on Artificial Intelligence*, 5(6), Jiao Shi, Tiancheng Wu, Alex Kai Qin, Yu Lei, Gwanggil Jeon, Self-Guided Autoencoders for Unsupervised Change Detection in Heterogeneous Remote Sensing Images, 2458–2471, Copyright (2024), with permission from IEEE.

J. Shi et al., *Computational Intelligence for Remote Sensing Image Change Detection*, SpringerBriefs in Computer Science,
https://doi.org/10.1007/978-981-92-1404-4_4

tions. First, initial unsupervised networks output an elementary change map that will be screened to obtain reliable pseudolabels. The selected pseudo-labeled samples will be used as the input of a supervised network to obtain another change map. Then, multiple change maps will be fused to refine the confidence of pseudo-labels again, obtaining new fused pseudolabeled samples for the self-guided network, which will be trained with pseudo-labeled samples and unlabeled samples. Finally, the above operations will be repeated to continuously optimize the net, which helps itself to extract the discriminative features for classification in self-guided iterations. Experiments on four datasets, comparing with several algorithms, show the effectiveness and robustness of the proposed SGAE-based method. It enables unsupervised models to improve feature extraction and classification performance with a more flexible learning approach.

4.1.1 Introduction

With the continuous advancement of remote sensing technology, the types of remote sensing data has become increasingly diverse. It encompasses synthetic aperture radar (SAR) images, optical images, multispectral images, and hyperspectral images. Given this trend, extensive research has been carried out in the field of remote sensing image processing, covering aspects such as target detection, change detection, and classification [1, 2].

Among these, remote sensing image change detection is a technique that identifies the changed areas by comparing two images acquired at different times over the same region. Currently, it has gained widespread applications across various fields, including land-cover change analysis, natural disaster assessment, agricultural evaluation, urban expansion and evolution monitoring, and environmental surveillance [3, 4]. Numerous change detection (CD) methods grounded in traditional machine learning have been put forward. Examples include principal component analysis (PCA) [5], Markov random fields [6, 7], and genetic algorithms [8, 9]. Nevertheless, the features learned by these methods are often too shallow, leading to sub-optimal detection performance.

In recent years, with the remarkable development of deep learning, the CD technology has witnessed substantial improvements. The deep neural network (DNN) is capable of extracting abstract features, thereby suppressing certain noise interference and significantly enhancing the performance of CD [10, 11]. Typically, CD can be categorized into change detection for homogeneous images and that for heterogeneous images [12]. Homogeneous remote sensing (RS) images refer to images captured by the same sensor under identical geometric, seasonal, and acquisition parameter conditions. In contrast, heterogeneous RS images refer to data acquired under discrepancies in environmental conditions, acquisition geometry, sensor settings, sensor modes, or sensor types [13, 14].

Currently, the majority of existing DNN-based algorithms are tailored for homogeneous images. These algorithms typically do not incorporate additional processing to account for the disparities in heterogeneous images [15]. Driven by the growing variety of remote sensing image types, the analysis of heterogeneous data has emerged as a prominent trend [16]. However, heterogeneous images pose significant challenges for change detection. The influence of diverse noise sources and varying sensor parameters results in substantial differences in image attributes, making it challenging to detect changes accurately [17, 18]. For instance, optical sensors are highly susceptible to the effects of light, while SAR sensors are primarily influenced by the reflection characteristics of objects [19]. Moreover, even RS images of the same area can exhibit large phase variations due to non-uniform interference [12, 20]. Consequently, there is an urgent necessity to develop methods to tackle these specific challenges.

For heterogeneous CD, a universal approach is to map the original data from different sources to a common domain through deep nonlinear transformations or by performing transmission and conversion tasks between different domains [13]. These methods share the same core objective of representing the original remote sensing data as deep abstract features prior to comparison [21, 22]. However, traditional frameworks face limitations. In the absence of true labels, they often attempt to mitigate the differences between images by devising transformation or alignment tasks. These can be regarded as auxiliary strategies formulated to facilitate a more effective analysis of heterogeneous images. Unfortunately, this approach leads to overly complex models that lack flexibility. For example, Liu et al. [23] proposed a symmetric convolutional coupling network (SCCN), which adopted a probability map to match the divergence between two images, which needs to repeatedly compare the probability map to refine the classification. Liu et al. [24] applied cycle consistency to obtain the subimage-to-subimage mapping relation, which requires complex image generation and cyclic image-to-image conversion in forward-inverse mapping and inverse-forward mapping way. Wu et al. [12] utilized a convolutional autoencoder (CAE) for feature extraction and then conducted feature transformation based on the abstract features in another commonality autoencoder. Luigi et al. [13] adopted four learning strategies of reconstruction, cycle consistency, weighted translation and code correlation to enforce alignment of the code spaces, whose total loss function can be very complicated. Although the auxiliary strategies mentioned above have been proven to be very effective in the alignment between images, it undoubtedly brings problems that too many tasks make the model enormous and difficult to train, and it is hard to achieve a balance between tasks of network loss training.

Consequently, this section aims to introduce a streamlined framework for heterogeneous CD. One viable approach is to leverage the initial autoencoder (AE) framework to conduct learning in a common domain, thereby generating pseudo labels. Pseudo labels can be described as the maximum predicted probability of a class assigned by a classifier to unlabeled data, and they are utilized as if they were actual true labels [25]. Once the pseudo-label information is obtained, it can be employed to drive a self-guided learning system. In the proposed method, self-guided learning is defined as using the pseudo-labels generated through unsupervised learning to direct the optimization of the network. During iterations, the network is continuously refined using both pseudo-labeled samples and unlabeled samples. By bypassing the need for explicit task formulation, this approach avoids complex auxiliary strategies, resulting in a more streamlined framework. In the field of remote sensing, obtaining labels is challenging. As a result, most of the traditional DNN-based change detection models are unsupervised frameworks. These unsupervised learning networks are mainly focused on the reconstruction or generation of source data. Even when the distance between the features extracted from the two images is reduced through various auxiliary strategies like cycle learning [24], the network's attributes still do not align with the true task, i.e. classification [26, 27]. Therefore, incorporating label guidance into the network can enhance this situation, enabling the network to better discern differences.

Given the lack of true labels, label guidance can be implemented via pseudo-labels. However, it is undeniable that the reliability of the pseudo-labels significantly impacts the performance of the proposed self-guided learning system. Hence, it is essential to enhance the confidence in the available information. The collaborative judgment method serves as an effective means of boosting the confidence of pseudo-labels. Specifically, pseudo-labels are generated under different judgment criteria using various methods. Subsequently, through collaborative analysis, more reliable pseudo-labels with higher confidence levels can be obtained. The main contributions of the proposed framework are as follows:

1. An unsupervised self-guided framework for CD in heterogeneous images is proposed. It can mine the discriminative information of unlabeled samples in an unsupervised manner and optimize pseudo-labels for higher confidence during iterations, which completely avoids label dependency and does not require additional auxiliary strategies to convert two images.
2. A collaborative judgment method is proposed to optimize the selection of reliable pseudo-labels. It can get different but collaborative judgment to prevent the interference of error label information. In addition, to make more efficient use of network computation, features extracted from unsupervised learning will be reused, which meanwhile suppresses the impact of noise on the original images.
3. The effectiveness of the proposed framework is demonstrated on four heterogeneous datasets. In terms of self-guided learning system, modules in the framework can be replaced by methods with similar functions, enhancing the proposed framework's universality and flexibility.

4.1.2 Methodology

4.1.2.1 Problem and Motivation

The change detection task for heterogeneous images typically involves generating a representation of the differences between a pair of RS images captured at different times, t_1 and t_2, over the same area. Due to the substantial variations in image attributes among heterogeneous image pairs, in DNN-based approaches, researchers commonly employ two deep neural networks to handle the heterogeneous images $\boldsymbol{I}_1$ and $\boldsymbol{I}_2$. The detailed implementation process is depicted in Fig. 4.1:

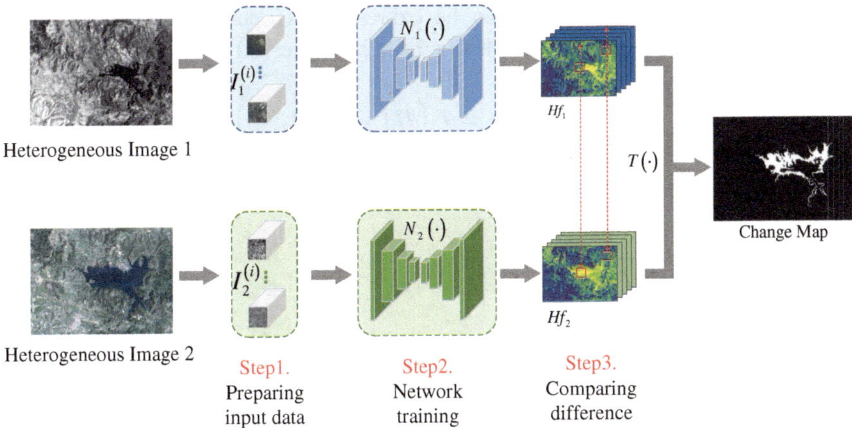

Fig. 4.1 Illustration of the process of change detection in heterogeneous image

The conventional processing flow can be divided into three steps:

- **Step 1. Preparing of Input Data:** For the given images $\boldsymbol{I}_1$ and $\boldsymbol{I}_2$, common registration has been performed to keep the image consistent, thus preventing the influence of registration error. Based on the processing scale of the difference measurement, the level of input data can be categorized into pixel-level, feature-level and object-level [28]. Taking the pixel-level $I^{(i,j)}$ as an example, assuming that the image sizes are $M * N$ with p bands in I_1 and q bands in I_2, the input data are

$$
\begin{aligned}
I_1 &= \left\{ I_1^{(i,j)} \middle| 1 \le i \le M, 1 \le j \le N \right\}, \\
I_2 &= \left\{ I_2^{(i,j)} \middle| 1 \le i \le M, 1 \le j \le N \right\}
\end{aligned}
\tag{4.1}
$$

where $I_1^{(i,j)}$ and $I_2^{(i,j)}$ represent the input data sampled from adjacent windows of p bands in I_1 and q bands in I_2 at (i, j) pixel position, respectively. They are stacked and one pixel has one set of data.
- **Step 2. Network Training:** Generally, two DNN structures of CD in heterogeneous image are basically the same, such as convolution networks and AE networks [12, 13, 23, 24]. Therefore, operation $N(\cdot)$ can be used to represent a trained network that processes each pixel to obtain abstract features $Hf_1{}^{(i,j)}$ and $Hf_2{}^{(i,j)}$:

$$
Hf_1{}^{(i,j)} = N_1\left(I_1{}^{(i,j)}\right), Hf_2{}^{(i,j)} = N_2\left(I_2{}^{(i,j)}\right) \tag{4.2}
$$

- **Step 3. Comparing Difference:** Finally, the difference representation of extracted features can be utilized for analysis, such as calculating the Euclidean distance between pixel pairs [29]. Then, threshold methods can be applied to divide the categories, which can be expressed as operation $T(\cdot)$. The final change detection result of a single pixel can be expressed as follows:

$$CM(i,j) = T\left(Hf_1^{(i,j)}, Hf_2^{(i,j)}\right) \tag{4.3}$$

The final change map is the accumulation of all pixel points:

$$CM = \left\{ \sum_{i,j} CM^{(i,j)} \middle| 1 \le i \le M, 1 \le j \le N \right\} \tag{4.4}$$

Conventional CD frameworks in heterogeneous images typically exist additional intricate conversion and alignment tasks before comparing the differences in step 3 of Fig. 4.1. Furthermore, these additional auxiliary tasks may constrain the network's adaptability to dynamic data variations. Consequently, this section put forward a streamlined framework that incorporates a self-guided learning paradigm. The detailed motivation is elucidated from two principal perspectives:

(1) To Guide the Flow of Identification Information in a Concise Structure

Due to the scarcity of true labels in RS images, the majority of CD frameworks in heterogeneous images are implemented using unsupervised learning. As depicted in Fig. 4.2a, researchers have devised auxiliary strategies, such as transformation and alignment, within the unsupervised network to minimize the differences between heterogeneous images. However, this significantly increases the network's

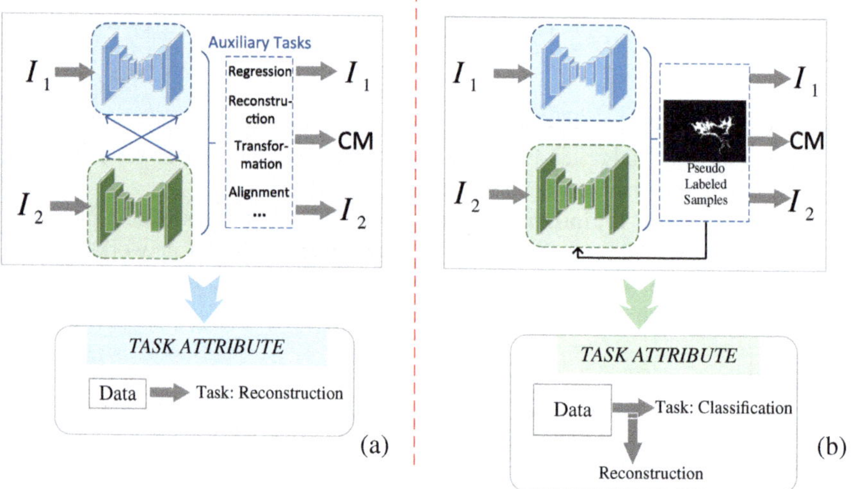

Fig. 4.2 Illustration of comparison of network task attributes: (**a**) traditional way (**b**) proposed way

complexity. Balancing multiple transformation and alignment tasks is challenging, often necessitating extensive manual trial and error.

To circumvent these adverse effects and learn features that are conducive to classification for CD, pseudo-labels are utilized instead of auxiliary strategies. These pseudo-labels guide the feature learning process for CD. Simultaneously, the confidence of the pseudo-labels is enhanced to optimize the network's performance. By constructing the proposed self-guided system, a more concise framework can be established.

Furthermore, when considering the task attributes of the traditional frameworks in the right-hand side of Fig. 4.2a, they are essentially AE networks, which rely on reconstructing I_1 and I_2 into their respective restored forms, I_1' and I_2'. Consequently, the task attribute is to restore the original images as accurately as possible at the decoding output. This results in the retention of sample information and even noise information, which inevitably hinders the extraction of difference features in CD.

Therefore, as illustrated in Fig. 4.2b, the proposed method uses pseudo-label information to replace the complex auxiliary tasks, rendering the network more lightweight. During the operation of the self-guided system, the pseudo-labels are refined through the flow of identification information. As a result, the task attribution gradually shifts more towards classification.

(2) To Obtain Collaborative Judgement and Reuse Abstract Features

Classifiers configured under different judgment criteria can collaborate to minimize generalization errors by maximizing their agreement [30]. As depicted in Fig. 4.3a, obtaining pseudo-labels solely through unsupervised learning can be regarded as a

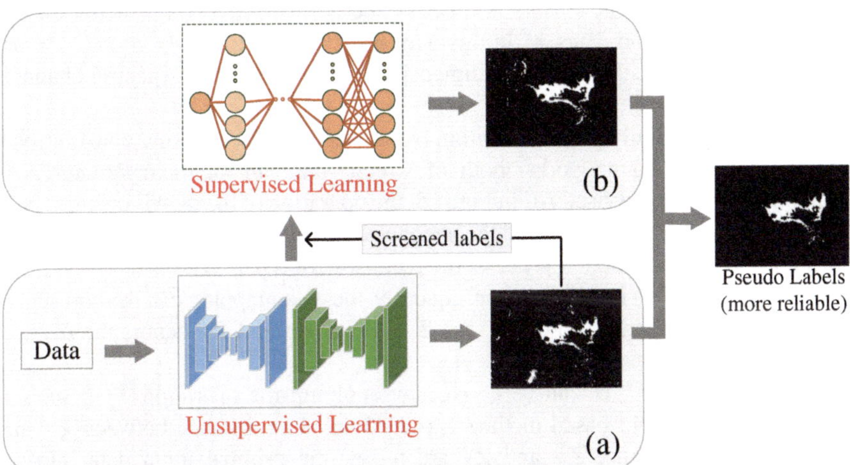

Fig. 4.3 Illustration of comparison of pseudo-labels acquisition: (**a**) unsupervised-only (single judgment); (**b**) supervised-supplemented (collaborative judgment)

single judgment, often lacking high confidence. Consequently, a supervised network is incorporated to supplement the judgment of unsupervised learning as illustrated in Fig. 4.3b. This approach is termed "collaborative judgment" . Evidently, the higher the confidence level of the pseudo results, the more effectively it can prevent the interference of mis-labeled information. Moreover, this effect can accumulate over time.

Furthermore, if the original image is employed as the input data for the supervised classifier, noise can severely impede the classification performance. Hence, it is worthwhile to consider using the features extracted from the initial unsupervised network as the input to the classification network. This not only mitigates the impact of interference in deep learning but also reuses the previously acquired hidden information. To some extent, it enables more efficient utilization of the networks, especially in large networks where features are often discarded after complex training processes.

In summary, unlike traditional CD frameworks for heterogeneous images that rely on complex auxiliary tasks, the proposed framework achieves a concise network structure by eliminating such strategies. Instead, it leverages comprehensive pseudo-label updates to facilitate iterative training, while employing a data-independent self-guided learning system to ensure flexibility.

4.1.2.2 The Data Flow of SGAE

The overview of proposed self-guided autoencoder (SGAE) in show in Fig. 4.4, which includes three modules: unsupervised AE, supervised net, self-guided AE. Taking one iteration as an example, the data flow of SGAE is shown in Fig. 4.5.

Let I_1 and I_2 denote coregistered and resampled RS images captured over the same region by different sensors at times t_1 and t_2, respectively. For better clarity, I_1 is defined as X and I_2 as Y. In this way, $I_1 \in X^{M*N*p}$ and $I_2 \in Y^{M*N*q}$ are obtained. They share the same size dimension, but the number of spectral channels p and q may be different.

Features are initially extracted within two unsupervised denoising convolutional autoencoder (dCAE) networks, both of which share an identical structure. As depicted in the unsupervised AE in Fig. 4.5, the operation of the dCAE network $N(\cdot)$ typically encompasses two stages: the encoder $E(\cdot)$ and the decoder $D(\cdot)$. However, during the feature extraction process, the reconstruction part $D(\cdot)$ is discarded, and only the encoder $E(\cdot)$ is utilized. Consequently, the data mapping can be represented as $E_X(\cdot) : X \rightarrow Z_X$ and $E_Y(\cdot) : Y \rightarrow Z_Y$, where Z_X and Z_Y denote the features extracted within the network.

On one hand, CM_U can be derived by applying the operation $T(\cdot)$, such as clustering or threshold-based methods, to the Euclidean distance between Z_X and Z_Y. On the other hand, Z_X and Z_Y are fed as the original input data into the supervised classification network. Then, CM_S can be obtained via the operation $C(\cdot)$, where a multilayer perceptron (MLP) [31] serves as the classification network. For these two change maps, they are fused together. Specifically, only the inter-

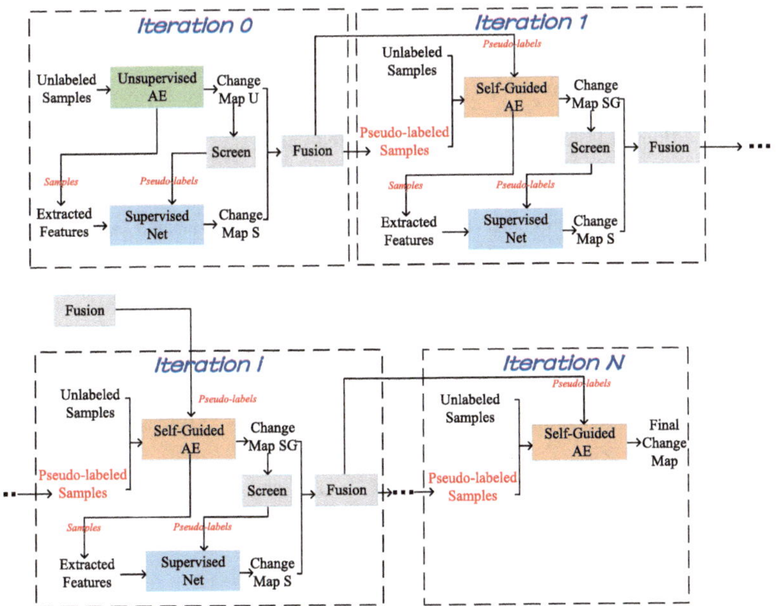

Fig. 4.4 Overview of the proposed SGAE. It includes three main modules: unsupervised AE, supervised AE and self-guided AE. Iterations will be stopped when the classification accuracy is less than the given value

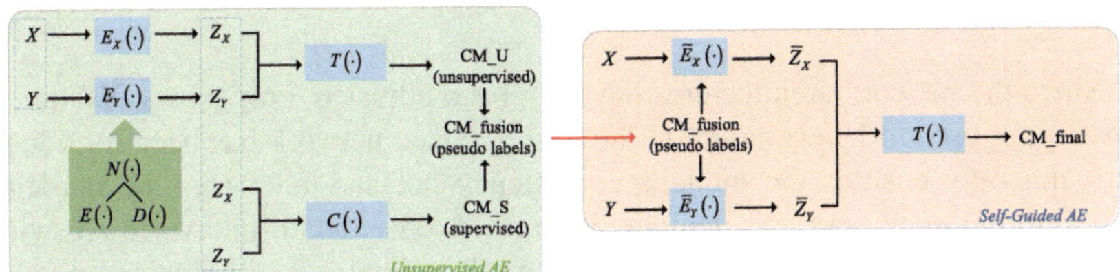

Fig. 4.5 Illustration pf the data flow of SGAE. It shows how the network changes from the unsupervised AE in iteration 0 to the self-guided AE in iteration 1

section of the changed areas is retained, and the remaining regions are designated as the unchanged area. This results in the generation of the pseudo change map CM_fusion, which exhibits a higher confidence level in the changed areas:

$$CM\_fusion = CM\_U \cap CM\_S \tag{4.5}$$

Here, only the implementation of CM_S using an MLP network is presented. In reality, additional judgment mechanisms can be incorporated to generate various pseudo change maps, such as CM_S_1, CM_S_2, etc., which can lead to a more refined CM_fusion. At this point, the first iteration of SGAE is concluded. Subsequently, this is utilized to retrain the dCAE network.

Algorithm 5 SGAE for change detection in heterogeneous images

Require: Remote sensing image datasets X and Y and iteration number N.
Ensure: A final change map CM_final.
Step 1) Iteration 0:
  i. Sample from X and Y to build unlabeled samples $X^{(i,j)}$ and $Y^{(i,j)}$.
  ii. Train the unsupervised AE net to obtain abstract features $Z_X^{(i,j)}$ and $Z_Y^{(i,j)}$ and change map CM_U.
  iii. Screen pseudo-labels from CM_U to obtain pseudo-labeled samples Z_{label}.
  iv. Train the supervised net with $Z_X^{(i,j)}$, $Z_Y^{(i,j)}$ and Z_{label} to obtain CM_S.
  v. Fuse CM_U and CM_S to obtain new pseudo-labeled samples $\bar{Z}_{label}$.
Step 2) Iteration 1-(N-1):
  i. Set $i = 1$ and define CM_SG, CM_S and $\bar{Z}_{label}$ as $(CM\_SG)^i$, $(CM\_S)^i$ and $\left(\bar{Z}_{label}\right)^i$ in iteration i .
while $i \leq (N-1)$ **do**
  ii. Train the self-guided net with unlabeled samples $X^{(i,j)}$ and $Y^{(i,j)}$ and pseudo-labeled samples $\left(\bar{Z}_{label}\right)^i$ to obtain $(CM\_SG)^{i+1}$.
  iii. Screen pseudo-labels from $(CM\_SG)^{i+1}$ and train the supervised net to obtain $(CM\_S)^{i+1}$.
  iv. Fuse $(CM\_SG)^{i+1}$ and $(CM\_S)^{i+1}$ to obtain new pseudo-labeled samples $\left(\bar{Z}_{label}\right)^{i+1}$.
  v. $i = i + 1$.
end while
Step 3) Iteration N:
  i. Train the self-guided net with unlabeled samples $X^{(i,j)}$ and $Y^{(i,j)}$ and pseudo-labeled samples $\left(\bar{Z}_{label}\right)^N$ to obtain CM_final.

Since the network architectures have not been adjusted, only a loss function for classifying pseudo-labels based on the unsupervised network has been introduced. This not only ensures the model's consistency but also alleviates the burden of redesigning the network. As depicted in Fig. 4.4, only the unsupervised AE within the green box has been transformed into the self-guided AE within the orange box. For the self-guided dCAE network augmented with pseudo-labeled information, the data mapping is defined as: $\bar{E}_X(\cdot) : X \rightarrow \bar{Z}_X$ and $\bar{E}_Y(\cdot) : Y \rightarrow \bar{Z}_Y$. Ultimately, the final change map CM_final can be obtained via the Otsu threshold method [32]. It is noteworthy that further iterations can be carried out to enhance the CD performance. However, based on experimental analysis, a single iteration suffices to acquire adequate pseudo-label information. Subsequently, the implementation details of the three modules will be elaborated. The pseudocode of the proposed method is presented in Algorithm 5.

4.1.2.3 Learning of Initial Supervised AE Net

(1) Extracting Features Through Two AE Network In the initial unsupervised network, two dCAE networks of identical structure are employed, each equipped with an encoder and a decoder to respectively carry out the operations of $E(\cdot)$ and $D(\cdot)$, as illustrated in Fig. 4.6.

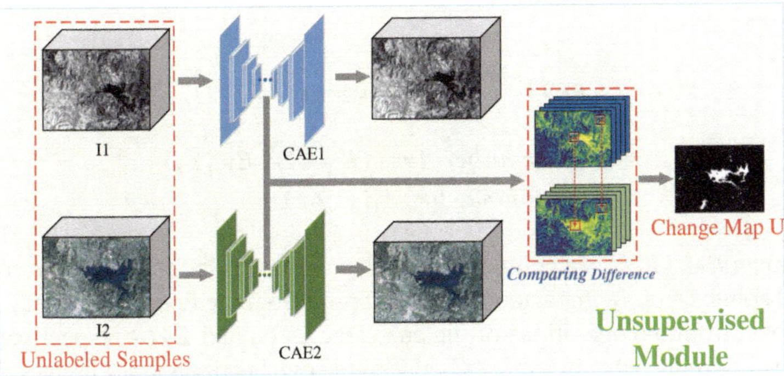

Fig. 4.6 Illustration of the initial unsupervised AE net

For the encoder, its first layer is a convolution layer having a kernel size of 3×3 and a stride of 1. This layer outputs a 20-dimensional feature vector [23], thereby completing an upsampling operation. Subsequently, there are two coupling layers, both with a kernel size of 1×1 and a stride of 1, where the output dimension remains unchanged. Finally, maintaining the same configuration, a coupling layer performs a downsampling process to reduce the feature dimension to 1, thereby preparing the data for the subsequent supervised classification network..

The decoding layer $D(\cdot)$ consists of two coupling layers and a deconvolution layer [12], forming a symmetric structure with the encoder. The first layer of the decoder has an output dimension of 20, and the last layer has an output dimension equal to the number of image channels. The two networks are trained simultaneously and operate independently of each other. Consequently, the loss constraints for data reconstruction are represented by the mean square error between the original data and the reconstructed data:

$$\begin{aligned} L_r(\theta) &= N_X\left(X, \dot{X}\right) + N_Y\left(Y, \dot{Y}\right) \\ &= \sum_{i,j}\left[\left\|X^{(i,j)} - \dot{X}^{(i,j)}\right\|^2 + \left\|Y^{(i,j)} - \dot{Y}^{(i,j)}\right\|^2\right] \end{aligned} \tag{4.6}$$

where $N_X(\cdot)$ and $N_Y(\cdot)$ represent the operation of network training for I_1 and I_2. X and Y are the raw images and $\dot{X}$ and $\dot{Y}$ denote the reconstructed images generated by the decoder.

(2) Mapping Loss to Shorten the Distance Simultaneously, given the substantial disparity between the two images, reducing the distance in the feature space between them is undoubtedly advantageous for facilitating the comparison in change detection. As a result, researchers have devised various task setups to aid in the alignment of the images. For instance, cycle learning can be implemented using the distance between X and $D_X(E_Y(Y))$. To streamline the network architecture and reduce the training burden, only the Huber loss between $E_X(X)$ and $E_Y(Y)$ is utilized to decrease the feature distance. Consequently, the final form of the training loss is:

$$\min L^{AE}(\theta) = L_r(\theta) + \alpha * L_h(\theta) \tag{4.7}$$

$$\begin{aligned} L_h(\theta) &= huber\_loss\left(E_X(X), E_Y(Y)\right) \\ &= huber\_loss\left(Z_X, Z_Y\right) \end{aligned} \tag{4.8}$$

where the $huber\_loss$ is a composite loss that combines the mean square error and mean absolute error. It characterizes the mapping from the feature Z_X to Z_Y, which are derived from the operations of the encoders $E_X(\cdot)$ and $E_Y(\cdot)$ respectively. This loss serves to reduce the differences between the two heterogeneous images. Similar loss functions aimed at minimizing image differences can be substituted. In the proposed approach, it merely acts as a function to help the unsupervised networks in feature extraction. α represents the weighting coefficient of the unsupervised mapping loss, which is determined based on manual experience.

Up to this point, the unsupervised network model has fulfilled the feature extraction function via the encoder $E(\cdot)$, while the decoder $D(\cdot)$ is no longer used. Evidently, other unsupervised models can also be applied here, as the primary goal is to obtain the hidden representation within $E(\cdot)$. After applying the Otsu thresholding operation, the pixel positions corresponding to changes are assigned a value of 1, and those representing unchanged positions are set to 0. Consequently, the final change map can be generated.

4.1.2.4 Learning of Supervised Classification Net

It is crucial to emphasize that the supervised classification network is designed to implement the modular function of collaborative judgment. This section focuses exclusively on fully-connected networks. Nevertheless, additional judgment methods can be incorporated, such as diverse sample-selection strategies and different classifiers. They can be learned from ensemble learning [33], which is another research field. The subsequent sections introduce the supervised classification network.

(1) Preparing of Input Data and Label Information Through the encoding layer of the unsupervised network, the extracted features Z_X and Z_Y, along with the pseudo-change map CM_U, can be acquired. Given that the final layer of the encoding layer is a reduced dimension representation with an output dimension of 1, a single original pixel $I_1^{(i,j)}$, $I_2^{(i,j)}$ corresponds to features $Z_X^{(i,j)}$, $Z_Y^{(i,j)}$, where $1 \le i \le M$ and $1 \le j \le N$. Consequently, for these two features, pixel vector pairs are obtained through adjacent-window extraction for each pixel point. Subsequently, these pairs are concatenated to form the final input data. Moreover, only the samples for which the pseudo-labels of the surrounding pixels obtained from adjacent window extraction are consistent with the pseudo-label of the central pixel are selected. This sample-selection approach ensures that the classification

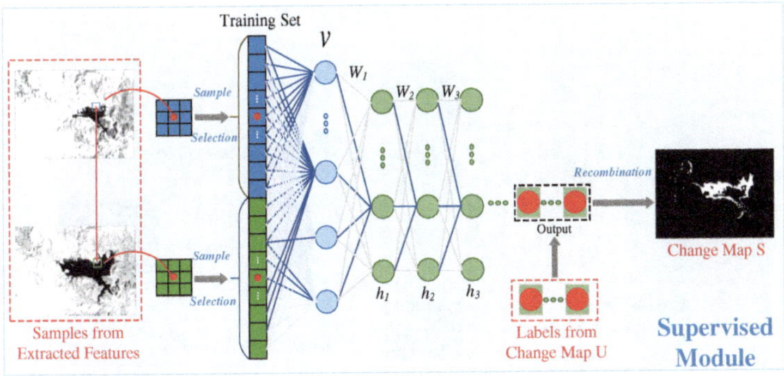

Fig. 4.7 Illustration of the supervised classification network

performed by the supervised network is not merely an approximation of the result obtained from the unsupervised AE.

(2) Classification of Fully-Connected Network As depicted in Fig. 4.7, the input data are fed into a fully-connected network featuring two hidden layers. Subsequently, this network is linked to the final classification layer, which has a dimension of 2. The cross-entropy loss between the output of the network and the label information of the pseudo change map is optimized using the back-propagation algorithm. Here, the label information 0 is extended to 01, and the label information 1 is extended to 10. Consequently, the loss form of the supervised classification network is derived as follows:

$$\begin{aligned} \min L^C(\theta) &= C\left(Z, Z_{label}\right) \\ &= \sum_{i,j}\left[-{Z_{label}}^{(i,j)} \log\left(Z^{(i,j)}\right)\right. \\ &\quad \left.+\left(1-{Z_{label}}^{(i,j)}\right)\log\left(1-Z^{(i,j)}\right)\right] \end{aligned} \tag{4.9}$$

where Z is the processed features with adjacent window extraction and combination in Z_X and Z_Y. Z_{label} is its labels, which are utilized for the supervised learning.

Finally, via the classification layer, the pseudo change map CM_S is obtained. The changed area of CM_S is then intersected with that of CM_U to yield the fused pseudo change map CM_fusion. Evidently, the detection of changed areas in CM_fusion is relatively weak since its confidence judgment is more stringent. This collaborative judgment approach aims to mitigate the false detection of unchanged areas. As positive samples, unchanged areas can have a more deleterious impact on network learning.

Simultaneously, the structure of the classification network significantly influences the classification performance. The two-layer fully-connected network employed here is designed based on empirical knowledge. Similar to the supervised network, the classification network can also be substituted with other comparable supervised learners.

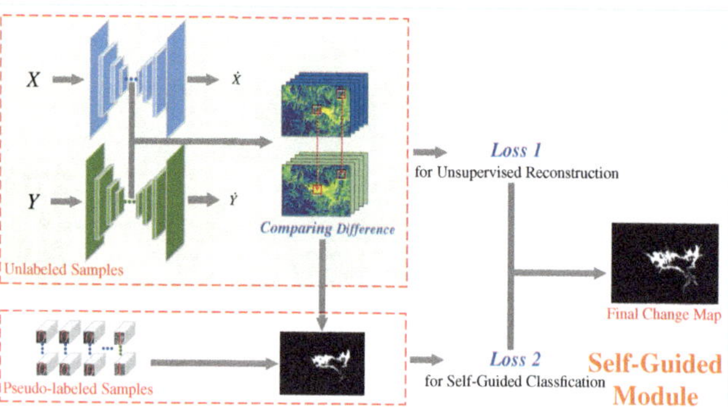

Fig. 4.8 Illustration of the self-guided AE network

4.1.2.5 Learning of Iterative Self-Guided AE Net

(1) Details in SGAE After the first iteration of the unsupervised AE network and the supervised classification network, the structure of the AE network remains unaltered. Only the learning mode of the network has been optimized, as depicted in Fig. 4.8. The features $\bar{Z}_X$ and $\bar{Z}_Y$ are not regarded as the new input for the AE. This is because the AE still needs to fulfill the reconstruction task. Although the abstract features eliminate noise and other interferences, they also disrupt the rich pixel and spatial information present in the original image.

(2) Retraining of AE Under Pseudo-Label Guidance Pseudo-label information is added by calculating the mean square error of the result of the Euclidean distance between the features $\bar{Z}_X$ and $\bar{Z}_Y$ with CM_fusion:

$$\min L^{SGAE}(\theta) = L_r(\theta) + \alpha * L_h(\theta) + \beta * L_n(\theta) \tag{4.10}$$

$$\begin{aligned} L_n(\theta) &= SG\left(\bar{Z}, \bar{Z}_{label}\right) \\ &= \sum_{i,j} \left\| \bar{Z}^{(i,j)} - \bar{Z}_{label}^{(i,j)} \right\|^2 \end{aligned} \tag{4.11}$$

where $SG(\cdot)$ denotes the operation of the self-guided network. $\bar{Z}$ represents the input data, which are I_1 and I_2, and $\bar{Z}_{label}$ is the labeled data. These are employed to specifically characterize the self-guided learning system in SGAE. β is the weighting coefficient of this system, determined through manual experience. It should be noted that α is already fixed at this stage since the classification task is the primary objective. Thus, the only parameter that requires adjustment is the weighting coefficient β.

The final change map is also derived through threshold-based judgment. Certainly, these iterations can be continued to further enhance the classification accuracy. However, experiments have demonstrated that the guidance function provided by the pseudo-label information can be essentially satisfied within two iterations.

In conclusion, the optimization of task attributes within the AE network is accomplished, and features are reused to boost the utilization rate of network information. It is important to note that the loss learning of the three networks is conducted independently in stages. This approach differs from the traditional CD framework for heterogeneous images, which typically involves the total optimization of the sum of numerous auxiliary strategies. Additionally, the three modules, consisting of the initial AE networks for obtaining elementary results, the supervised networks for collaborative judgment, and the self-guided AE networks for mining pseudo-labeled information, can be substituted with methods having similar functions. This is because such substitutions will not disrupt the proposed self-guided learning system.

4.1.3 Experimental Study

Four RS image datasets are put to the test, with their sources and sizes presented in Table 4.1. Each pair of images has undergone radiometric correction and co-registration to guarantee maximum comparability. These datasets span a diverse range of geographic regions and imaging modalities, incorporating multispectral, optical, and SAR imagery. The performance of the proposed framework is quantitatively assessed using a set of standard metrics, including Overall Accuracy (OA), the Kappa coefficient κ, the F1-score, and the Area Under the Curve (AUC). All these metrics are computed by comparing the predicted change map with the ground truth at the pixel level. More detailed information regarding the dataset description and metric definition can be found in Chap. 2.

4.1.3.1 Experimental Setup

(1) Setting of Unsupervised dCAE Network The unsupervised network framework is a fully convolutional neural network. It consists of four encoding layers: $Conv(3 \times 3 \times 20) - ReLU - Coup(1 \times 1 \times 20) - ReLU - Coup(1 \times 1 \times 20) - ReLU - Coup(1 \times 1 \times 1) - Sigmoid$, and two decoding layers: $Coup(1 \times 1 \times$

Table 4.1 Introduction to four test datasets

Dataset	Image 1	Image 2
D1: California	Multispectral (875×500×11)	SAR (875×500×3)
D2: Italy	Near Infrared (412×300×1)	Optical (412×300×3)
D3: Shuguang	SAR (549×411×1)	Optical (549×411×3)
D4: Yellow River	SAR (291×343×1)	Optical (291×343×1)

20) $- ReLU - Coup(1 \times 1 \times p$ or $1 \times 1 \times q) - Tanh$. Here, $3 \times 3 \times 20$ indicates that the kernel size is 3×3 and the output dimension is 20. Before being fed into the network, the original data is normalized within the range from -1 to 1. Finally, the Adam optimizer is chosen to minimize the loss over 350 epochs, with a learning rate of 10^{-4}.

(2) Setting of Supervised MLP Classification Network The input of the supervised network is based on 9-dimensional feature vectors extracted from 3×3 adjacent windows. These vectors are then tiled and combined to ultimately obtain the input data with a dimension of 18×1. The size of the adjacent window is set manually. If it is too small, there will be insufficient spatial information; conversely, if it is too large, there may be excessive interference from boundary pixels. For instance, when a pixel is at the changed boundary, its adjacent window block contains both the changed and unchanged areas. In the experiment, it is set to 3×3 based on experience.

(3) Comparison Methods and Implementation Details To validate the effectiveness of the proposed method, several representative change detection methods are compared, including RFR [34], a ResNet-based classification network [35], an MLP-based classification network [36], CAN [37], SCCN [23], ACE-Net [38], and X-Net [38]. Among them, RFR, ResNet, and MLP are implemented in a supervised setting, using 60% of the ground-truth labels for training. The remaining methods follow the unsupervised or weakly-supervised protocols as described in their original works. For a fair comparison, all baseline methods adopt the experimental configurations recommended in [38], with the exception that the training epochs for ACE-Net and X-Net are limited to 60 due to hardware constraints. All experiments are carried out on a machine equipped with an Intel(R) Core(TM) i5-1035G1 CPU @ 1.00 GHz (1.19 GHz boost), 16 GB RAM, and run on Python 3.6.10 with TensorFlow 1.4.

4.1.3.2 Performance of SGAE Compared with Other Methods

(1) D1—Flood in California For the California dataset, the change detection results are shown in Fig. 4.9 and the test metrics are displayed in Table 4.2. As can be observed from Fig. 4.9, the supervised methods of RFR, ResNet, and MLP all exhibit severe overfitting. Consequently, numerous unchanged areas are misclassified as changed areas, which are highlighted in green. In contrast, among the unsupervised methods, there are numerous instances where changed areas remain undetected, marked in red. Specifically, SCCN misidentifies a large number of regions as changed in the rural part of the raw images in the lower-right corner. However, this issue is unique to this dataset. Due to the large size of the California dataset, a downsampling operation is carried out when it is fed into the network for processing. As a result, the image appears a certain zigzag shape, adding challenges to change detection. Furthermore, at the boundaries between changed and unchanged areas, ACE-Net and X-Net encounter difficulties in detection due

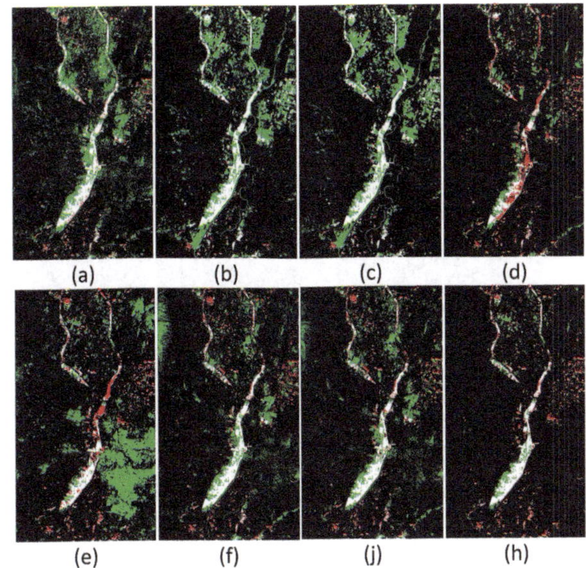

Fig. 4.9 Change detection results of D1—Flood in California achieved by (**a**) RFR, (**b**) Resnet, (**c**) MLP, (**d**) CAN, (**e**) SCCN, (**f**) ACE-Net, (**g**) X-Net, (**h**) proposed. (*TP* white, *TN* black, *FP* green, *FN* red)

Table 4.2 Experimental results of D1—Flood in California

D1	Methods	Metrics					
		FP	FN	OA	κ	F1	AUC
Supervised	RFR	61,399	6573	0.845	0.311	0.374	0.871
	Resnet	53,529	2124	0.873	0.418	0.471	0.916
	MLP	50,796	2491	0.878	0.426	0.478	0.918
Unsupervised	ACE-Net	34,767	9795	0.898	0.385	0.434	0.875
	CAN	17,241	15,598	0.925	0.368	0.408	0.858
	SCCN	60,163	15,201	0.828	0.162	0.237	0.700
	X-Net	31,837	10,207	0.904	0.395	0.443	0.879
	Proposed	8868	11,781	0.953	0.570	0.594	0.899

to the presence of fine and misclassified pixels. Across the entire image, these fine, misclassified points are also prevalent. To a certain degree, the downsampling operation discards some spatial and spectral information, exacerbating this misdetection problem. As demonstrated in Table 4.2, the proposed method achieved the best results in terms of OA, the κ, and the F1-score, with the lowest FP coefficient. This validates the effectiveness of the proposed method.

(2) D2—Lake Overflow in Italy For Italy dataset, the change detection results are shown in Fig. 4.10 and test metrics are displayed in Table 4.3. It can be noticed that the detection of the D2 dataset presents two major challenges. Firstly, the lower-half of the changed area is extremely slender. This causes nearly all methods to fail in detecting this changed area, which is indicated in red. However, in the supervised methods, both ResNet and MLP exhibit a more pronounced over-fitting

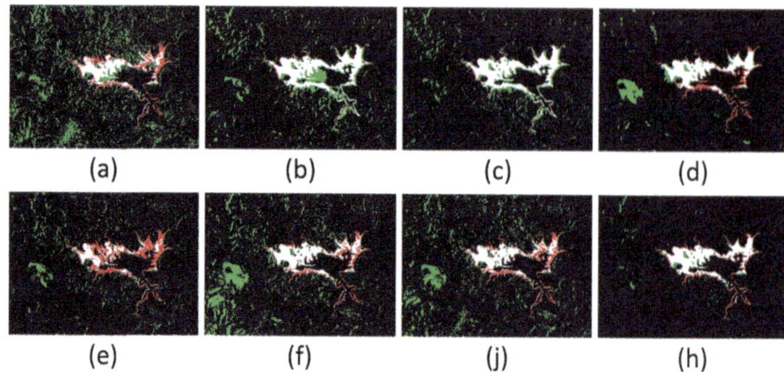

Fig. 4.10 Change detection results of D2—Lake overflow in Italy achieved by (**a**) RFR, (**b**) Resnet, (**c**) MLP, (**d**) CAN, (**e**) SCCN, (**f**) ACE-Net, (**g**) X-Net, (**h**) proposed. (*TP* white, *TN* black, *FP* green, *FN* red)

Table 4.3 Experimental results of D2—lake overflow in Italy

D2	Methods	Metrics					
		FP	FN	OA	κ	F1	AUC
Supervised	RFR	13,980	2776	0.864	0.306	0.367	0.866
	Resnet	8085	689	0.929	0.578	0.613	0.959
	MLP	5529	652	0.950	0.667	0.693	0.971
Unsupervised	CAN	3291	2203	0.956	0.640	0.664	0.922
	SCCN	3947	4456	0.932	0.394	0.430	0.844
	ACE-Net	9543	2294	0.904	0.427	0.474	0.894
	X-Net	7861	2826	0.914	0.429	0.473	0.872
	Proposed	1258	1925	0.974	0.768	0.782	0.955

tendency in the changed region. As a result, their change maps have almost no undetected changed pixels marked in red, as clearly reflected by the lowest FP value in Table 4.3. Secondly, there is the issue of noise interference. The proposed method manages to avoid false detection, as can be seen from the land terrain in the left-hand half of the images. Due to varying imaging mechanisms, the land geomorphic areas covered with green plants severely disrupt the detection process. Ultimately, although the FN coefficient of the proposed method is not the lowest, it still attains the best values for OA, κ, and other metrics. This showcases the effectiveness and superiority of the proposed approach.

(3) D3—Farmland in Shuguang For the Shuguang dataset, the change detection results are presented in Fig. 4.11, and the test metrics are shown in Table 4.4. As depicted in Fig. 4.11e, f, horizontal and vertical lines of the changed area respectively appear in their change detection results. Thus, the challenge in detecting the Shuguang dataset stems from the fact that I_1 and I_2 feature different geomorphic types within the same changed areas. This causes algorithms to tend to fit one of the landforms, leading to inaccurate detection results. In the supervised methods,

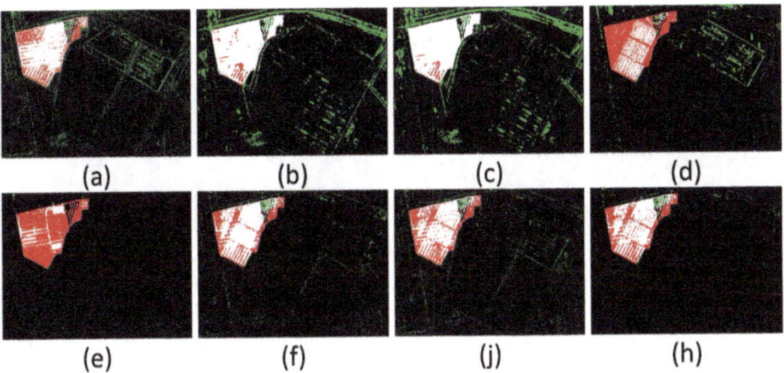

Fig. 4.11 Change detection results of D3—Farmland in Shuguang achieved by (**a**) RFR, (**b**) Resnet, (**c**) MLP, (**d**) CAN, (**e**) SCCN, (**f**) ACE-Net, (**g**) X-Net, (**h**) proposed. (*TP* white, *TN* black, *FP* green, *FN* red)

Table 4.4 Experimental results of D3—Farmland in Shuguang

D3	Methods	Metrics					
		FP	FN	OA	κ	F1	AUC
Supervised	RFR	16,234	4727	0.907	0.575	0.626	0.940
	Resnet	19,485	1369	0.908	0.618	0.667	0.949
	MLP	21,577	801	0.901	0.606	0.657	0.945
Unsupervised	CAN	6872	12,832	0.913	0.443	0.489	0.872
	SCCN	195	17,452	0.922	0.327	0.351	0.788
	ACE-Net	3706	5773	0.958	0.753	0.776	0.967
	X-Net	6096	7050	0.942	0.666	0.698	0.953
	Proposed	1434	7274	0.961	0.754	0.775	0.950

since 60% of the labeled samples can basically meet the differential assimilation of different landforms, the detection performances of RFR, ResNet, and MLP are relatively better to some extent. Among the unsupervised methods, aside from the CAN method, the others exhibit a distinct under-fitting phenomenon. These methods sacrifice the detection of the changed region to enhance the overall algorithm performance, meaning they prefer to miss detections rather than make incorrect detections. Consequently, their FN coefficients are quite high. In the case of the CAN method, it is evident that it has a stronger bias to fit I_1, resulting in a prominent display of the original landform type of I_1. Moreover, there is a hollow-shaped unchanged area in the upper-right corner of the changed area, where the detection performance of all methods is rather poor. However, when compared with ACE-Net, considering the balance between the FP and FN coefficients, the proposed method ultimately achieves the best performance in terms of OA and κ.

(4) D4—Flood in Yellow River For Yellow River dataset, the change detection results are shown in Fig. 4.12 and test metrics are displayed in Table 4.5. From Fig. 4.12i, it can be seen that the changed area of the Yellow River forms an S-

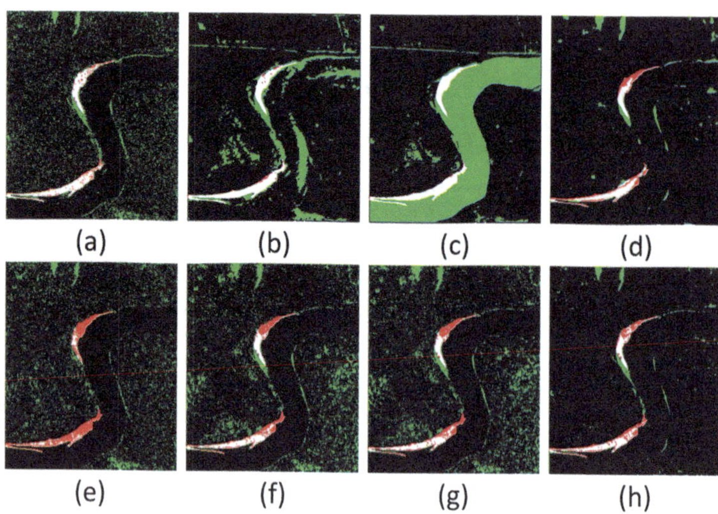

Fig. 4.12 Change detection results of D4—Flood in Yellow River achieved by (**a**) RFR, (**b**) Resnet, (**c**) MLP, (**d**) CAN, (**e**) SCCN, (**f**) ACE-Net, (**g**) X-Net, (**h**) proposed. (*TP* white, *TN* black, *FP* green, *FN* red)

Table 4.5 Experimental results of D4—Flood in Yellow River

D4	Methods	Metrics					
		FP	FN	OA	κ	F1	AUC
Supervised	RFR	8527	674	0.908	0.318	0.351	0.917
	Resnet	9080	328	0.906	0.343	0.376	0.947
	MLP	24,269	162	0.755	0.149	0.197	0.867
Unsupervised	CAN	2370	1447	0.962	0.454	0.474	0.922
	SCCN	6958	2363	0.907	0.107	0.147	0.737
	ACE-Net	8628	1464	0.899	0.214	0.252	0.838
	X-Net	5945	1393	0.927	0.294	0.326	0.868
	Proposed	1831	1417	0.968	0.502	0.519	0.927

shaped curve, representing the flood-related changes in the Yellow River. However, the imaging mechanisms for representing the river in I_1 and I_2 are nearly opposite. As a result, there are severe misdetection issues in such marginal changed areas. The most prominent example is that the two sharp-corner areas in the top-right corner of each change map in Fig. 4.12 should not be part of the flood-detection range. Due to the inconsistency in the regions of I_1, over-fitting occurs in the detection results. Furthermore, since the river is not a continuously connected changed area while being physically continuous, most algorithms struggle to perform the required cut-off detection. This makes it difficult to eliminate the green-colored area in the middle part. Similarly, by balancing the FP and FN coefficients in Table 4.5, the proposed algorithm attains the best detection performance in terms of OA, κ, F1-score and AUC.

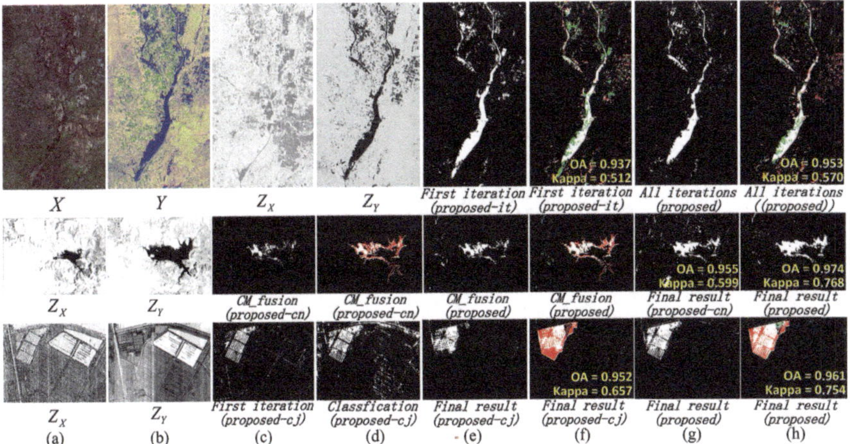

Fig. 4.13 Display of results in ablation experiments. The first line represents the comparison of proposed-it and SGAE. The second line represents the comparison of proposed-cn and SGAE. The third line represents the comparison of proposed-cj and SGAE. Different datasets are exhibited for comparison to show fairness. (*TP* white, *TN* black, *FP* green, *FN* red)

4.1.4 Ablation Study

The effectiveness of three main strategies proposed in SGAE will be verified in this subsection.

(1) Proposed-It (Iterative Training in Self-Guided Way) As an iterative framework, SGAE can perform repeated training. But only in the first iteration, it is a pure unsupervised framework composed of the basic AE network. The subsequent iterations are trained through self-guided AE networks with pseudo-labeled information after collaborative judgment. To verify the effectiveness of iterations, the results of the first iteration and the last iteration is compared in this part.

As shown in the first line of Fig. 4.13, Z_x in (c) and Z_y in (d) are the hidden features extracted from autoencoders, which take one of the dimensions for presentation. In the last four figures of (e)–(h), it shows that the values of OA and Kappa all have a certain increase, because the proportion of FN has decreased, which is shown in reduction of red scatter. With more available pesudo labeld during iterations, FP in green scatter also disappeared a lot. It demonstrates that the labeled guidance information can make SGAE take into account the strong fitting effect of supervised methods. Consequently, the guidance information derived from pseudo-labels can be expanded and purified in the self-guided way, thereby optimizing the performance of network for change detection.

(2) Proposed-cn (Different Inputs for Classification Network) For the classification network, the features extracted from the initial AE network are used as the input, which makes better use of the complex trained network. Therefore, to verify

Table 4.6 Test metrics in ablation experiments

Metric	Proposed	Proposed-it	Proposed-cn	Proposed-cj
D3—Farmland in Shuguang				
OA	0.961	0.934	0.955	0.952
Kappa	0.754	0.546	0.695	0.657
F1	0.775	0.579	0.718	0.681
AUC	0.950	0.842	0.946	0.944
D4—Flood in Yellow River				
OA	0.968	0.947	0.963	0.952
Kappa	0.502	0.247	0.450	0.288
F1	0.519	0.274	0.469	0.313
AUC	0.927	0.813	0.905	0.856

the effectiveness of using extracted features, the raw data (I_1 and I_2) and the abstract features are input into the classification network, respectively, to explore whether the features are more conducive to classification than the original data after suppressing the interference.

As illustrated in the second row of Fig. 4.13, Z_x in (c) and Z_y in (d) demonstrate that the two heterogeneous images are converted to the common domain in network learning for direct comparison. It can be observed that the CM_fusion of proposed-cn obviously fails to detect more changed areas, resulting in less pseudo-label information available in Fig. 4.13c. This also results in a significant number of wrong-detected areas in the final output of proposed-cn, attributed to an under-fitting effect caused by insufficient discriminative information. Since there are almost no false positive samples, the coefficient of FN increases substantially. This phenomenon is visually evidenced by the reduction in red scatter points, ultimately leading to poor detection performance.

(3) Proposed-cj (Collaborative Judgment to Screen Pseudo-labels) To verify the effectiveness of the collaborative judgment for pseudo-label screening, this part compares the effect of the pseudo change map obtained only by the AE network and the pseudo change map obtained by the collaborative judgment when they are input to the self-guided AE network in the next iteration.

The third line of Fig. 4.13 showsthe obvious over-fitting phenomenon in proposed-cj. Similar to the limited detection capability of the fused change map in proposed-cn, numerous changed regions remain undetected, as illustrated in (c) and (d). In contrast, SGAE incorrectly identifies unchanged pixels in the upper-right corner of the changed region as changes. However, after collaborative judgment, the FP rate is significantly mitigated.

Finally, take the D3 dataset and D4 dataset as examples, Table 4.6 shows the numerical results of the three strategies. The integration of all strategies demonstrates that the proposed method achieves superior performance.

4.1.5 Conclusions

In this section, a framework of self-guided autoencoders (SGAE) is presented for unsupervised change detection in heterogeneous remote sensing images. Unlike traditional CD models that rely on numerous additional auxiliary strategies, such as transformation and alignment, the proposed model is a simple yet effective network with a concise structure. Its primary objective is to extract discriminative features that guide the network's learning process for change detection. Moreover, it continuously enhances the confidence of pseudo-labels to optimize the utilization of available effective information. The flow of effective identification information is independent of data, ensuring the flexibility of this framework.

Specifically, the basic AE network serves as a common feature extractor to conduct the unsupervised classification. Based on the initial change map derived from the AE, a certain number of pseudo-labelled samples are screened to train the supervised network, forming collaborative judgements and obtaining the fused change map. After intersection, the fused results with higher confidence are re-input into the self-guided AE with training of pseudo-labeled samples and unlabeled samples. Specially, modules in such a self-guided learning system can be replaced by methods with similar functions, showing the excellent universality of the proposed method.

It should be noted that in the proposed self-guided learning system, the negative migration effect of misclassified labeled samples cannot be overlooked. Hence, it is worthwhile to incorporate more remedial measures into the framework to boost the confidence of pseudo-labels. This could be a central focus of the future work.

4.2 Multi-layer Composite Autoencoders for Semi-supervised Heterogeneous Remote Sensing Images Change Detection

4.2.1 Introduction

With the increasing complexity of application scenarios, the fusion of different remote sensing data types has gradually become a trend, which can greatly improve the utilization of massive remote sensing data.[2]

While the problem of change detection for heterogeneous remote images can be much more complicated than the traditional change detection for homologous remote sensing images, there are huge differences between heterogeneous images caused by factors such as the light sensitivity, object reflection properties, etc. [12,

[2] **Acknowledgement**: Reprinted from *Science China Information Sciences*, 66(4), Jiao Shi, Tiancheng Wu, Hanwen Yu, A. K. Qin, Gwanggil Jeon, Yu Lei, Multi-layer composite autoencoders for semi-supervised change detection in heterogeneous remote sensing images, 140308, Copyright (2023), with permission from Springer Nature.

39]. So the common methods are meant to align the images from two different domains and then compare the original data in the common domain to highlight the difference [21].

However, most traditional heterogeneous change detection frameworks have complex alignment tasks due to their unique design [13, 24]. However, these additional auxiliary tasks will deepen the network's complexity, and it is difficult to balance multiple tasks such as the mentioned loss learning of cycle consistency, weighted translation, etc.

Therefore, it is hoped to propose a concise network framework. One method is to use a small amount of label information to spread its guiding role in network learning. Thus, it is not required to complete the additional tasks of transformation and alignment of two images in the model. On the other hand, by making more use of the discriminant difference information extracted from the traditional framework that has not been fully utilized, it can complete the difference learning only by mapping the labeled samples, avoiding complex additional operations.

4.2.2 Methodology

Figure 4.14 shows the structure of proposed multi-layer composite autoencoders (MLCAE) for change detection:

Step 1 For heterogeneous images, two AE networks with same set are used to extract discriminative features of $I1$ and $I2$. It completes the reconstruction of unsupervised data. In this way, their identification information will be more prominent in hidden higher-order space. So the unsupervised loss is shown as follows:

$$L_u(\theta) = N_{I1}\left(I1, \dot{I1}\right) + N_{I2}\left(I2, \dot{I2}\right) \tag{4.12}$$

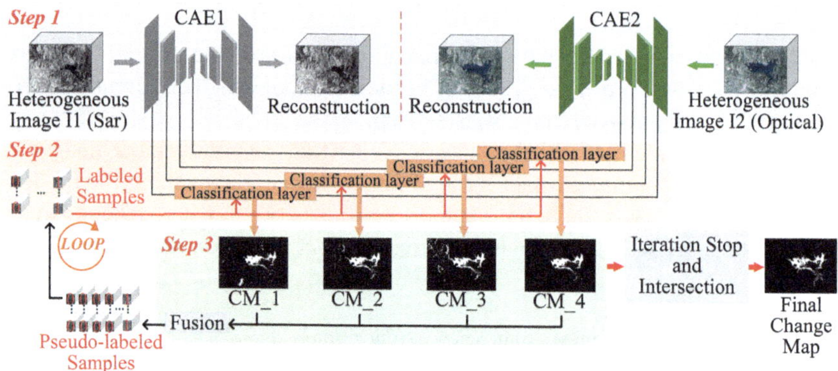

Fig. 4.14 Overview of the proposed MLCAE

where $N_{I1}(\cdot)$ and $N_{I2}(\cdot)$ represent the operation of network training to $I1$ and $I2$ respectively, which are $CAE1$ and $CAE2$ in Step 1 of Fig. 4.4. $\dot{I}1$ and $\dot{I}2$ are the output of the decoder, which are meant for reconstruction. It represents the unsupervised part of MLCAE.

Step 2 The combination of multi-layer composite features is carried out in the multi-layer outputs, which are CM_1, CM_2, CM_3, CM_4. To obtain independent change detection results, each corresponding layer of the two AE networks will be combined to connect a classification layer:

$$\begin{aligned} L_s(\theta) = & -I_{label} \log(Z) \\ & + (1 - I_{label}) \log(1 - Z) \end{aligned} \tag{4.13}$$

where Z is the extracted high-order features in the process of unsupervised learning in Step 2 of Fig. 4.14 and I_{label} are the true-labels, being used for the supervised learning in comparison to Z. The supervised loss is the classical cross entropy loss.

So the total training loss can be expressed as follows:

$$\min L(\theta) = L_u(\theta) + \sum_{i=1}^{4} L_s^i(\theta) \tag{4.14}$$

where $L_s^1(\theta)$, $L_s^2(\theta)$, $L_s^3(\theta)$, $L_s^4(\theta)$ represent the losses of the classification layer connected to each layer of the encoders. Although network training appears to have many losses, it does not require any additional manual parameter settings because it is a mapping of label information.

Step 3 After voting of multiple change detection results from multi-layer composite features, the pseudo-labeled samples with higher confidence are selected, which is shown in Step 3 of Fig. 4.14. And it is re-added to the 0.1% true-labeled training samples to obtain a new training data set to re-train the network. By adding high-confidence pseudo-labeled samples, it can not only avoid the over-fitting problem caused by a small number of true-labeled samples but also mine the information of unlabeled samples more effectively, optimizing the process of change detection.

Finally, when the change degree of the pseudo-labeled training sample is less than a fixed value, the iteration can be stopped. From the experimental results, generally, the global label pool can be diffused after one iteration of the pseudo-labels, and the final change map can be output.

4.2.3 Experimental Study

Similar to Sect. 4.1.3, the experimental evaluation is conducted on four widely used heterogeneous remote sensing image pairs: California, Italy, Shuguang, and the Yellow River. All image pairs have undergone radiometric correction and co-registration to ensure maximum comparability, and each dataset is accompanied by a manually annotated ground truth map. The proposed framework is quantitatively assessed using six standard metrics: False Positives (FP), False Negatives (FN), Overall Accuracy (OA), Kappa coefficient κ, F1-score, and Area Under the Curve (AUC).

4.2.3.1 Experimental Setup

(1) Processing Flow The proposed framework uses a small number of labeled samples to complete the initial detection task, and then captures the difference information of optimized features in a large number of unlabeled data. By filtering with high confidence selection, large amount of new pseudo labeled data set can be obtained in multi-layer composite judgment and then be added to the original true-labeled training set to form new training set. Finally, the final change detection result is iteratively optimized to attain.

The iteration can be stopped when the change degree of the pseudo-labeled training sample is less than a fixed value. The fixed value is set by artificial experience according to the experimental results. Specifically, the degree of change refers to the number change of pseudo-labeled samples and the position repetition of the screened pixels. In the experiment, the number of labels screened after one iteration is usually about 90%, and the pixel position repeats greatly with the second iteration, so the network can basically complete the final output after one iteration

In addition, when the pixel position of the vote is consistent with the position of a true label, the label value of the true label will be directly retained, regardless of whether the result of the pseudo label voting is consistent. When there is no true label of one position, the pixel will vote for screening.

(2) Network Parameters The proposed framework is composited of two autoencoders(AE). Each AE is a fully convolution neural networks, composed of four encoding layers: $Conv(3*3*20) - ReLU - Coup(1*1*20) - ReLU - Coup(1*1*20) - ReLU - Coup(1*1*1) - Sigmoid$. At the same time, the decoder has the opposite structure. The learning rate is 10e-4, batch size is 1000, epoch set is 100, weight decay is 0.9, and optimizer is based on Adam algorithm. The experiments are performed on Intel(R) Core(TM) i7-4790 CPU @3.60GHz 3.60 GHz with 16 GB of RAM. Tensorflow 1.4 framework with Python 3.6.10 is as the programing language.

(3) Comparison Methods and Implementation Details The metrics of FP, FN, OA, κ, F1 and AUC will be shown in the exhibition compared with unsupevised methods of SCCN [23], ACE-Net [38] and X-Net [38], supervised methods of RFR [34], classification network based on Resnet [35] and classification network based on multilayer perceptron (MLP) [36] and semi-supervised method of Semi-GAN [40]. Besides, in experiments, a systematic comparison of the classification performance between pure supervised and semi-supervised methods was conducted under the same 60% label quantity.

And the experiment of 0.1% label quantity is used to prove that, due to the scarcity of true labels in the remote sensing field, the compared unsupervised models are able to get rid of the label dependency of remote sensing images. And though the proposed model is a semi-supervised network, it only needs 0.1% labeled training samples. So the cost of labeled samples is similar to the unsupervised one. Specially, the experimental result of 0.1% label amount is the result of the minimum label amount that combines the algorithm cost and the experimental performance. The other experimental setup of the comparison algorithms is consistent with Luigi er al. proposed in [38]. But the training epoches of ACE-Net and X-Net were set to 60 due to the limitation from the test platform.

4.2.3.2 Experimental Results

(1) D1—Flood in California For California dataset, the change detection results are shown in Fig. 4.15 and test metrics are displayed in Table 4.7. From the comparison between unsupervised methods and supervised methods, it is obvious that unsupervised methods such as SCCN, ACE-Net and X-Net do not have the guidance of true-labeled samples, so a large number of red undetected areas appear in the changed areas. Other methods with labels have a large number of

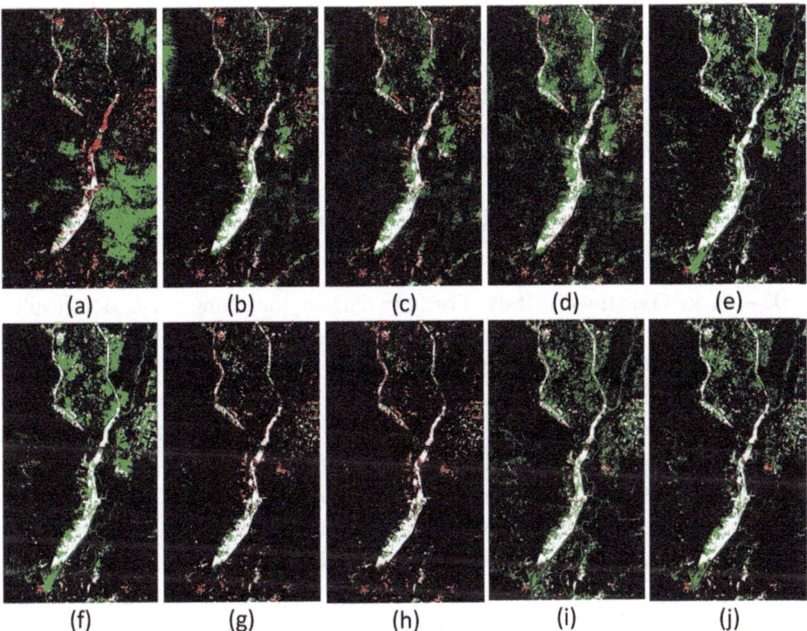

Fig. 4.15 Change detection results of D1—Flood in California achieved by (**a**) SCCN, (**b**) ACE-Net, (**c**) X-Net, (**d**) RFR, (**e**) Resnet, (**f**) MLP, (**g**) Semi-GAN (60%), (**h**) proposed (60%), (**i**) Semi-GAN (0.1%) and (**j**) proposed (0.1%). (*TP* white, *TN* black, *FP* green, *FN* red)

Table 4.7 Experimental results of D1—Flood in California

D1	Methods	FP	FN	OA	κ	F1	AUC	Time cost
Unsupervised	SCCN	60,163	15,201	0.828	0.162	0.237	0.700	925.7
	ACE-Net	34,767	9795	0.898	0.385	0.434	0.875	6918.3
	X-Net	31,837	10,207	0.904	0.395	0.443	0.879	3419.4
Supervised (60%)	RFR	61,399	6573	0.845	0.311	0.374	0.871	299.3
	Resnet	53,529	2124	0.873	0.418	0.471	0.916	387.2
	MLP	50,796	2491	0.878	0.426	0.478	0.918	179.5
Semi-supervised (60%)	Semi-GAN	7146	9624	0.961	0.652	0.672	0.812	3654.1
	Proposed	5356	10,873	0.963	0.645	0.664	0.791	2951.4
Semi-supervised (0.1%)	Semi-GAN	47,102	3949	0.883	0.421	0.472	0.869	865.9
	Proposed	33,248	4339	0.914	0.505	0.546	0.879	592.6

green false detected change areas in the upper part of each change map in the Fig. 4.15. However, by using the information of unlabeled samples, it can be seen in Fig. 4.15i, j that the false detected phenomenon has been weakened. On the whole, at the nearly cost of unsupervised models,the proposed framework achieves the performance of 0.914 in OA and 0.505 in κ which is shown in Table 4.7. And under the unified 60% label usage, the semi-supervised method is obviously superior to the pure supervised method, and the proposed method achieves the best results of OA under the initial network startup with a larger number of labels. For the time cost, the cost of supervised machine learning methods is the least, because they do not include a lot of training time for unlabeled data. In addition to them, the time complexity of the proposed method with 0.1% label amount is the lowest, which proves that the proposed framework is a concise network. However, as the number of labels increases, the time cost of the framework will also increase dramatically. It can be seen that the time cost of proposed method with 60% labels is almost twice that of the one with 0.1% labels, which is more obvious in the large data set D1 data set, for they contain more classification feedback of labeled data.

(2) D2—Lake Overflow in Italy For Italy dataset, the change detection results are shown in Fig. 4.16 and test metrics are displayed in Table 4.8. The phenomenon of missing detection and false detection is the most obvious in the Italy dataset of all results. For example, in unsupervised methods, SCCN has a large number of undetected changed areas in Fig. 4.16a, while ACE-Net and X-net has fewer undetected changed areas, but then a large number of green false detected areas appear in the lower left corner area, which is shown in Fig. 4.16b, c. This means that unsupervised methods are difficult to balance changed and unchanged identification information. In contrast, the proposed framework makes good use of unsupervised information and the coarse-and-fine features to fuse and filter a large number of noise points with 0.1% label quantity. So it achieves excellent change detection results. At the same time, with 60% label quantity, Semi-GAN and the proposed framework almost perfectly detect the changes in the Italy dataset, leading the Table 4.8.

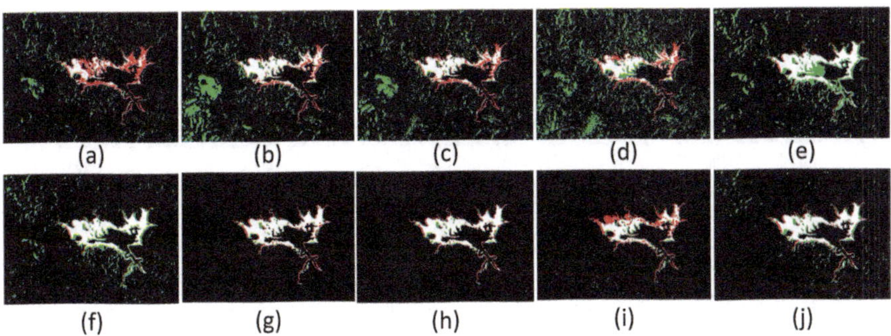

Fig. 4.16 Change detection results of D2—Lake Overflow in Italy achieved by (**a**) SCCN, (**b**) ACE-Net, (**c**) X-Net, (**d**) RFR, (**e**) Resnet, (**f**) MLP, (**g**) Semi-GAN (60%), (**h**) proposed (60%), (**i**) Semi-GAN (0.1%) and (**j**) proposed (0.1%). (*TP* white, *TN* black, *FP* green, *FN* red)

Table 4.8 Experimental results of D2—Lake overflow in Italy

D2	Methods	FP	FN	OA	κ	F1	AUC	Time cost
Unsupervised	SCCN	3947	4456	0.932	0.394	0.430	0.844	397.3
	ACE-Net	9543	2294	0.904	0.427	0.474	0.894	6374.3
	X-Net	7861	2826	0.914	0.429	0.473	0.872	3327.8
Supervised (60%)	RFR	13980	2776	0.864	0.306	0.367	0.866	16.5
	Resnet	8085	689	0.929	0.578	0.613	0.959	112.2
	MLP	5529	652	0.950	0.667	0.693	0.971	54.1
Semi-supervised (60%)	Semi-GAN	796	1641	0.980	0.820	0.831	0.889	447.6
	Proposed	812	1523	0.981	0.829	0.839	0.897	393.1
Semi-supervised (0.1%)	Semi-GAN	871	3210	0.967	0.667	0.684	0.786	247.6
	Proposed	2491	1367	0.969	0.748	0.764	0.900	197.1

(3) D3—Farmland in Shuguang For Shuguang dataset, the change detection results are shown in Fig. 4.17 and test metrics are displayed in Table 4.9. The detection difficulty of shuguang dataset is that $I1$ and $I2$ have different surface types in the changed area on the upper left corner. This leads to either a horizontal test result close to $I2$ in Fig. 4.17a or an obvious vertical test result close to $I1$ in Fig. 4.17b, c. In addition, because the imaging mechanisms of the two heterogeneous images in Shuguang dataset are different, the uppermost road area is often over-detected into a changed area, which is particularly obvious in the labeled supervised methods such as Fig. 4.17e, f, i, j. This over-fitting phenomenon occurs because the model excessively learns the characteristics of changed samples. However, when the number of labeled samples is increased, Semi-GAN and the proposed method can achieve a better balance between changed features and unchanged features. In general, the proposed method achieves the best results at 60% label amount, and achieves the best detection performance at 0.1% label amount near the condition of no label.

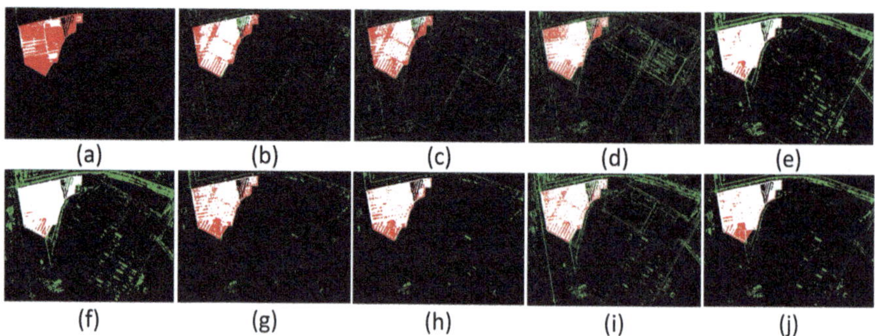

Fig. 4.17 Change detection results of D3—Farmland in Shuguang achieved by (**a**) SCCN, (**b**) ACE-Net, (**c**) X-Net, (**d**) RFR, (**e**) Resnet, (**f**) MLP, (**g**) Semi-GAN (60%), (**h**) proposed (60%), (**i**) Semi-GAN (0.1%) and (**j**) proposed (0.1%). (*TP* white, *TN* black, *FP* green, *FN* red)

Table 4.9 Experimental results of D3—Farmland in Shuguang

D3	Methods	FP	FN	OA	κ	F1	AUC	Time cost
Unsupervised	SCCN	195	17,452	0.922	0.327	0.351	0.788	684.1
	ACE-Net	3706	5773	0.958	0.753	0.776	0.967	6455.2
	X-Net	6096	7050	0.942	0.666	0.698	0.953	3093.4
Supervised (60%)	RFR	16,234	4727	0.907	0.575	0.626	0.940	49.4
	Resnet	19,485	1369	0.908	0.618	0.667	0.949	189.3
	MLP	21,577	801	0.901	0.606	0.657	0.945	84.9
Semi-supervised (60%)	Semi-GAN	2499	5211	0.966	0.796	0.815	0.877	565.9
	Proposed	2493	4224	0.970	0.826	0.843	0.900	517.5
Semi-supervised (0.1%)	Semi-GAN	17,952	2566	0.908	0.608	0.657	0.898	375.9
	Proposed	9814	2852	0.944	0.723	0.754	0.912	308.4

(4) D4—Flood in Yellow River For Yellow River dataset, the change detection results are shown in Fig. 4.18 and test metrics are displayed in Table 4.10. It can be seen from Fig. 4.18a–c that the YellowRiver dataset is prone to global noise in the image, because $I1$ image has many hollow scattered points due to lighting and other reasons, while $I2$ as an optical image is more smooth. Therefore, there is serious interference when comparing the two. In addition, due to the subtle texture differences on the optical image $I2$, there are wrong-detected place in triangular areas on the left half and river areas on the right half in Fig. 4.18e, i, j. So how to convert and eliminate the difference between heterogeneous images is the key to change detection of heterogeneous images. And even if 60% of the labels are used, Semi-GAN is still difficult to reduce the influence of fine horizontal lines in the upper part of the optical image $I2$. However, the proposed framework finally achieves the best change detection results through the fusion of multiple change maps, which is shown in Table 4.10, the highest OA of 0.981 and κ of 0.691.

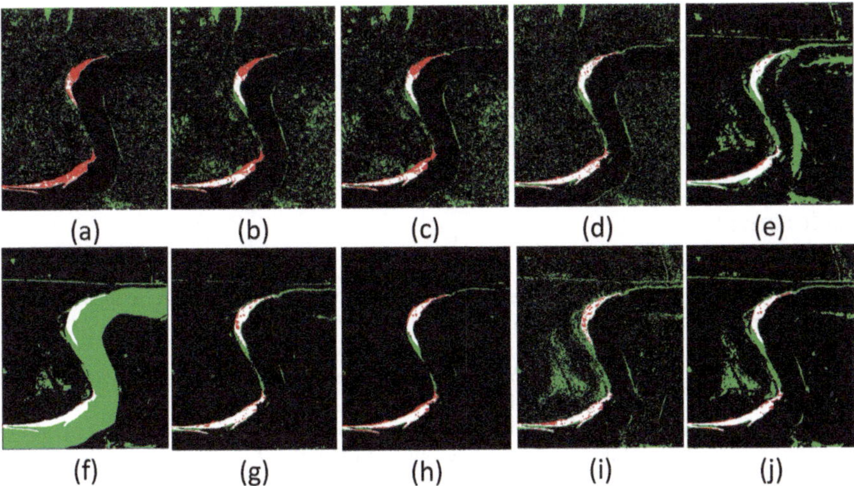

Fig. 4.18 Change detection results of D4—Flood in Yellow River achieved by (**a**) SCCN, (**b**) ACE-Net, (**c**) X-Net, (**d**) RFR, (**e**) Resnet, (**f**) MLP, (**g**) Semi-GAN (60%), (**h**) proposed (60%), (**i**) Semi-GAN (0.1%) and (**j**) proposed (0.1%). (*TP* white, *TN* black, *FP* green, *FN* red)

Table 4.10 Experimental results of D4—Flood in Yellow River

D4	Methods	FP	FN	OA	κ	F1	AUC	Time cost
Unsupervised	SCCN	6958	2363	0.907	0.107	0.147	0.737	194.6
	ACE-Net	8628	1464	0.899	0.214	0.252	0.838	5911.6
	X-Net	5945	1393	0.927	0.294	0.326	0.868	3113.0
Supervised (60%)	RFR	8527	674	0.908	0.318	0.351	0.917	14.9
	Resnet	9080	328	0.906	0.343	0.376	0.947	87.5
	MLP	24,269	162	0.755	0.149	0.197	0.867	34.2
Semi-supervised (60%)	Semi-GAN	1758	613	0.976	0.670	0.682	0.894	413.7
	Proposed	806	1027	0.981	0.691	0.700	0.834	350.2
Semi-supervised (0.1%)	Semi-GAN	8647	636	0.906	0.318	0.352	0.854	220.7
	Proposed	5891	465	0.936	0.433	0.459	0.896	181.1

4.2.4 Conclusions

Traditional heterogeneous change detection methods often rely on complex cross-modal alignment or image translation, which increases model complexity and limits robustness. In this section, the Multi-Layer Composite Autoencoder is proposed to address these issues in a semi-supervised manner. By leveraging minimal labeled data (only 0.1) and fusing multi-layer features from dual autoencoders, MLCAE enables effective difference learning without explicit alignment. A voting-based pseudo-label selection strategy further refines supervision by exploiting high-confidence unlabeled samples.

Experimental results on four heterogeneous datasets show that MLCAE achieves performance comparable to or better than fully supervised methods while operating at near-unsupervised labeling cost, demonstrating its efficiency and practicality for real-world remote sensing applications.

References

1. Kalita, I., Roy, M.: Deep neural network-based heterogeneous domain adaptation using ensemble decision making in land cover classification. IEEE Trans. Artif. Intell. **1**(2), 167–180 (2020)
2. Yu, H., Yang, T., Zhou, L., Wang, Y.: PDNet: a lightweight deep convolutional neural network for InSAR phase denoising. IEEE Trans. Geosci. Remote Sens. **60**, 1–9 (2022)
3. Yousif, O., Ban, Y.: Improving SAR-based urban change detection by combining MAP-MRF classifier and nonlocal means similarity weights. IEEE J. Sel. Top. Appl. Earth Obs. Remote Sens. **7**(10), 4288–4300 (2014)
4. Zhou, L., Yu, H., Lan, Y., Xing, M.: Artificial intelligence in interferometric synthetic aperture radar phase unwrapping: a review. IEEE Geosci. Remote Sens. Mag. **9**(2), 10–28 (2021)
5. Deng, J., Wang, K., Deng, Y.H., Qi, G.: PCA-based land-use change detection and analysis using multitemporal and multisensor satellite data. Int. J. Remote Sens. **29**(15–16), 4823–4838 (2008)
6. Kasetkasem, T., Varshney, P.K.: An image change detection algorithm based on Markov random field models. IEEE Trans. Geosci. Remote Sens. **40**(8), 1815–1823 (2002)
7. Moser, G., Serpico, S.B., Benediktsson, J.A.: Land-cover mapping by Markov modeling of spatial—contextual information in very-high-resolution remote sensing images. Proc. IEEE **101**(3), 631–651 (2013)
8. Celik, T.: Change detection in satellite images using a genetic algorithm approach. IEEE Geosci. Remote Sens. Lett. **7**(2), 386–390
9. Wang, Q., Li, H., Gong, M., Su, L., Jiao, L.: A multiobjective optimization method based on MOEA/D and fuzzy clustering for change detection in SAR images. In: 2014 IEEE Congress on Evolutionary Computation, pp. 3024–3029 (2014)
10. Jiao, L., Chen, J., Liu, F., Yang, S., You, C., Liu, X., Li, L., Hou, B.: Graph representation learning meets computer vision: a survey. IEEE Trans. Artif. Intell. **4**(1), 2–22 (2023)
11. Zhou, L., Yu, H., Pascazio, V., Xing, M.: PU-GAN: a one-step 2-D InSAR phase unwrapping based on conditional generative adversarial network. IEEE Trans. Geosci. Remote Sens. **60**, 1–10 (2022)
12. Wu, Y., Li, J., Yuan, Y., Qin, A.K., Miao, Q., Gong, M.: Commonality autoencoder: learning common features for change detection from heterogeneous images. IEEE Trans. Neural Netw. Learn. Syst. **33**, 4257–4270 (2021)
13. Luppino, L.T., Hansen, M.A., Kampffmeyer, M., Bianchi, F.M., Moser, G., Jenssen, R., Anfinsen, S.N.: Code-aligned autoencoders for unsupervised change detection in multimodal remote sensing images. IEEE Trans. Neural Netw. Learn. Syst., **35**, 60–72 (2022)
14. Touati, R., Mignotte, M., Dahmane, M.: Multimodal change detection in remote sensing images using an unsupervised pixel pairwise-based Markov random field model. IEEE Trans. Image Process. **29**, 757–767 (2020)
15. Jimenez-Sierra, D.A., Quintero-Olaya, D.A., Alvear-Muñoz, J.C., Benítez-Restrepo, H.D., Florez-Ospina, J.F., Chanussot, J.: Graph learning based on signal smoothness representation for homogeneous and heterogeneous change detection. IEEE Trans. Geosci. Remote Sens. **60**, 1–16 (2022)
16. Yu, H., Cao, N., Lan, Y., Xing, M.: Multisystem interferometric data fusion framework: a three-step sensing approach. IEEE Trans. Geosci. Remote Sens. **59**(10), 8501–8509 (2021)

17. Brunner, D., Lemoine, G., Bruzzone, L.: Earthquake damage assessment of buildings using VHR optical and SAR imagery. IEEE Trans. Geosci. Remote Sens. **48**(5), 2403–2420 (2010)
18. Mercier, G., Moser, G., Serpico, S.B.: Conditional copulas for change detection in heterogeneous remote sensing images. IEEE Trans. Geosci. Remote Sens. **46**(5), 1428–1441 (2008)
19. Touati, R., Mignotte, M., Dahmane, M.: A reliable mixed-norm-based multiresolution change detector in heterogeneous remote sensing images. IEEE J. Sel. Top. Appl. Earth Obs. Remote Sens. **12**(9), 3588–3601 (2019)
20. Luppino, L.T., Bianchi, F.M., Moser, G., Anfinsen, S.N.: Unsupervised image regression for heterogeneous change detection. IEEE Trans. Geosci. Remote Sens. **57**(12), 9960–9975 (2019)
21. Su, L., Gong, M., Zhang, P., Zhang, M., Liu, J., Yang, H.: Deep learning and mapping based ternary change detection for information unbalanced images. Pattern Recognit. **66**, 213–228 (2017)
22. Gong, M., Niu, X., Zhan, T., Zhang, M.: A coupling translation network for change detection in heterogeneous images. Int. J. Remote Sens. **40**(9), 3647–3672 (2019)
23. Liu, J., Gong, M., Qin, K., Zhang, P.: A deep convolutional coupling network for change detection based on heterogeneous optical and radar images. IEEE Trans. Neural Netw. Learn. Syst. **29**(3), 545–559 (2018)
24. Liu, Z., Zhang, Z., Pan, Q., Ning, L.: Unsupervised change detection from heterogeneous data based on image translation. IEEE Trans. Geosci. Remote Sens. **60**, 1–13 (2022)
25. Lee, D.: Pseudo-label: The simple and efficient semi-supervised learning method for deep neural networks. In: ICML 2013 Workshop: Challenges in Representation Learning (WREPL), pp. 1–6 (2013)
26. Valpola, H.: From neural PCA to deep unsupervised learning. In: Advances in Independent Component Analysis and Learning Machines, pp. 143–171. Academic (2015)
27. Rasmus, A., Raiko, T., Valpola, H.: Denoising autoencoder with modulated lateral connections learns invariant representations of natural images. Comput. Sci. **31**(4), 555–563 (2014)
28. Zhang, P., Gong, M., Zhang, H., Liu, J., Ban, Y.: Unsupervised difference representation learning for detecting multiple types of changes in multitemporal remote sensing images. IEEE Trans. Geosci. Remote Sens. **57**(4), 2277–2289 (2019)
29. Gong, M., Zhan, T., Zhang, P., Miao, Q.: Superpixel-based difference representation learning for change detection in multispectral remote sensing images. IEEE Trans. Geosci. Remote Sens. **55**(5), 2658–2673 (2017)
30. Zhou, Z., Li, M.: Tri-training: exploiting unlabeled data using three classifiers. IEEE Trans. Knowl. Data Eng. **17**(11), 1529–1541 (2005)
31. Ruck, D., Rogers, S., Kabrisky, M., Oxley, M., Suter, B.: The multilayer perceptron as an approximation to a Bayes optimal discriminant function. IEEE Trans. Neural Netw. **1**(4), 296–298 (1990)
32. Li, Y., Gong, M., Jiao, L., Li, L., Stolkin, R.: Change-detection map learning using matching pursuit. IEEE Trans. Geosci. Remote Sens. **53**(8), 4712–4723 (2015)
33. Khurana, M., Saxena, V.: A unified approach to change detection using an adaptive ensemble of extreme learning machines. IEEE Geosci. Remote Sens. Lett. **17**(5), 794–798 (2020)
34. Tuia, D., Verrelst, J., Alonso, L., Perez-Cruz, F., Camps-Valls, G.: Multioutput support vector regression for remote sensing biophysical parameter estimation. IEEE Geosci. Remote Sens. Lett. **8**(4), 804–808 (2011)
35. He, K., Zhang, X., Ren, S., Sun, J.: Deep residual learning for image recognition. In: 2016 IEEE Conference on Computer Vision and Pattern Recognition (CVPR), pp. 770–778 (2016)
36. Shi, J., Liu, X., Lei, Y.: SAR images change detection based on self-adaptive network architecture. IEEE Geosci. Remote Sens. Lett. **18**(7), 1204–1208 (2021)
37. Niu, X., Gong, M., Zhan, T., Yang, Y.: A conditional adversarial network for change detection in heterogeneous images. IEEE Geosci. Remote Sens. Lett. **16**(1), 45–49 (2019)
38. Luppino, L.T., Kampffmeyer, M., Bianchi, F.M., Moser, G., Serpico, S.B., Jenssen, R., Anfinsen, S.N.: Deep image translation with an affinity-based change prior for unsupervised multimodal change detection. IEEE Trans. Geosci. Remote Sens. **60**, 1–22 (2022)

39. Luppino, L.T., Bianchi, F.M., Moser, G., Anfinsen, S.N. (2019) Unsupervised image regression for heterogeneous change detection. IEEE Trans. Geosci. Remote Sens. **57**(12), 9960–9975
40. Jiang, F.L., Gong, M.G., Zhan, T., et al.: A semisupervised GAN-based multiple change detection framework in multi-spectral images. IEEE Geosci. Remote Sens. Lett. **17**, 1223–1227 (2020)

Chapter 5
Network Architecture Search-Based Remote Sensing Image Change Detection

Abstract The preceding chapters have demonstrated the effectiveness of deep learning in both homogeneous and heterogeneous remote sensing change detection. However, reliance on fixed, manual architectures limits adaptability across diverse sensors, scenes, and modalities. Neural architecture search (NAS) offers a promising solution by automatically discovering task-specific network architectures in a data-driven manner, leading to more discriminative representations for change detection. In this chapter, two self-adaptive neural architecture search frameworks are presented to enhance the flexibility and robustness of change detection systems. First, an evolutionary NAS framework is introduced, which employs adaptive gene encoding, specialized genetic operators, and a self-adaptive selection mechanism to automatically discover simple, efficient networks for SAR images change detection. Second, a semi-supervised adaptive ladder network is introduced that adjusts its dual-input architecture and generates pseudo-labels by fusing semi-supervised and unsupervised outputs, enabling effective adaptation to homogeneous and heterogeneous image pairs with minimal labeled data.

Keywords Change detection · Evolutionary algorithm · Neural network · Neural architecture search · Semi-supervised learning

5.1 Self-Adaptive Network Architecture for SAR Images Change Detection

In recent years, neural networks have been introduced into change detection to enhance the interpretation and analysis of remote sensing imagery.[1] However, the design of these networks has largely relied on time-consuming trial-and-error

[1] **Acknowledgement:** Reprinted from *IEEE Geoscience and Remote Sensing Letters*, 18(7), Jiao Shi, Xiaodong Liu, Yu Lei, SAR Images Change Detection Based on Self-Adaptive Network Architecture, 1204–1208, Copyright (2021), with permission from IEEE.

J. Shi et al., *Computational Intelligence for Remote Sensing Image Change Detection*, SpringerBriefs in Computer Science,
https://doi.org/10.1007/978-981-92-1404-4_5

processes, often lacking systematic validation of their effectiveness and theoretical soundness. Thus, a simple and efficient change detection method based on NAS in terms of evolutionary algorithm is proposed to deal with SAR images change detection problems. In the proposed method, an efficient gene encoding is applied to represent the unpredictable optimal depth and the number of neurons in each hidden layer. Besides, a combinatorial evaluation strategy and a self-adaptive network solution selection are designed for effective and reasonable network architectures. What's more, a hidden layer random alignment crossover operator and a drawing lots mutation operator are designed for the enhancement of diversity of network architectures. Experimental results on a few SAR image datasets demonstrate that the proposed method can generate appropriate networks to solving SAR images change detection.

5.1.1 Introduction

SAR images change detection has been attracting an increasingly interests along with the development of SAR systems. Benefit from its potential characteristics of all-weather and full-time working, SAR systems have been applied in many fields, like disaster monitoring and resource exploration [1–3]. The widespread applications of SAR systems has generated abundant SAR image resources for change detection research, thereby promoting the rapid development and diversification of SAR image change detection methods.

Change detection is a technique that distinguish changed and unchanged objects between a pair of multi-temporal images derived at the same region. With respect to change detection in remote sensing imagery, the process can generally be divided into three stages [4]: image preprocessing, which primarily involves the co-registration of bi-temporal images; the generation of a difference image; and the subsequent analysis of the difference image. Among these stages, the third step (difference image analysis) has attracted the most research attention in recent years [5–7]. There are also some change detection methods that perform well without difference images and play an important role in the advance of change detection [8].

In the recent years, neural networks are introduced to change detection because of its good performance in classification tasks [9–11]. Compared with traditional machine learning approaches, neural networks are capable of extracting higher-level and more discriminative representations from remote sensing imagery, thereby improving the overall accuracy of change detection. In [9], Zhang et al. used stacked denoising auto-encoders to learn high-level representation of local features of remote sensing images and built a mapping network to explore inner relationship between features come from difference images. In [10], Gong et al. proposed a method based on DNNs for solving SAR images change detection problems, which achieved a better performance than conventional change detection methods.

However, there are some problems hindering the practical implementation of these neural network based change detection methods. These methods typically employ fixed network architectures to perform change detection across different remote sensing datasets. However, given that datasets often vary significantly in their structural characteristics and analytical complexity, such rigid architectures may lead to performance degradation when applied to diverse data scenarios. Besides, these methods need to be adjusted again and again when they were designed, which costed a lot of time. Furthermore, if a network is designed for each of remote sensing dataset specifically, the overhead cannot be afforded.

Therefore, this section introduces a simple yet efficient NAS-based change detection method designed to search for optimal fully connected neural network architectures for change detection in SAR images. In the proposed method, there are three contributions highlighted.

1. Firstly, an efficient gene encoding is applied to represent the unpredictable optimal depth and the number of neurons in each hidden layer in fully connected neural networks.
2. Secondly, a combinatorial evaluation strategy and a self-adaptive network solution selection are designed for urging networks to improve their performances.
3. Thirdly, a hidden layer random alignment crossover (HLRAC) operator and a drawing lots mutation (DLM) operator are designed for the enhancement of diversity of network architectures.

The proposed method eliminates the reliance on empirical design of network architecture and instead establishes an evaluation index to guide the network generation, thereby yielding an interpretable and structurally sound architecture.

5.1.2 Methodology

The proposed Evolving Fully Connected Neural Network (EVONN) framework for change detection will be described in detail. Within this framework, an optimal neural network architecture is first automatically derived through the evolutionary mechanism of EVONN, after which change detection is performed based on the constructed network. Figure 5.1 illustrates the procedure of searching a promising architecture of neural networks for SAR images change detection.

5.1.2.1 Gene Encoding and Population Initialization

Gene encoding plays a pivotal role in evolutionary algorithms. In EVONN, an efficient and intuitive encoding scheme is developed to flexibly represent variable network depths and neuron quantities. Because the input size and output size of all neural networks have been customized according to the need of change detection problems, only the structures of hidden layers are encoded in the evolutionary algorithms. For example, an architecture of having three hidden layers where the number of neurons are 5, 9 and 12 respectively can be encoded by a list [**5 9 12**].

During individual initialization, the number of hidden layers is first randomly determined, followed by the random assignment of the number of neurons in each

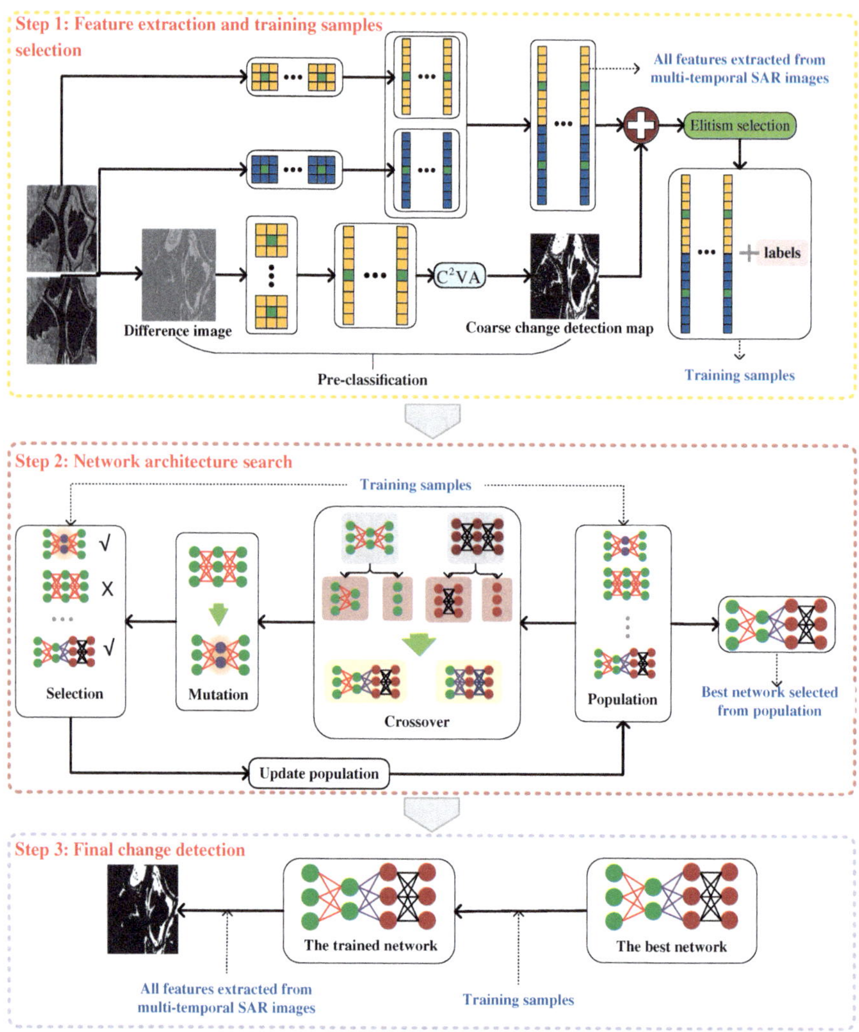

Fig. 5.1 The proposed SAR images change detection framework

hidden layer. Obviously, the initialization of a population of having N individuals is composed of N times of an individual initialization.

5.1.2.2 Combinatorial Evaluation Strategy

In order to give a quantitative measure of each individual in the population, a combinatorial evaluation strategy is designed in this method. Theoretically, a test dataset with true labels is used for evaluating the quality of training process.

However, obtaining fully accurate ground-truth labels for SAR images in change detection tasks is extremely challenging. Consequently, researchers often assign pseudo-labels to extracted features for supervised network training [10, 11], thereby exploiting the inherent capability of deep networks to learn informative and discriminative representations from the data. Therefore, training error is chosen to be an evaluation index to quantify the performance of candidate networks, in which a small training error is preferred.

Nevertheless, generalization cannot be promised without validation of test dataset in the training process, instead easily resulting in over-fitting. For this, an incomplete training strategy is applied on the candidate networks to avoid over-fitting. Specifically, each candidate network is trained with a small number of epochs less than normal to relieve the over-fitting problem, unexpectedly improving efficiency of evolutionary process. Furthermore, network complexity is carefully considered to ensure generalization capability and enhance heuristic search efficiency, with a preference for relatively simple architectural configurations to avoid overfitting and excessive computational burden. The combinatorial evaluation strategy composed of training error and network's complexity forms a basis for the evolutionary direction of networks.

Algorithm 5.1 Self-adaptive network selection

Require: Two individuals, the self-adaptive threshold α.
Ensure: The selected individual.
$s_1 \leftarrow$ the individual with larger training error.
$s_2 \leftarrow$ the other individual.
$t_1, t_2 \leftarrow$ the training errors of s_1 and s_2.
$c_1, c_2 \leftarrow$ the number of neurons of s_1 and s_2.
if $t_1 - t_2 \geq \alpha$ **then**
    return s_2
else
    if $c_1 \leq c_2$ **then**
        return s_1
    else
        return s_2
    end if
end if

5.1.2.3 Self-Adaptive Network Selection

In this section, a self-adaptive network selection strategy tailored to change detection tasks is proposed for selecting parent solutions while maintaining population diversity during evolution. The detailed procedure is presented in Algorithm 5.1. Note that the threshold α is formulated as Eq. (5.1).

$$\alpha = (T_{max} - T_{min}) * \frac{1}{N} \tag{5.1}$$

where T_{max} and T_{min} are the maximum training error and minimum training error of current population respectively and N is the population size.

5.1.2.4 Genetic Operation

In order to prompt the diversity of the architectures, genetic operations are designed based on the efficient gene encoding strategy. In general, the crossover operation is performed between two parent solutions randomly selected from the mating pool, and the resulting offspring are subsequently refined through a mutation operator.

(1) Hidden Layers Random Alignment Crossover The crossover operator, hidden layers random alignment crossover (HLRAC) depicted in Fig. 5.2, is designed to recombine the chromosome fragments of parent solutions for generating offspring solutions. To fully exploit the genetic potential contained within a pair of parent solutions, chromosomes are aligned and paired to the greatest extent possible during crossover. This random alignment strategy constitutes the core mechanism of the crossover operation, facilitating effective genetic recombination and diversity generation. The second step selects crossover points and third step exchange the chromosomes at crossover points.

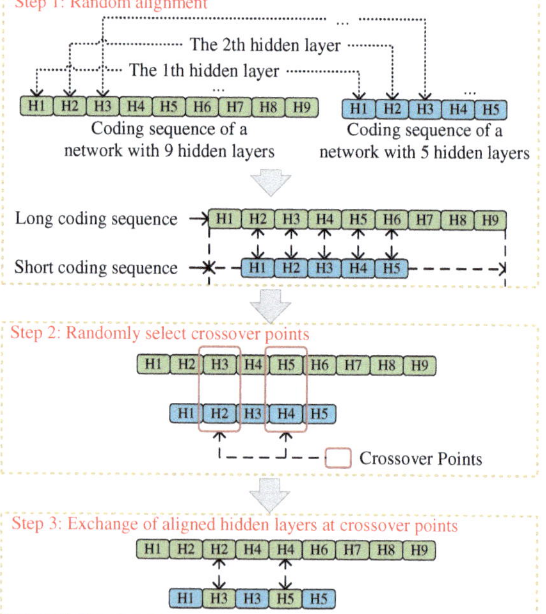

Fig. 5.2 An example to illustrate the crossover process

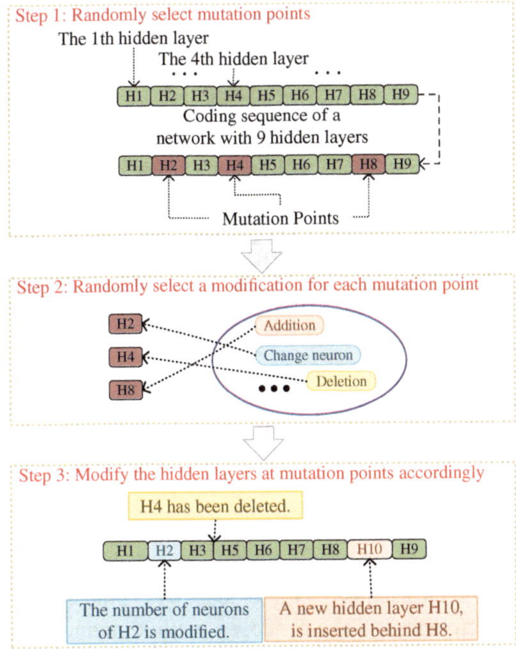

Fig. 5.3 An example to illustrate the mutation process

(2) Drawing Lots Mutation A drawing lots strategy is designed to modify hidden layers, in which three types of modification that are involved, including adding a hidden layer, delete a hidden layer and change the number of neurons. To satisfy the predefined constraints during mutation, a drawing lots pool composed of a limited set of distinct modification operations is constructed. This pool is used to determine the specific type of modification applied to selected mutation points. Specifically, in the pool, the addition operators size cannot exceed the number of the hidden layers that are allowed to be modified while the sum of the addition operators size and the length of the current individual cannot exceed the maximum hidden layer size. In addition, the number of deletion operations and change neuron number operations should be equal to the number of the remaining hidden layers that are allowed to be modified on the present moment. Figure 5.3 show an visual example for giving an intuitive insight.

5.1.2.5 Change Detection with Best Neural Network

After the second stage of the proposed method, the best-performing individual is selected and decoded into a neural network architecture, which is regarded as superior to the remaining candidate solutions. The network should be fine-tuned with training samples because it does not fully trained to be evaluated in the second stage. After fine-tuned, the network can be used to analyze the features extracted in the first stage and produce a final change detection map.

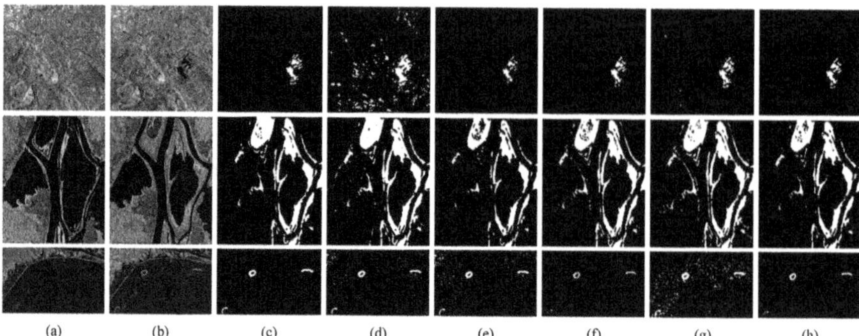

Fig. 5.4 SAR images datasets and change detection results. (**a**) SAR image I_1, (**b**) SAR image I_2, (**c**) reference map, and change detection result achieved by (**d**) GGKI, (**e**) RFLICM, (**f**) DNN, (**g**) MSSDNN, (**h**) EVONN

5.1.3 Experimental Study

In the experiments, three real SAR image datasets are employed to validate the effectiveness of the proposed method, namely the Bern dataset, the Ottawa dataset, and the Yellow River dataset. Besides, there are two multi-temporal SAR images and one ground truth image to shown real changed regions for a reference in each SAR image dataset, which are displayed in Fig. 5.4a–c. Except intuitively visual way of showing change detection images, PCC and Kappa coefficient κ are used to quantify the performance of the proposed method.

5.1.3.1 Performances on SAR Image Datasets

Figure 5.4d–h show the change detection results achieved by generalized Gaussian Kittler & Illingworth method (GGKI), reformulated fuzzy local-information c-means algorithm (RFLICM) [12], deep neural network method, multiscale superpixel segmentation based DNN method (MSSDNN) [13] and the proposed method, respectively. In the change results on Bern dataset, DNN method and the proposed method have similarly good performances visually. However, the change detection results produced by GGKI and MSSDNN are significantly affected by speckle noise, with GGKI exhibiting particularly severe noise contamination. Although the result obtained by RFLICM on the Bern dataset is relatively free from noise interference, it fails to identify all changed regions. In contrast, for both the Ottawa and Yellow River datasets, the proposed method demonstrates stronger robustness to speckle noise and yields more complete and coherent detection of changed areas compared with the competing approaches. Furthermore, the neural networks generated by the proposed method to achieve change detection against aforementioned SAR image datasets have only one hidden layer while the DNN and MSSDNN methods use

Table 5.1 The evaluation indexes of change detection results

Datasets	Index	Methods				
		GGKI	RFLICM	DNN	MSSDNN	EVONN
Bern	PCC	0.9608	0.9964	**0.9968**	0.9960	0.9965
	κ	0.3796	0.8377	**0.9968**	0.8545	0.8589
	Hidden layers	–	–	250-200-100	100-50-20	142
Ottawa	PCC	0.9799	0.9733	0.9809	0.9719	**0.9845**
	κ	0.9276	0.8935	0.9278	0.8981	**0.9845**
	Hidden layers	–	–	250-200-100	100-50-20	150
Yellow River	PCC	0.9915	0.9878	0.9958	0.9669	**0.9963**
	κ	0.6916	0.5998	0.7651	0.3567	**0.7999**
	Hidden layers	–	–	250-200-100	100-50-20	149

three hidden layers [10], which is detailed in Table 5.1. Although deep networks can generate more representative features to promote the performance of classification than shallow ones in general, reasonable design is more meaningful than simply increasing the depth of the network in practice.

In order to conduct a direct comparison between these methods, PCC and κ are used to quantify their performances. Table 5.1 indicates that the proposed method achieved the best performances on Ottawa and Yellow River datasets and approximately best performance on Bern dataset. Furthermore, the proposed method adopts a relatively simpler architecture compared with conventional DNN approaches, implying that it requires fewer computational resources while achieving comparable performance.

5.1.4 Conclusions

In SAR image change detection tasks, network architectures are typically designed based on researchers' empirical knowledge. However, manually crafted networks often struggle to maintain consistently strong performance across diverse SAR change detection scenarios. Thus, a SAR images change detection framework based on NAS in terms of evolutionary algorithm is proposed in this section. For a fast heuristic search, an efficient gene encoding is applied to represent the unpredictable optimal depth and the number of neurons in each hidden layer. Besides, a hidden layers random alignment crossover and a drawing lots mutation are designed for the diversity of solutions. Through the proposed framework, network architectures can be designed in terms of specific SAR images change detection problems. Experimental results on SAR image datasets demonstrate that the proposed method can generate appropriate networks targeted for different SAR images change detection problems to promise good performances.

5.2 Semi-supervised Adaptive Ladder Network for Remote Sensing Image Change Detection

In recent years, as the acquisition of true labels is challenging, semi-supervised neural networks have demonstrated significant potential for change detection (CD) in remote sensing images.[2] Nevertheless, most traditional semi-supervised detection frameworks suffer from high training complexity and a reliance on additional structural analysis, while their rigid architectures limit universality. This section presents a semi-supervised adaptive ladder network (SSALN) for remote sensing image change detection, enabling dual-input label-incremental architecture search with a concise and variable structure. First, SSALN is suitable for CD from two remote sensing images of any types with the characteristic of minimal label dependency and automatic network structure adjustment. The network can generate more reliable pseudo labels through continuous iterations to help limited real labels exploit implicit information, identify the most effective network and form the ascending network structure optimization. Second, the acquisition of pseudo labels is the fusion of semi-supervised and unsupervised CD approaches, which ensures the multi-perspective information supplement. Multiple CD maps are fused to generate labels for next iteration, making the predicting more reliable. Finally, both homogenous images and heterogenous images are tested with experiments. Even if the detection object is switched, it can be well adaptive and compatible without manual modification of the network. Experimental results show that the proposed method can promote the flow of label information through structure search and self-circulation in the ascending network optimization, thereby achieving outstanding performance in remote sensing image change detection tasks.

5.2.1 *Introduction*

Remote sensing image change detection aims to identify changes in the same region at different times by comparing and processing a pair of remote sensing images. With the development of remote sensing technology, the types of remote sensing images are gradually diversifying, including synthetic aperture radar (SAR), optical, very high-resolution (VHR), multispectral, hyperspectral, and heterogeneous images, providing more abundant remote sensing image information. Nowadays, driven by the capacity to leverage abundant remote sensing image information, remote sensing image change detection is widely applied in diverse land-surface change analyses, such as land-cover change, natural-disaster assessment, agri-

[2] **Acknowledgement:** Reprinted from *IEEE Transactions on Geoscience and Remote Sensing*, 60, Jiao Shi, Tiancheng Wu, A. K. Qin, Yu Lei, Gwanggil Jeon, Semisupervised Adaptive Ladder Network for Remote Sensing Image Change Detection, 1–20, Copyright (2022), with permission from IEEE.

cultural assessment, urban expansion and evolution, environmental monitoring, etc. [14].

In the past, many traditional methods have been employed for remote sensing image change detection. Typically, pre-acquired difference maps are further processed by methods that can effectively analyze variation characteristics and highlight changes. Most of these methods are thresholding and clustering techniques. Thresholding methods, such as Otsu [15], the Kittler-Illingworth minimum-error thresholding algorithm [16], and the change vector analysis (CVA) [17], attempt to balance thresholds between changed and invariant pixels. However, they are often noise-sensitive, resulting in degraded performance in many cases. Meanwhile, in the clustering technology applied to remote sensing image change detection, the change detection based on the fuzzy c-means algorithm [12] can preserve more useful information compared to traditional hard-clustering methods. Additionally, principal component analysis [18], Markov random fields [19], and genetic algorithm [20] have also been extensively used to address the change detection problem. However, the above methods all operate directly on the original pixels, and their detection performance may be significantly weakened in complex scenarios. In contrast, neural networks can extract high-level abstract features from the original pixel data, making it possible to enhance the effectiveness of remote sensing image change detection.

As previously noted, the volume of remote sensing image information has experienced explosive growth. This growth has opened up new opportunities for a wider range of technological applications in the area of change detection [21]. Leveraging the availability of large-scale data, deep learning techniques can effectively extract high-level features from remote sensing images [22, 23]. Through layer-wise nonlinear transformation, deep neural networks (DNNs) can learn more profound difference representations. Simultaneously, this process can mitigate the impact of noise and redundant information [24]. However, DNN models are highly reliant on substantial amounts of annotated training samples. These samples usually require manual generation, involving expert knowledge and tedious effort. In the field of remote sensing, the number of publicly available annotated datasets is extremely limited [25]. Consequently, remote sensing image processing, including the task of remote sensing image change detection, can be considered a few-sample problem [26]. Among various approaches, neural network models that utilize a significant proportion of unlabeled data to compensate for the scarcity of supervised information fall under the category of semi-supervised learning [27]. Recently, emerging semi-supervised techniques, implemented with deep neural networks, have found success in the image processing tasks, such as object detection and semantic segmentation [28].

Currently, several deep learning-based semi-supervised methods have been applied to the remote sensing image change detection task. Examples include the generative adversarial network and graph-based networks. In generative models, the discriminator serves as an appropriate feature extractor for discriminative remote sensing image change detection tasks. Meanwhile, the generator aims to simulate the information distribution of remote sensing images to generate false objects [29]. Nonetheless, in practical applications, it is challenging to obtain both well-performing generators and excellent semi-supervised classifiers simultaneously. This limitation affects their utility in semi-supervised learning tasks, particularly in remote sensing image change detection tasks where data is severely scarce [30]. On the other hand, graph-based network change detection models use graph-based methods to establish connections between similar samples within the dataset [31]. In the remote sensing image change detection task, this approach makes the extracted graph structures highly sensitive to penalties in both changed and unchanged regions. Moreover, these methods often necessitate the analysis of a complex and time-consuming Laplacian matrix, thereby restricting the scope of their application in remote sensing [32].

Existing semi-supervised frameworks, struggling to strike a balance between discrimination and generation or being overly sensitive to variable graph structures, are in urgent need of a concise, rapid, and effective enhancement. Inspired by the ladder network [33], labeled data directly guides the similarity learning of unlabeled data. This approach aims to ease the complexity of unified training in the semi-supervised remote sensing image change detection task [34]. By jointly learning labeled and unlabeled data, the training complexity of the network is reduced. However, the original ladder network does not fare well in complex remote sensing image change detection tasks. Even in binary classification for remote sensing image change detection, there are more changes compared to the digital changes in the MNIST datasets, which were used to test the ladder network. The insufficient utilization of data results in incomplete and sub-optimal network learning. Thus, a circular incremental information-supplementation mode is desired, where the detection performance gradually improves through self-training [35].

Simultaneously, existing semi-supervised remote sensing image change detection frameworks employ fixed architectures, which leads to an unforeseen burden of manual parameter adjustment whenever the dataset changes. Manually redesigning the network is time-consuming and labor-intensive, rendering the semi-supervised framework insufficiently intelligent. Hence, an automatic method for searching the optimal network structure is highly appealing. Even when datasets are switched, the network should be able to adaptively achieve optimal performance after undergoing structural adjustments. An effective approach to obtaining the optimal neural-network architecture is structure searching based on the evolutionary algorithm. This algorithm can perform efficient gene coding for the network through a fast heuristic search [36]. For instance, in the previous SAR-image change detection task, Shi et al. [37] applied an efficient gene-encoding method to represent the network depth and the number of network nodes. This method can achieve effective and reasonable network architectures through mutation and other evolutionary operations. Nevertheless, it has a tendency to select shallower networks, thereby weakening the ability to utilize the high-level information extracted from the middle layers of the network.

Furthermore, unsupervised analysis methods will be employed to complement the semi-supervised classification by reusing the middle-layer feature information extracted by the network. The current semi-supervised classification for change detection is in a single perspective and lacks stability. Therefore, unsupervised analysis is designed to obtain predictive results independently, assisting the semi-supervised network in determining regional changes. By making multiple judgments in the same region, this approach ensures the reliability of the pseudo labels to a greater extent.

In this section, a semi-supervised adaptive ladder network (SSALN) for remote sensing image change detection with label-incremental architecture searching is proposed. The main contributions can be summarized as follows:

1. A SSALN is proposed for CD from two remote sensing images of any type, captured over the same scene at different times, which is capable of handling insufficient labeled data and avoids manual network configuration. In SSALN, pseudo labels are updated iteratively. In each iteration, they are used together with limited real labels to automatically identify the most effective ladder network in terms of both architecture and parameters.
2. A pseudo label updating strategy is devised that combines the strengths of semi-supervised and unsupervised change detection approaches, where unsupervised change detection is applied to the output of each hidden layer in the main branch of the ladder network to generate multiple CD maps. These CD maps are then fused with the CD map generated by the semi-supervisedly trained ladder network to produce the updated pseudo labels to be used in the next iteration.
3. The proposed method is applied to several pairs of homogenous images (e.g., both optical or both SAR images) and also several pairs of heterogenous images (e.g., optical and SAR images), leading to the superior performance over existing CD techniques.

5.2.2 *Methodology*

The overview of the proposed SSALN is shown in Fig. 5.5, which will be described in detail in three parts: (1) The overall model will be summarized with circular and learning part; (2) The dynamic network optimization based on evolutionary algorithms is discussed; (3)The label-selection strategy with detailed screening operation is talked in combinatorial way.

5.2.2.1 Semi-supervised Adaptive Ladder Network

(1) Introduction of Autoencoder Network It is notable that the proposed method is founded on the autoencoder (AE) network. As depicted in Fig. 5.6, in the ladder network, Ns denotes the added noise, and X^i represents all the input data. Y^{super} is the classification result of the labeled data, while $Y^{unsuper}$ is the sum of the unsupervised results at each layer.

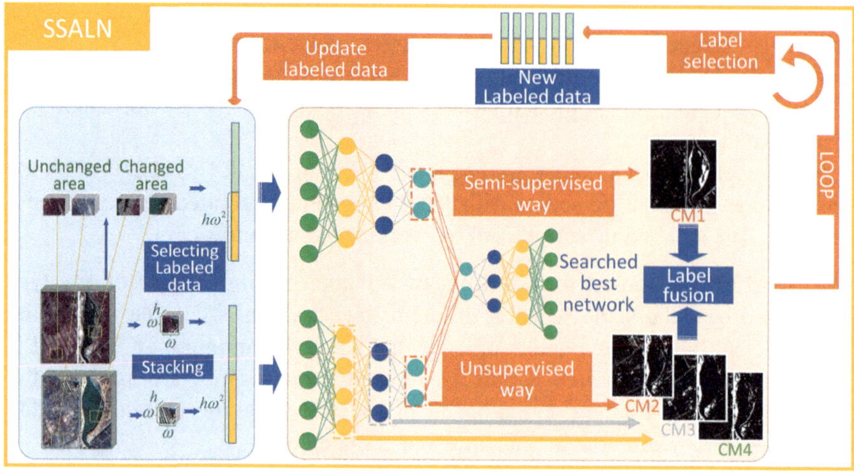

Fig. 5.5 Overview of the proposed SSALN, a semi-supervised framework for remote sensing image change detection task

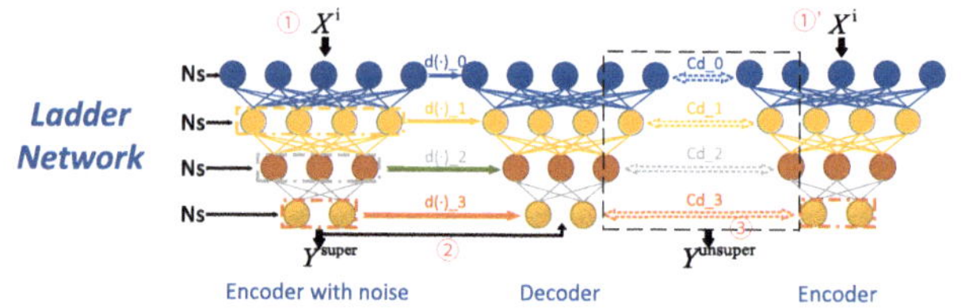

Fig. 5.6 Ladder network compared with traditional AE

The AE network [38] is one of the most fundamental and widely adopted architectures in deep learning. It consists of an encoder and a decoder. As shown in Fig. 5.6a, it operates by minimizing the error between the input X and the reconstruction values Y, and updates the weights and biases using the gradient-descent method [39]. Currently, the AE network has found extensive applications in the field of remote sensing image processing. For example, Geng et al. [40] designed a deep convolutional autoencoder to extract representative features. Wang [41] proposed a stacked sparse autoencoder with virtual adversarial regularization for PolSAR image classification.

As a variant of the AE network, the ladder network is illustrated in Fig. 5.6b. Unlike the traditional AE network, the ladder network's structure is composed of two encoders and one decoder. The standard implementation of the ladder network involves the following steps:

1. An encoder is constructed by injecting noise into each layer, facilitating supervised learning on labeled data via a connected classification head.

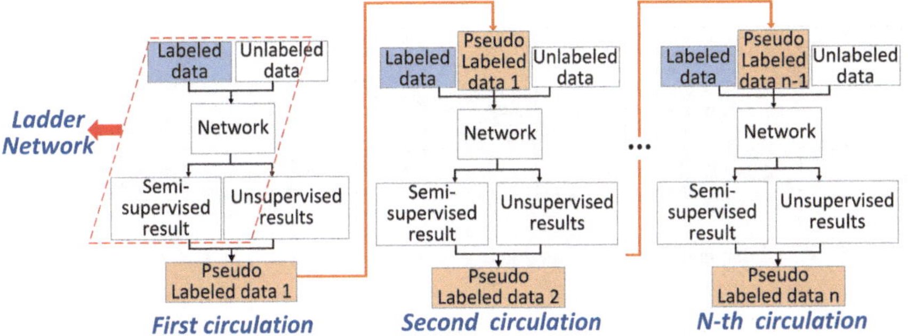

Fig. 5.7 Illustration of overall circulation framework

2. A decoder performs reconstruction using a denoising function $d(\cdot)_i$, which implements the inverse mapping of the encoder's layers.
3. An encoder without noise is restored to maintain a one-to-one correspondence Cd_i with the decoder, enabling unsupervised learning across all data.
4. The total objective function, comprising both supervised and unsupervised loss terms, is minimized.

(2) Introduction of SSALN While based on ladder network which is the "Network" part in every circulation in Fig. 5.7, the proposed framework makes use of the unsupervised restore part in the net.

1. It is then divided into supervised part and unsupervised part. In the supervised part, labeled data are classified by appending a classification layer after the feature extraction of the encoder with noise.
2. The outputs from both parts will be fused to generate pseudo labeled dataset, facilitating circulation-training.

Based on the low-density assumption, the proposed framework aims to obtain similar classified outputs from inputs with similar change attributes. This is achieved by adding noise to the unlabeled data and minimizing the reconstruction error through the reconstruction Cd_i of the labeled data at each layer in the ladder network [33]. The noise interference $d(\cdot)\_i$ at each layer renders the model less sensitive to the perturbations of the training data. In essence, this encourages the decision boundary to lie within the low-density region.

The original ladder network was initially tested on the MNIST and CIFAR-10 datasets. However, it did not perform well in remote sensing image change detection. In the case of MNIST, the structure and shape of the digits are relatively consistent, enabling the neural network to easily extract their key features. Conversely, the regional changes in remote sensing images are far more intricate, leading to often unsatisfactory initial classification accuracies. Owing to the complexity of change differences in remote sensing images, the limited number of labels in

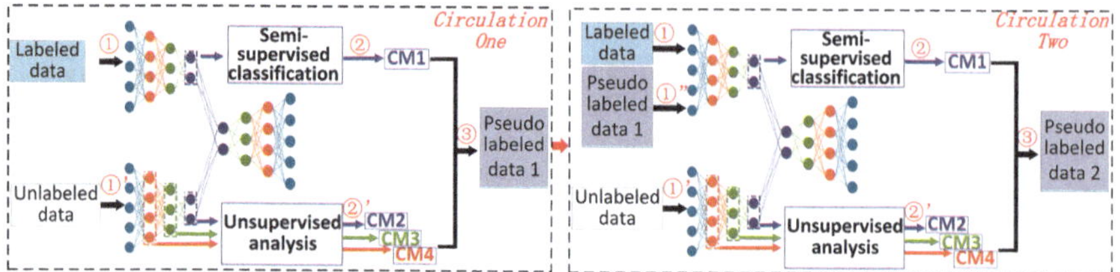

Fig. 5.8 Visual display of sample selection

the semi-supervised network frequently results in over-fitting of the classification outcomes.

Therefore, a circular information-reuse approach is proposed, which involves the outcomes of the change map generated by both the semi-supervised network and the unsupervised method. This aims to fully exploit the existing classification structure features. A combinatorial label selection strategy is employed to ensure the reliability of the predictive classification. Through the incremental supplementation of potential information, the performance of differentiating changes has been notably enhanced.

(3) Semi-supervised Annotation Case In SSALN, pseudo labels are updated iteratively. As shown in Fig. 5.8, after the semi-supervised annotation, the labels has been updated:

1. Labeled data and unlabeled data are inputted into network;
2. Semi-supervised and unsupervised results can be obtained.
3. After fusing two kinds of results such as CM1(Change Map 1), CM2, CM3 and CM4, the pseudo labeled data is selected.

In the iterative process, pseudo-labeled data is incorporated into the labeled data set, which is presented as the third type of input data in the "Pseudo labeled data 1" step. The two-fold predictive outcomes from the semi-supervised and unsupervised methods are beneficial in supplementing classification information from different viewpoints.

(4) Circular Sample Selection There exists a problem where the number of manually-labeled samples is too limited to comprehensively capture the characteristics of the changed and unchanged regions in remote sensing images. Thus, it is reasonable to consider making better use of the classified labels to expand the prior knowledge.

Consequently, the aim is to enrich the information through two perspectives. The first prediction results of the network are combined with several classification results derived from the unsupervised method. Subsequently, the principle of "the minority is subordinate to the majority" is applied to screen out relatively reliable pseudo-labels, thereby increasing the confidence level of the labels. Following this, the network is retrained through iterative operations.

Ultimately, as the quantity of available labeled data grows, the re-predictive result is undeniably more reliable. However, even though the obtained labels are more trustworthy, there remains a possibility of error. To prevent the continuous interference of misclassified labels on the network, only the last network prediction result is reused. Experiments have demonstrated that most of the remote sensing image labels can be acquired through the first sample-selection process, and these labels are reliable.

As illustrated in Fig. 5.8, the labels selected under multi-layer monitoring are deemed reliable. In this manner, more pseudo labels can guide the network training once again. Abundant prior knowledge can undoubtedly enhance the network's classification performance through self-training. Additionally, if highly accurate results are not essential, the circular part of the network can be omitted to accomplish rapid change detection operations.

(5) Learning of Framework In the proposed framework, circular structure is pivotal to classification task. Algorithm 5.2 shows the learning process of SSLAN.

Algorithm 5.2 Learning process of SSLAN

Input: X:Remote image datasets; X_{all}:all data; $X_{labeled}$:data with true labels; $iter_{max}$:the number of iterations.

Output: CM: change map.

Step 1) Data X adjacent-window processing.

Step 2) Preparation of X_{all} and $X_{labeled}$.

Step 3) **while** $i < iter_{max}$ **do**

  if $i > 1$ **then**

   $X_{labeled} = X_{labeled} + X_{pseudo}$

  i. Ladder network training;

  ii. Outputting semi-supervised CM: CM_{semi};

  iii. Extracting hidden-layers information;

  iv. Outputting unsupervised CMs: CM_i;

  v. CMs fusion and selecting pseudo labels:

   $X_{pseudo} = CM_{semi} \cap CM_i$;

  vi. $i = i + 1$;

  end while

Step 4) **return** The final semi-supervised CM.

In the proposed iterative framework, the losses L over all time steps $t \in \{t \mid t = 1, 2, ..., T\}$ can be accumulated and formulated as:

$$\min_{l,n,\{\lambda_i\}} L(x; x_{label}) = \sum_{t=1}^{T} L^t(x; x_{label}) \tag{5.2}$$

At stage t, the loss function of SSALN can be formulated as follows. Notably, at the final stage, noise n will not be added in network training.

$$
\begin{aligned}
L^{t}(x; x_{label}) &= C_c + C_d \\
&= C_c + \sum_{i=0}^{l-1} \lambda_i \cdot C_d^i \\
&= -\frac{1}{n} \sum_{i=1}^{n} \log P\left(g(x_{label}) | y_{label}\right) \\
&+ \frac{1}{n} \sum_{i=0}^{l-1} \frac{\lambda_i}{m_i} \sum_{j=1}^{n} \left\| f(x)_i^j - (x+n)_i^j \right\|^2
\end{aligned}
\tag{5.3}
$$

where C_c represents the supervised loss, and C_d denotes the unsupervised loss at each layer. The variable n is the number of training samples. The function $P(\cdot)$ calculates the average negative log-probability of the noisy output $g(x_{label})$ with respect to the prior labels y_{label}. The parameter l indicates the number of network layers. λ_i is the unsupervised penalty factor for each layer, and m_i represents the number of nodes in each layer. Moreover, $f(x)_i^j$ is the unsupervised output, and x_i^j is the processed pixel pair in each sample j of each layer i.

Based on these elements, a semi-supervised circulative remote sensing image change detection framework is proposed. This framework is capable of obtaining the final change map by using only a small number of manually identified labels. Additionally, the classification performance was evaluated using the minimum number of pre-obtained labels, revealing the remarkable practicality of this approach.

5.2.2.2 Dynamic Framework with Self-Variable Structure

The incorporation of structure searching is primarily aimed at addressing the issues of large-scale, time-consuming, and inefficient manual parameter adjustment. Pseudo-codes are utilized to depict the flow of adaptive structure training within circular networks. As illustrated in Fig. 5.9, an optimal structure can be obtained through self-adaptive searching. The entire network structure search is grounded in the evolutionary algorithm. This algorithm adopts a specialized combinatorial off-

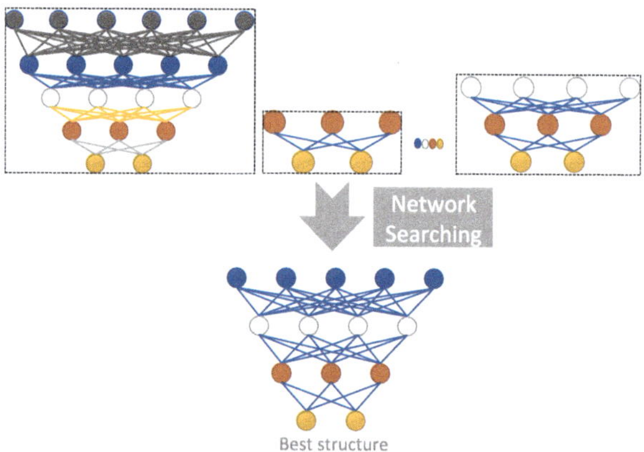

Fig. 5.9 Illustration of network searching

spring selection method that focuses on the utilization of intermediate information across multiple hidden layers.

(1) Dynamic Network Structure During the evolutionary selection process, the search is confined to the number of network layers and nodes, thus reducing the overall evolutionary search space.

The number of network layers and nodes for the coding layer of the auto-encoder network are encoded within the network. The decoding layer is in one-to-one correspondence with the coding layer, eliminating the need for additional coding operations. Step 1 of Fig. 5.10 depicts this process with two example networks. For instance, if net 2 has 4, 3, and 2 nodes in its first, second, and third layers respectively, it is encoded as [4, 3, 2]. In Algorithm 5.3, the initial population

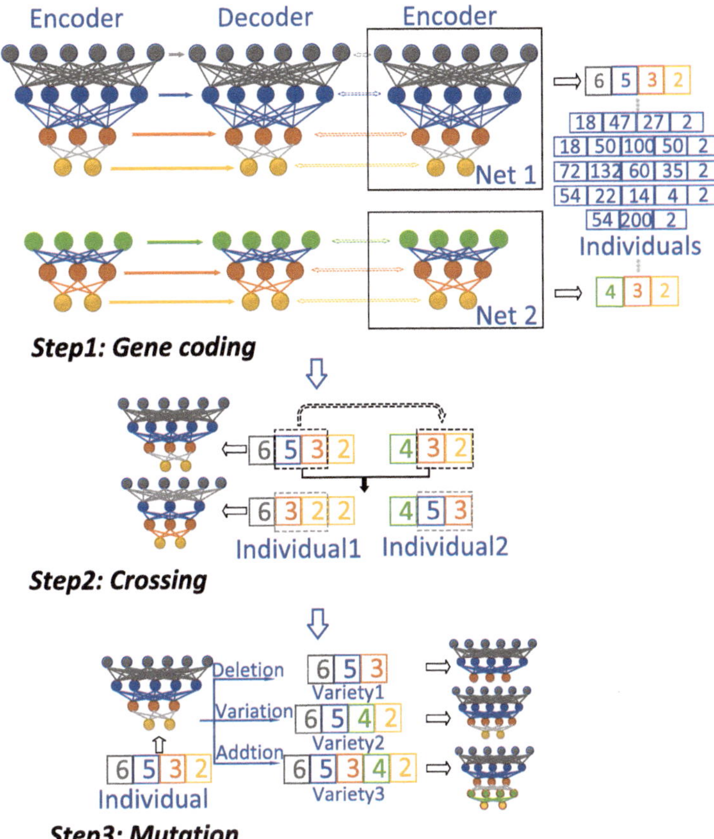

Fig. 5.10 Population evolution of network

of SSALN individuals is configured with varying numbers of layers and different numbers of nodes in each layer. Subsequently, corresponding evolutionary operations such as crossing and mutation, as depicted in step 2 and step 3 of Fig. 5.10, are performed. Finally, the offspring individuals with the highest classification accuracy are selected. Additionally, each network cycle triggers a new search for the neural architecture, as the increased information from predictive labels can lead to unforeseen changes.

Algorithm 5.3 Dynamic compatible structure adjustment

Input: X:Remote image datasets; n:popsize; $iter_{max}$:the number of iterations.
Output: The better architecture.

Step 1) Population initialization.
Step 2) Calculate fitness L^t of each individual.
Step 3) **while** $i < iter_{max}$ **do**
  i. Generation of offsprings;
  ii. Comparative fitness;
  if no better elimination **then**
    break
  iii. Evolutionary selection;
  iv. $i = i + 1$;
  end while
Step 4) **return** Better architecture.

(2) Fitness Evaluation Combined with Average Unsupervised Loss During the network architecture searching process, a vast number of network individuals are generated. To assess the quality of these network individuals, a set of criteria needs to be established. Three factors are taken into account: the average level α, the total loss L^t, and the loss of the unsupervised layers L_u^t. Firstly, the average level α serves as a fundamental metric for evaluating the basic merit of two individuals. It ensures that each selected individual meets or exceeds this average benchmark:

$$\alpha = \left(L^t(x; x_{label})_{\max} - L^t(x; x_{label})_{\min}\right) \big/ N \tag{5.4}$$

where L^t is the loss of step t, and N represents the number of network individuals.

Secondly, high-order features are utilized for unsupervised analysis to complement the semi-supervised analysis. Therefore, when making selections, the unsupervised attributes L_u^t are also considered to ensure an adequate amount of labeled information within the unsupervised part of the model:

$$L_u^t = \sum_{i=0}^{l-1} C_d^i \Big/ l \tag{5.5}$$

$$
\begin{array}{c} better \\ individual \end{array} = \begin{cases} A, & \begin{array}{c} (L^t)_B - (L^t)_A \geq \alpha \\ or \\ (L^t)_A - (L^t)_B \geq \alpha \& (L^t_u)_B \geq (L^t_u)_A \end{array} \\ B, \; otherwise & \end{cases} \tag{5.6}
$$

In Eq. (5.6), it is assumed that the overall loss L^t of individual B is greater than that of individual A by default. If this is not the case, the positions of individuals A and B are interchanged. When the difference $((L^t)_B - (L^t)_A)$ is less than the average level α, the individual A with the lower unsupervised loss $(L^t_u)_A$ is more likely to be selected. This implies a preference for better reconstruction-based classification. Algorithm 5.4 encapsulates the entire evolutionary selection process.

Algorithm 5.4 Combinatorial strategy of evolution under unsupervised control

---

Input: p:Crossover rate; q:variation rate; pop:Network population.
Output: Optimal individual.
Step 1) Crossing and mutation to get offspring off_{pop}.
Step 2) Calculate the fitness value L^t of each offspring, including total loss a and average unsupervised loss b.
Step 3) Calculation $\alpha = (L^t{}_{max} - L^t{}_{min}) \, / \, n$.
Step 4) **if** $a_1 - a_2 > \alpha$ **then**
  return a_2
 else
  if $b_1 > b_2$ **then**
   return a_2
  else
   return a_1
  end
 end
Step 5) **return** Optimal individual.

---

(3) Prevention of Population Degradation To avoid meaningless network evolution, the "stop without better offspring" principle is implemented. This implies that if the classification performance of the offspring in the subsequent three generations of the network is inferior to that of the worst-performing network individual in the parent generation, the iterative process is halted immediately, and the optimal network individual at that moment is preserved.

5.2.2.3 Combinatorial Label-Selection Strategy

(1) Unsupervised Clustering Operation Besides the direct prediction results of the initial network, a set of high-order features that have been extracted are reused. It is noted that a simple unsupervised AE network tends to extract features that are beneficial for reconstruction and restoration. In contrast, a dual-input label-incremental network, under the guidance of labeled data, can extract high-order features that are more conducive to classification, with their characteristics being modified.

Subsequently, an unsupervised clustering method is applied to the high-order features extracted from each layer. This helps to mitigate the impact of redundant information and noise, making the features more suitable for classification. Finally, for the feature-extraction results of each layer, a corresponding change map can be obtained, enabling classification results to be derived from an unsupervised perspective.

(2) Selection of New Predictive Labels For the unsupervised prediction results nl and the semi-supervised network results nl_{semi} at each layer, the same percentage of points is assigned. Thus, the total score NL_j can be formulated as follows:

$$(NL)_j = \sum_{i=0}^{l-1} nl_i + nl_{semi} \tag{5.7}$$

where l is the number of network layers, and the scores for the changed and unchanged areas are as follows:

$$nl_i, nl_{semi} = \begin{cases} 0, \; predictive\ unchanged \\ 1, \; predictive\ changed \end{cases} \tag{5.8}$$

The following rules are employed to filter for reliable changed and unchanged pseudo labels:

$$(NL)_j = \begin{cases} l \;,\; changed\ sample \\ 0 \;,\; unchanged\ sample \\ otherwise,\ uncertain\ sample \end{cases} \tag{5.9}$$

In this manner, sample selection is carried out from the perspectives of semi-supervised network prediction and unsupervised clustering classification. Subsequently, the network is retrained to enhance accuracy. However, despite multi-layer control, misclassified samples may still exist and flow into the network. Therefore, the sample selection results are only utilized after the final screening.

5.2.3 *Experimental Study*

5.2.3.1 Datasets and Evaluation Metrics

In the experiments, five types of remote sensing images presented in Table 5.2 are employed to assess the performance of the proposed method. Each image pair has undergone radiometric correction and co-registration to maximize their

Table 5.2 The introduction of test data

Category	SAR	Optical	Heterogeneous	VHR	Multispectral
Dataset	Bern	Mexico City	Wuhan	Guangzhou	Hongqi
	Ottawa	Sardinia	Sardinia	Montpellia	Minfeng
	Yellow River		Shuguang	Shanghai	Yandu
Pixel Size	301 × 301	512 × 512	503 × 495	877 × 738	539 × 543
	290 × 350	412 × 300	412 × 300	451 × 426	651 × 461
	450 × 280		921 × 593	873 × 782	322 × 266

comparability. The test indicators will be presented in the subsequent tables corresponding to each type of remote sensing image dataset. In the experimental evaluations, the Pearson Correlation Coefficient (PCC) and the Kappa coefficient κ are utilized to quantify the performance of remote sensing image change detection.

5.2.3.2 Experiment Setting

The whole framework is based on one-time network training and circulative part. Some detailed parameters will be described as follows.

(1) One-Time Network Training Remote sensing images are sampled in local neighborhoods of size $w \times w \times h$, where each neighborhood centered at a pixel constitutes a single sample. Here, h denotes the number of bands in the image. A total of 100 pixels are selected as semi-supervised training labels. For the auto-encoder part, the noise factor is set to 0.3, and the weights of the reconstruction layer are set as [1000.0, 0.10, 0.010, 0.0010, 0.00010].

(2) Circulative Training To prevent over-fitting and to actively learn the variable difference information in remote sensing images when the detection objects are switched, the complexity of the structure searching algorithm is kept lower than that of the complete network training. Regarding the network architecture design, an overly large and complex neural network is not recommended. The ideal network structure should have a relatively small number of nodes in each layer and tend to be deeper, facilitating multi-layer unsupervised feature extraction.

5.2.3.3 Performance of SSALN Compared with Other Methods

In the experiments, all performance comparisons are categorized into three types: unsupervised, semi-supervised, and supervised. This categorization helps in understanding the detection capabilities in relation to labeled and unlabeled methods. The supervised approach includes a comparison of ResNet [42] with a fully-connected structure applied to remote sensing images [43], which uses 100, 60%, and 100% labeled data respectively. Simultaneously, SSALN with the same 60% labeled data

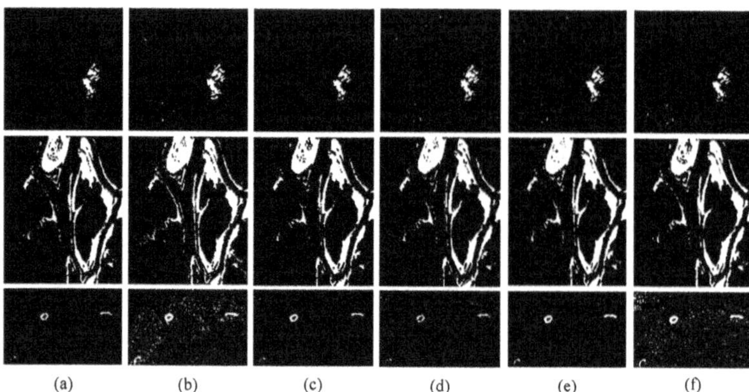

Fig. 5.11 SAR images datasets and change detection results. (**a**) DNN, (**b**) MSSDNN, (**c**) EVONN, (**d**) Semi-GAN, (**e**) SSALN (100), (**f**) Resnet (100%)

Table 5.3 Performance comparison of different methods on SAR datasets

		Bern		Ottawa		Yellow River	
Method type	Method	PCC	κ	PCC κ	PCC	κ	
Unsupervised	RFLICM	0.9964	0.8377	0.9733	0.8935	0.9878	0.5998
	MSSDNN	0.9960	0.8545	0.9719	0.8981	0.9669	0.3567
	EVONN	0.9965	0.8589	0.9845	**0.9845**	0.9963	0.7999
Semi-supervised	Semi-GAN(100)	0.9947	0.8073	0.9738	0.8994	0.9928	0.5933
	SSALN (100)	0.9964	0.8634	0.9851	0.9444	0.9975	0.8778
	SSALN (60%)	**0.9970**	**0.8838**	**0.9889**	0.9588	**0.9977**	**0.8901**
Supervised	Resnet (100)	0.1878	0.0841	0.1096	0.0528	0.2578	0.0190
	Resnet (60%)	0.9871	0.8173	0.9576	0.8771	0.8593	0.1732
	Resnet (100%)	0.9960	0.8434	0.9736	0.9029	0.9726	0.4142

is utilized as the semi-supervised method under a unified standard for performance comparison. Additionally, to address the fixed limited labels, only SSALN (100) is elaborated upon in the experimental analysis section.

(1) SAR Image For SAR remote sensing images, Fig. 5.11 shows Bern, Ottawa and Yellow River data set from top to bottom compared with RFLICM [12], MSSDNN [13], EVONN [37] and Semi-GAN [44] methods. And index results are shown in Table 5.3.

Subjectively, the detection performance of each method appears satisfactory. This can be attributed to the relatively simple internal change structure of the Bern dataset and the simplicity of the SAR image. Regarding the Ottawa dataset, all methods have managed to detect the main change areas. However, the key challenge of this dataset lies in the presence of a small number of unchanged points within large change areas, particularly in the upper-left corner of the large change region shown in Fig. 5.11f. The proposed method ensures extremely-fine classification performance. The Yellow River dataset is significantly affected by noise, making change detection difficult. Nevertheless, in the comparison of PCC and κ, the proposed method has achieved the best results. Simultaneously, it is highly successful in restoring the details of the lower-left corner, outperforming the DNN and EVONN methods in Column 3 of Fig. 5.11.

Furthermore, SSALN, when using 100 labeled training data, already attains a very good result. When provided with more training samples (i.e., 60% of the total available labeled data), its performance improves even further. Notably, the proposed method can even outperform the supervised ResNet trained with 100% of the available labeled data. Since SSALN combines supervised and unsupervised approaches, it can make full use of the vast amount of unlabeled information, which is an advantage over the supervised method (i.e., ResNet). Moreover, the supervised network with 100% labels is prone to problems such as over-fitting, resulting in inferior results.

(2) Optical Image For Optical remote sensing images, Fig. 5.12 shows Mexico City and Sardinia data set from top to bottom compared with SCCN [45], EVONN [37] and Semi-GAN [44] methods. And index results are shown in Table 5.4.

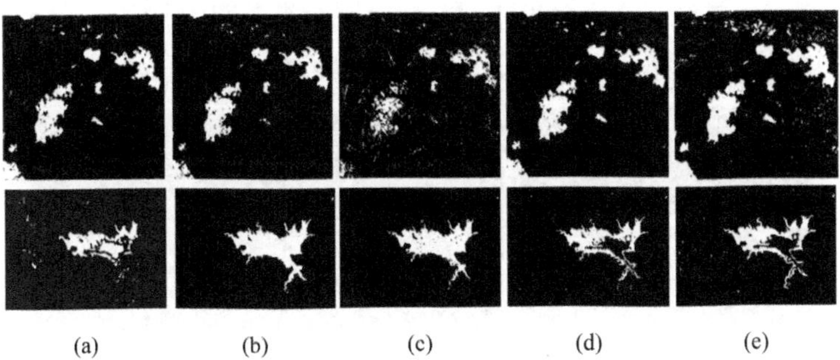

Fig. 5.12 Optical images datasets and change detection results. (**a**) SCCN, (**b**) EVONN, (**c**) Semi-GAN, (**d**) SSALN (100), (**e**) Resnet (100%)

Table 5.4 The evaluation indexes of optical image

Method type	Method	Mexico City		Sardinia	
		PCC	κ	PCC	κ
Unsupervised	SCNN	0.9826	**0.9011**	0.9618	0.6796
	EVONN	0.9910	0.8247	0.9546	0.7007
Semi-supervised	Semi-GAN(100)	0.9731	0.4763	0.9601	0.7219
	SSALN(100)	0.9933	0.8785	0.9836	0.8702
	SSALN(60%)	**0.9934**	0.8833	**0.9905**	**0.9205**
Supervised	Resnet(100)	0.1584	0.1453	0.1852	0.2399
	Resnet(60%)	0.9382	0.7354	0.9359	0.6801
	Resnet(100%)	0.9716	0.8571	0.9816	0.8602

As is evident, the proposed method exhibits the lowest false-detection rate in Table 5.4. This is because it effectively manages the boundary between the changed and unchanged regions. In the Mexico City dataset, the over-fitting of the unchanged area is relatively minor. Regarding the Sardinia dataset, it is clear that the proposed method outperforms other detection methods. As depicted in Fig. 5.12d, the outline is more distinct. This is further corroborated by the fact that the detection coefficients of the PCC and κ rank first for the Sardinia dataset in Table 5.4.

(3) Heterogeneous Image For Heterogeneous remote sensing images, Fig. 5.13 shows Wuhan, Yellow Sardinia and Shuguang data set from top to bottom compared with ALSC-O [46], PSGM [47] and Semi-GAN [44] methods. And index results are shown in Table 5.5.

For the Wuhan dataset, while the proposed method can suppress noise interference to a certain degree, this also results in a weakening of detection performance in the main change areas. This is the reason why it obtains a relatively lower score in the κ coefficient in Table 5.5. Around the changed area of the Sardinia dataset, all methods are inevitably encountered with the issue of noise. The proposed method

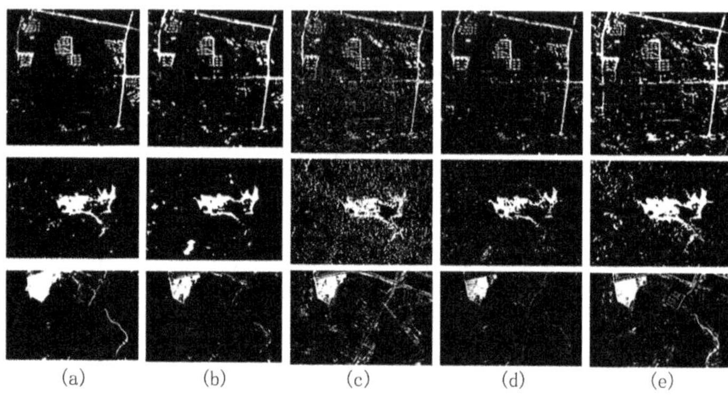

Fig. 5.13 Heterogeneous images datasets and change detection results. (**a**) ALSC-O, (**b**) PSGM, (**c**) Semi-GAN, (**d**) SSALN (100), (**e**) Resnet (100%)

Table 5.5 The evaluation indexes of heterogeneous image

		Wuhan		Sardinia		Shuguang	
Method type	Method	PCC	κ	PCC	κ	**PCC**	κ
Unsupervised	ALSC-O	0.9540	0.5950	0.9620	0.6983	0.9580	0.6410
	PSGM	0.9532	0.6858	0.9610	0.6821	0.9766	0.7438
Semi-supervised	Semi-GAN (100)	0.8973	0.3957	0.8867	0.3908	0.9257	0.4629
	SSALN (100)	0.9579	0.6556	0.9670	0.7115	0.9777	0.7295
	SSALN (60%)	**0.9725**	**0.7113**	**0.9842**	**0.8571**	**0.9795**	**0.7522**
Supervised	Resnet (100)	0.1985	0.0921	0.2091	0.1204	0.2402	0.2116
	Resnet (60%)	0.8257	0.4897	0.9197	0.4981	0.9155	0.5901
	Resnet (100%)	0.9124	0.5393	0.9423	0.6307	0.9498	0.6142

is capable of suppressing noise in a large unchanged area. However, this is achieved at the expense of missing some changed regions, as depicted in Fig. 5.13e. In the Shuguang dataset, both over-fitting and under-fitting occur simultaneously. Visually, there is no substantial difference among the methods. In terms of the κ value, the proposed method is slightly lower than the PSGM method in the Shuguang dataset of Table 5.5, due to the presence of more discontinuous black false-detection areas in Fig. 5.13b.

(4) VHR Image For VHR remote sensing images, Fig. 5.14 shows Guangzhou, Montpellia and Shanghai data set from top to bottom compared with DCVA [48], DBN [49], MSDRL [50] and Semi-GAN [44] methods. And index results are shown in Table 5.6.

For the three small middle parts of the change regions, only the proposed method demonstrates the best detail-retention ability. This is the reason it attains the highest PCC and κ in the Guangzhou dataset presented in Table 5.6. Compared to the Guangzhou dataset, the Montpellia dataset has numerous scattered changed

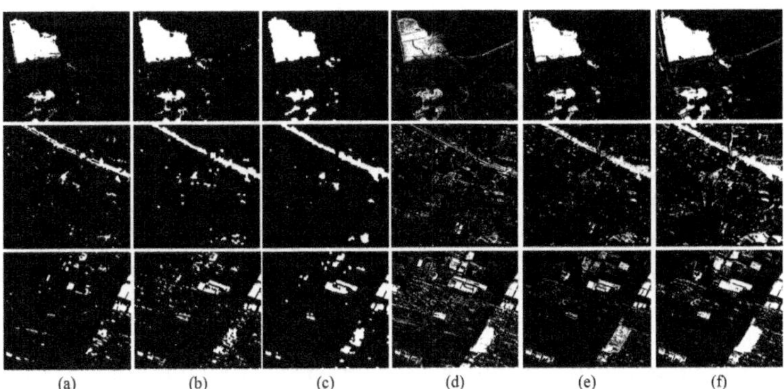

Fig. 5.14 VHR images datasets and change detection results. (**a**) DCVA, (**b**) DBN, (**c**) MSDRL, (**d**) Semi-GAN, (**e**) SSALN (100), (**f**) Resnet (100%)

Table 5.6 The evaluation indexes of VHR image

		Guangzhou		Montpellia		Shanghai	
Method type	Method	PCC	κ	PCC	κ	PCC	κ
Unsupervised	DCVA	0.9606	0.8343	0.9425	0.6101	0.9233	0.5729
	DBN	0.9666	0.8572	0.9514	0.5557	0.9339	0.5145
	MSDRL	0.9752	0.9007	0.9694	0.7339	0.9524	0.6768
Semi-supervised	Semi-GAN (100)	0.9247	0.6654	0.9118	0.2977	0.8889	0.5010
	SSALN (100)	0.9781	0.9118	0.9591	0.6404	0.9553	0.7117
	SSALN (60%)	**0.9796**	**0.9189**	**0.9709**	**0.7424**	**0.9714**	**0.8144**
Supervised	Resnet (100)	0.3914	0.2985	0.2319	0.2310	0.3981	0.1953
	Resnet (60%)	0.9385	0.8571	0.8692	0.4932	0.8962	0.6294
	Resnet (100%)	0.9701	0.8873	0.9248	0.5741	0.9386	0.6977

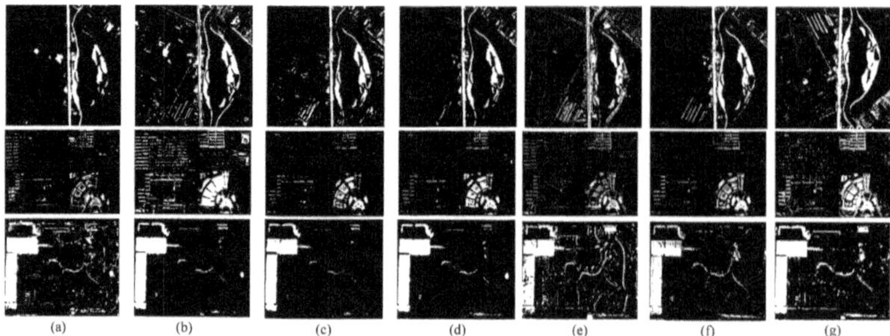

Fig. 5.15 Multispectral images datasets and change detection results. (**a**) IR-MAD, (**b**) DNN, (**c**) GAND, (**d**) GDCN, (**e**) Semi-GAN, (**f**) SSALN(100), (**g**) Resnet (100%)

Table 5.7 The evaluation indexes of multispectral image

Method type	Method	Hongqi		Minfeng		Yandu	
		PCC	κ	PCC	κ	PCC	κ
Unsupervised	IR-MAD	0.9491	0.6856	0.9376	0.5221	0.9141	0.6817
	DNN	0.9532	0.7231	0.8810	0.4531	0.9446	0.7693
	GAND	0.9476	0.7252	0.9533	0.6151	0.9449	0.7538
	GDCN	0.9697	0.8107	0.9526	0.6421	0.9058	0.7909
Semi-supervised	Semi-GAN (100)	0.9077	0.4846	0.9269	0.4529	0.9058	0.6308
	SSALN (100)	0.9713	0.8297	0.9563	0.6668	0.9523	0.7978
	SSALN (60%)	**0.9751**	**0.8491**	**0.9679**	**0.6714**	**0.9540**	**0.8029**
Supervised	Resnet (100)	0.3091	0.2712	0.1842	0.2011	0.3099	0.2549
	Resnet (60%)	0.8593	0.6767	0.8875	0.5491	0.8591	0.6771
	Resnet (100%)	0.9439	0.7292	0.9243	0.6063	0.9279	0.7255

regions. This gives rise to over-fitting, as observable in Column 2 of Fig. 5.14. In the Shanghai dataset, the highest PCC and κ values confirm that the proposed method outperforms others. Subjectively, the results in Table 5.6 are consistent.

(5) Multispectral Image For multispectral remote sensing images, Fig. 5.15 shows Hongqi, Minfeng and Yandu data set from top to bottom compared with IR-MAD [51], DNN [52], GAND [4], GDCN [53] and Semi-GAN [44] methods. And index results are shown in Table 5.7.

From the detection results, it is evident that the proposed method can preserve the best details across the entire remote sensing image and suppress noise in the middle area, achieving the best PCC and κ as presented in Table 5.7. Compared to the Hongqi dataset, change detection in the Minfeng dataset is more challenging. Evidently, the proposed method performs better, outperforming other change detection methods with the highest PCC and κ in the Minfeng dataset of Table 5.7. As depicted in Fig. 5.15f, a good detection result is obtained in the unchanged area within the changed area. For the Yandu dataset, an overly strong fitting effect weakens the detection of the middle road, which resembles a clothes rack in Fig. 5.15e. Clearly, the proposed method achieves the best change detection results with the highest PCC and κ.

5.2.3.4 Extra Comparison of Uncalibrated Objects: UAV as an Example

Previously, the remote sensing images were all matched and aligned, ensuring no additional pixel-pair misalignment. However, UAV images, captured by cameras mounted on UAVs, are acquired from different viewpoints and angles. Thus, it is a relevant question to explore whether the proposed semi-supervised framework can still accomplish the detection task when guided by a small number of labels in unregistered images.

Figure 5.16 showcases the relevant UAV image dataset, and Fig. 5.17a–g displays the change detection results of the UAV dataset in comparison with classification-based [54], superpixel-based [55], and BDNN [56] methods. From the results, it is evident that the performance of the traditional methods in Fig. 5.17b, d, f is suboptimal, as they are restricted to a consistent coordinate system and are thus subject to various interferences. BDNN method employs content comparison, enabling it to extract holistic features from unchanged regions, thereby achieving good results.

Notably, even when compared to the specially-designed BDNN for UAV images, the proposed method can largely suppress the surrounding noise. The contour edges of the main change areas are effectively detected. This demonstrates that, even in unregistered images, the proposed SSALN can effectively utilize the labeled data to

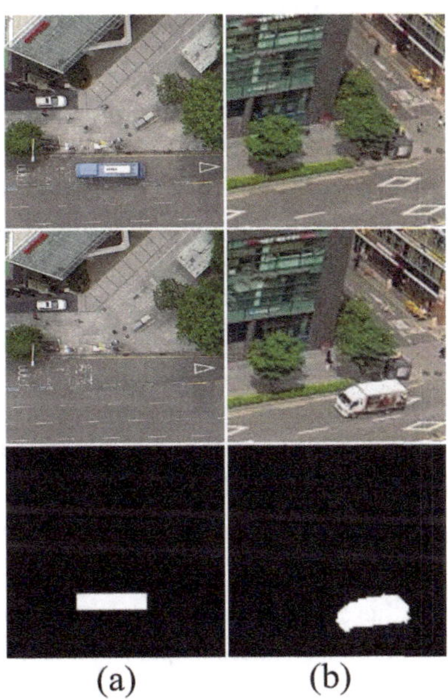

Fig. 5.16 (**a**) UAV image 1, (**b**) UAV image 2

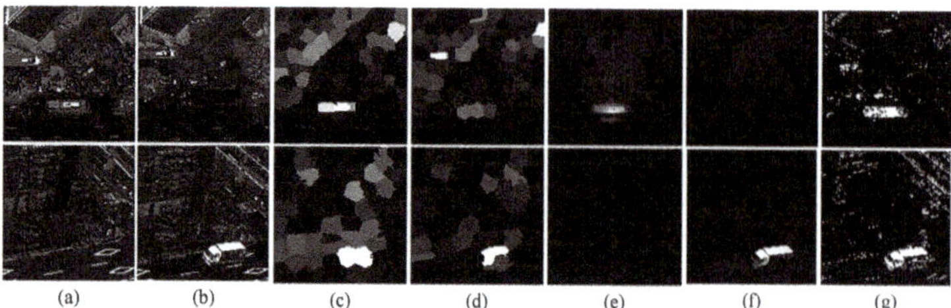

Fig. 5.17 Difference images generated on the UAV data set by (**a**) and (**b**) classification-based, (**c**) and (**d**) superpixel-based, (**e**) and (**f**) BDNN, change detection result achieved by (**g**) SSALN

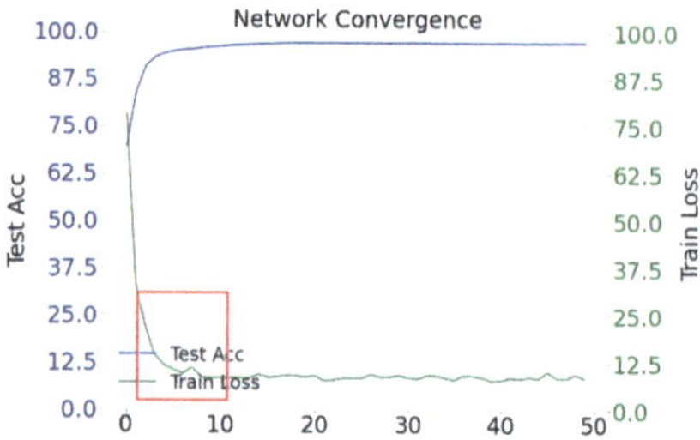

Fig. 5.18 Illustration of network convergence in Bern data set of SAR image

actively learn the difference information related to changes. This remarkable feature is attributed to the model's low reliance on true labels and the high reliability of the updated pseudo-labels obtained through a combinatorial approach.

5.2.3.5 Effect of Network Circulation

Overall, as the core of the framework, it is necessary to prove the validity and reliability of circular part.

(1) The Convergence of Network in One Circulation As shown in Fig. 5.18, the experiment is conducted on the first image pair: the Bern dataset of SAR images, with 50 iterations serving as an example. Here, the stability of the test accuracy is used as the criterion. The network is considered to have converged when the loss oscillation is within a certain range. Essentially, the network converges within five iterations, as indicated by the red box in Fig. 5.18. The training loss and test accuracy have stabilized, meeting the requirements.

Regarding network circulation, after obtaining more reliable pseudo-labels, the overall network should demonstrate an upward trend in performance improvement. This issue will be analyzed from two perspectives as follows.

(2) The Number of Available Labels in Network Training The pseudo labels of the entire framework are selected based on the classification prediction labels generated by the unsupervised method and the semi-supervised network.

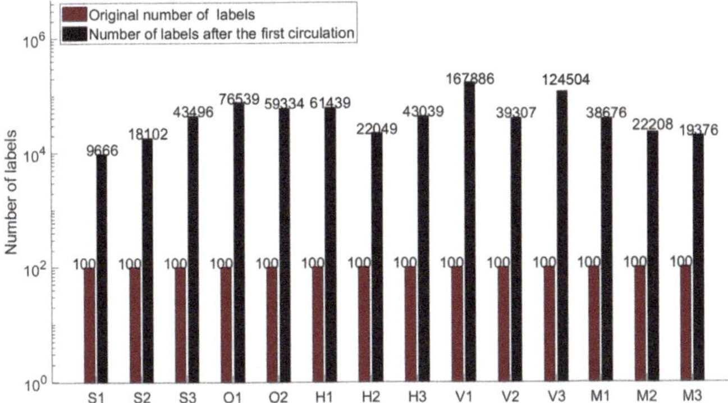

Fig. 5.19 The number of new pseudo labels added after the first circulation on each remote sensing image dataset. Note: S1 means the first dataset of SAR image, and O2 is corresponding to the second dataset of Optical image. A similar meaning can be applied on H1, V1, M1 and so on

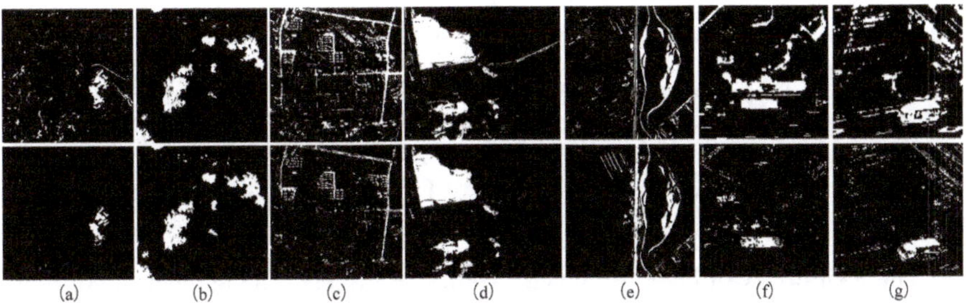

Fig. 5.20 The first column and the second column are the change detection results of the first and last circulation respectively. (**a**) SAR image, (**b**) optical image , (**c**) heterogeneous image, (**d**) VHR image, (**e**) multispectral image, (**f**) UAV1 image, (**g**) UAV2 image

To examine the degree to which the number of reliable labels increases after the circulation, the number of labels obtained after the first circulation is compared with the 100 initial real labels. Figure 5.19 depicts a remarkable increase in the number of available labels. The quantity of available labels has achieved a qualitative leap, significantly enriching the information that the neural network can process. This also validates that the framework can effectively exploit the potential information in unlabeled data. As can be observed, for the first dataset of the Bern dataset in SAR images, the original number of labels used in network learning is 100. However, after the first circulation, the number of pseudo-labels that can be utilized increases to 9666. A similar substantial increase is also evident in other images.

Figure 5.20 clearly illustrates that the model's change detection performance ultimately improves as the network undergoes circulation. In the first circulation, with only 100 labels, this quantity is insufficient to detect complex marginal areas, leading to a more severe and inevitable over-fitting problem. However, after multiple iterations, as the number of available labels increases, the detailed detection areas

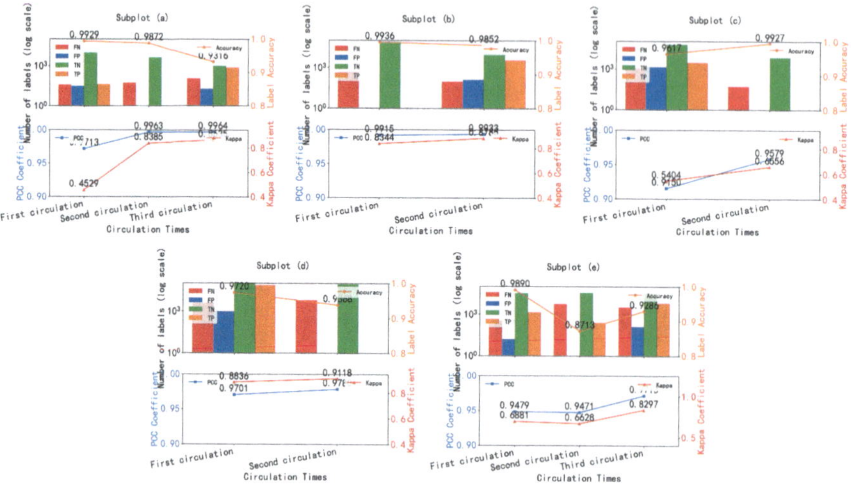

Fig. 5.21 Exhibition of the necessity of circulation on the increase of label number and accuracy and the coefficient of PCC and κ based on the first set of different datasets. (**a**) SAR dataset, (**b**) optical dataset, (**c**) heterogeneous dataset, (**d**) VHR dataset, (**e**) multispectral dataset

yield better results, as shown in Column 2 of Fig. 5.20. This is because the model's ability to suppress noise and preserve details has been significantly enhanced.

(3) The Reliability of New Achieved Predictive Labels The number of correctly detected samples in the unchanged and changed areas, as well as the incorrectly detected samples in these areas (TN, TP, FN and FP) in the predictive results, along with the accuracy with respect to the ground-truth maps, are presented in Column 1 of Fig. 5.21. It can be observed that TN and TP constitute the majority of all predictive labels, and the quality of the predictive labels is generally over 90%. This indicates that most of these labels are reliable. Consequently, these pseudo labels can be reused to train the neural network iteratively to achieve better classification capabilities, as verified by the high PCC and κ values in Column 2 of Fig. 5.21. Additionally, when the label accuracy, PCC, and κ essentially remain unchanged, the circulation process is halted. Based on numerous experiments, the network performance stabilizes after three circulations.

5.2.3.6 Effect of SSALN: Network Structure Adjustment

To prove the effective of structure searching, the performance of autonomous-searched net and artificial-designed net on the first dataset in different type of remote sensing image is showed in Fig. 5.22.

As depicted in Fig. 5.22a–e, models with different network structures exhibit varying performance on the same image. The comparison between the better network structure identified by SSALN and other empirically-designed networks

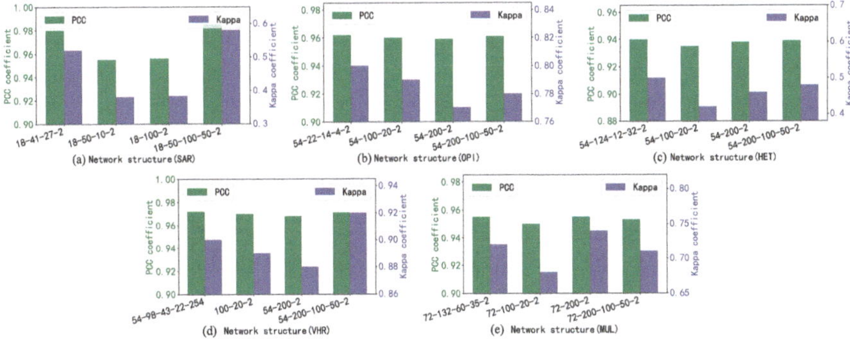

Fig. 5.22 Exhibition of the effective of SSALN on the several network structures based on each of the first set of different datasets. (**a**) SAR dataset, (**b**) optical dataset, (**c**) heterogeneous dataset, (**d**) VHR dataset and (**e**) multispectral dataset

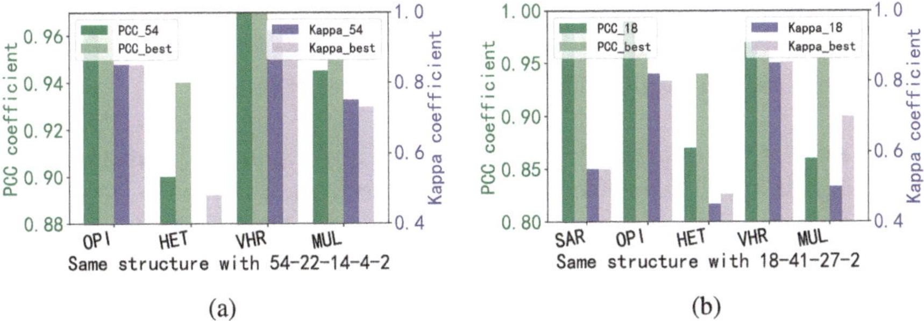

Fig. 5.23 Exhibition of the same net structure of SSALN on the different datasets. (**a**) The same network structure based on all of the first set of different datasets. (**b**) The same network structure based on datasets with multiple spectral bands

validates the efficacy of network architecture search for a single image. For instance, in the SAR image of Fig. 5.22a, the network with the searched 18-41-27-2 structure demonstrates performance comparable to that of the manually-defined empirical network with a 18-50-100-50-2 structure, outperforming the ordinary manually-defined structures of 18-50-10-2 and 18-100-2. Consequently, the performance of the network structure found by SSALN is either on par with or superior to that of an empirically-designed artificial network. Moreover, SSALN addresses the issue where a single network fails to adaptively and intelligently learn different information when the detection objects change. This is evident in the situation where a particular network may perform well on SAR datasets but poorly on heterogeneous images.

Furthermore, to investigate the necessity of network structure adjustment when switching between different data types, an experiment was conducted in Fig. 5.23, where the same searched network structure was applied to different types of remote sensing images.

Figure 5.23a indicates that the network with an 18-41-27-2 structure, which is specifically searched for SAR images, performs well within the SAR image dataset but poorly for other remote sensing image types. Since SAR images have only one spectral segment, their processed dimension differs from that of other image types. Hence, on this basis, remote sensing image data types with the same number of spectral segments are considered for measurement. The network structure of 54-22-14-4-2, which is separately searched for optical images, is applied to heterogeneous images, VHR images, and multispectral images, as presented in Fig. 5.23b. The results demonstrate that, despite having consistent input dimensions, the network that performs optimally in optical images fails to achieve outstanding results in other remote sensing image types. This reveals the complexity of difference information among different remote sensing image datasets. Nevertheless, SSALN can actively learn the difference information and autonomously complete the search for the most suitable structure without human intervention, thereby attaining the best detection performance for a specific remote sensing image data type.

5.2.3.7 Network Feasibility on Minimum Number of Labels

(1) The Effectiveness of the Presented Pseudo Label Updating Strategy Before analyzing the minimum number of labels, the effectiveness of pseudo label update strategy is verified. From the accuracy of pseudo labels, the proposed pseudo-label updating strategy is grounded in semi-supervised classification and unsupervised analysis. The unsupervised analysis plays an additional role in assisting the presented SSALN in pseudo-label updating, offering a completely distinct perspective. To investigate this, the following metrics were evaluated: FN, FP, TN, TP, and the accuracy of new pseudo-labels generated without unsupervised analysis, as depicted in Fig. 5.24.

The results clearly indicate that with the implemented pseudo-label updating strategy, although the quantity of available labels has decreased, the accuracy has increased to a certain degree. It is remarkable that in the case without the strategy, the number of FPs is larger than that of TPs. This implies that in the area detected as

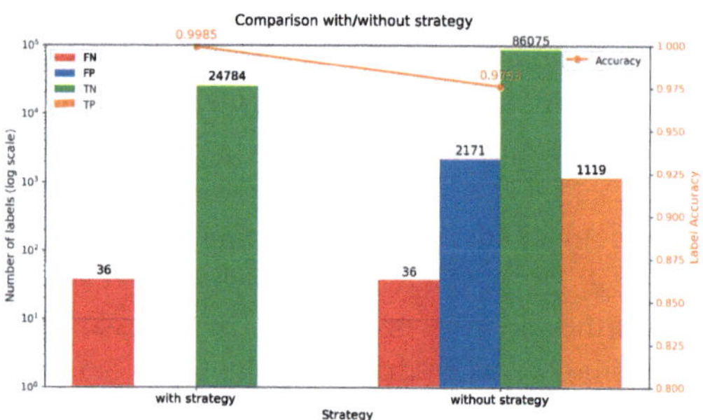

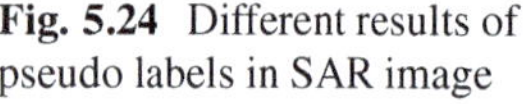
Fig. 5.24 Different results of pseudo labels in SAR image

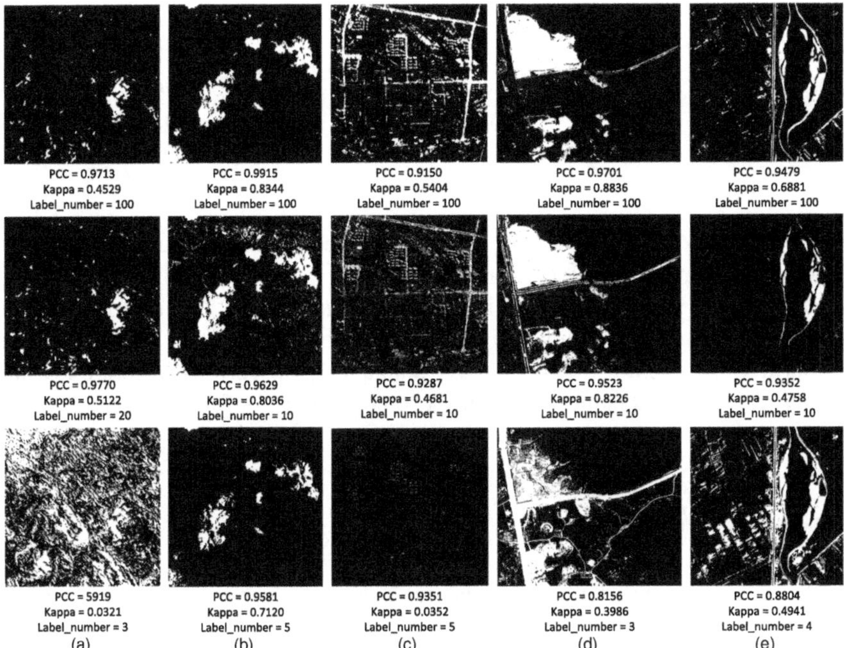

Fig. 5.25 The test of minimum number of true labels adopted in the network training based on the first set of different datasets. (**a**) SAR dataset, (**b**) optical dataset, (**c**) heterogeneous dataset, (**d**) VHR dataset, (**e**) Multispectral dataset

changed, the error part dominates, which significantly weakens the network's ability to learn the difference information between the changed and unchanged areas.

(2) The Possible Minumum Number of Label Assumption The pseudo-label updating strategy's effectiveness depends on the availability of labels. Initially, the proposed framework was executed based on 100 true labels. To explore the network's greater practicality, experiments were conducted by reducing the number of labels used. As can be observed in Fig. 5.25, the test results for the minimum label amount vary across different types of remote sensing images. After more than ten rounds of retraining, a stable minimum number of labels for network use can be determined to avoid accidental outcomes. The final test reveals that even with as few as 10 labels, the network remains relatively stable. The classification accuracy of the initial training reaches up to 90%, enabling the completion of the iterative processes.

In reality, apart from the complexity of remote sensing images, the pixel-size of such images serves as a crucial metric for gauging the number of true labels required by the proposed semi-supervised network. As depicted in Fig. 5.25a, it is evident that a SAR image with a relatively small number of pixels can still accomplish the change detection task with as few as three labels. In contrast, other images

Table 5.8 The new compared evaluation indexes of heterogeneous image

Method	Wuhan		Sardinia		Shuguang	
	PCC	κ	PCC	κ	PCC	κ
SSALN (100)	0.9579	0.6556	0.9816	0.6877	0.9612	0.7764
SSALN (0.5%)	**0.9722**	**0.7081**	**0.9820**	**0.7288**	**0.9656**	**0.8057**

may yield sub-optimal results even when provided with 100 labels. As presented in Table 5.8, further testing indicates that approximately 0.5% of the total data in a remote sensing image can generally meet the requirements of the change detection task. The SSALN demonstrates significantly better performance under 0.5% label scenario. Consequently, the challenge of maintaining the network's feature-learning ability with a limited number of labels becomes an area for future research.

5.2.4 Conclusions

In this section, a semi-supervised adaptive ladder network (SSALN) is introduced for remote sensing image change detection. Featuring an iterative framework, this network is applicable to change detection across diverse types of remote sensing images. Following sample selection and network circulation, the latent information within the labeled data undergoes global diffusion during network training. This enables the high-level features extracted from unlabeled data to be simultaneously conducive to classification, without the need for complex structure generation and analysis. As a result, complex remote sensing image change detection tasks can be accomplished using only a small number of labels, significantly alleviating the burden of manual annotation. Besides, semi-supervised and unsupervised change detection approaches are combined together to guarantee the reliability of the predictive labels to support dynamic structural adjustment for incremental prior information. Multiple change detection maps are fused to generate labels for next iteration and the disposable principle also prevents the incorrect-divided labels from polluting the network, improving the process of label prediction. Finally both the fundamental and derivative analyses on five types of remote sensing image and UAV images have verified the universality and effectiveness of the SSALN and the ability to learn variable differences of multi-type remote sensing images proactively. Even if the detection object is switched, it can be well adaptive and compatible without manual modification of the network.

However, the detection results of misaligned UAV images reveal that while SSALN performs well on calibrated images, its performance deteriorates significantly for unregistered images. This is attributed to the substantial difficulty in label selection when the image is not calibrated. Therefore, the focus of the future work will be on maintaining the network's classification ability and enhancing its stability in the absence of image alignment.

References

1. Rikka, S., Pleskachevsky, A., Uiboupin, R., Jacobsen, S.: Sea state in the Baltic Sea from spaceborne high-resolution synthetic aperture radar imagery. Int. J. Remote Sens. **39**(4), 1256–1284 (2018)
2. Benassai, G., Luccio, D.D., Corcione, V., Nunziata, F., Migliaccio, M.: Marine spatial planning using high-resolution synthetic aperture radar measurements. IEEE J. Ocean. Eng. **43**(3), 586–594 (2018)
3. Yan, H., Liao, G., Zhang, Y., Xu, J., Li, J.: Effective baseline estimation in dual-channel synthetic aperture radar for moving target imaging and relocation. Digit. Signal Process. **78**, 1–10 (2018)
4. Gong, M., Niu, X., Zhang, P., Li, Z.: Generative adversarial networks for change detection in multispectral imagery. IEEE Geosci. Remote Sens. Lett. **14**(12), 2310–2314 (2017)
5. Meng, J., Lei, W.: Novel class-relativity non-local means with principal component analysis for multitemporal SAR image change detection. Int. J. Remote Sens. **39**(4), 1068–1091 (2018)
6. Shang, R., Zhang, W., Yuan, Y., Jiao, L.: Markov-Potts prior model and fuzzy membership based nonparametric SAR image change detection. In: International Conference on Bio-inspired Computing: Theories and Applications, pp. 1–6 (2017)
7. Zhuang, H., Deng, K., Fan, H., Mei, Y.: Strategies combining spectral angle mapper and change vector analysis to unsupervised change detection in multispectral images. IEEE Geosci. Remote Sens. Lett. **13**(5), 681–685 (2017)
8. Zhang, H., Gong, M., Zhang, P., Su, L., Jiao, S.: Feature-level change detection using deep representation and feature change analysis for multispectral imagery. IEEE Geosci. Remote Sens. Lett. **13**(11), 1666–1670 (2017)
9. Zhang, P., Gong, M., Su, L., Liu, J., Li, Z.: Change detection based on deep feature representation and mapping transformation for multi-spatial-resolution remote sensing images. ISPRS J. Photogramm. Remote Sens. **116**, 24–41 (2016)
10. Gong, M., Zhao, J., Liu, J., Miao, Q., Jiao, L.: Change detection in synthetic aperture radar images based on deep neural networks. IEEE Trans. Neural Netw. Learn. Syst. **27**(1), 125–138 (2017)
11. Liu, F., Jiao, L., Tang, X., Yang, S., Ma, W., Hou, B.: Local restricted convolutional neural network for change detection in polarimetric SAR images. IEEE Trans. Neural Netw. Learn. Syst. **30**(3), 818–833 (2018)
12. Gong, M., Zhou, Z., Ma, J.: Change detection in synthetic aperture radar images based on image fusion and fuzzy clustering. IEEE Trans. Image Process. **21**(4), 2141–2151 (2012)
13. Lei, Y., Liu, X., Shi, J., Lei, C., Wang, J.: Multiscale superpixel segmentation with deep features for change detection. IEEE Access **7**, 36600–36616 (2019)
14. Liang, B., Weng, Q.: Assessing urban environmental quality change of Indianapolis, United States, by the remote sensing and GIS integration. IEEE J. Sel. Top. Appl. Earth Obs. Remote Sens. **4**(1), 43–55 (2011)
15. Otsu, N.: A threshold selection method from gray-level histograms. IEEE Trans. Syst. Man Cybern. **9**(1), 62–66 (1979)
16. Kittler, J., Illingworth, J.: Minimum error thresholding. Pattern Recognit. **19**(1), 41–47 (1986)
17. Bovolo, F., Bruzzone, L.: A theoretical framework for unsupervised change detection based on change vector analysis in the polar domain. IEEE Trans. Geosci. Remote Sens. **45**(1), 218–236 (2007)
18. Deng, J.S., Wang, K., Deng, Y.H., Qi, G.J.: PCA-based land-use change detection and analysis using multitemporal and multisensor satellite data. Int. J. Remote Sens. **29**(16), 4823–4838 (2008)
19. Moser, G., Serpico, S.B., Benediktsson, J.A.: Land-cover mapping by Markov modeling of spatial–contextual information in very-high-resolution remote sensing images. Proc. IEEE **101**(3), 631–651 (2013)

20. Celik, T.: Change detection in satellite images using a genetic algorithm approach. IEEE Geosci. Remote Sens. Lett. **7**(2), 386–390 (2010)
21. Lei, P., Zheng, T., Wang, J., Bai, X.: A joint convolutional neural network for simultaneous despeckling and classification of SAR targets. IEEE Geosci. Remote Sens. Lett. **18**(9), 1610–1614 (2021)
22. Li, X., Du, Z., Huang, Y., Tan, Z.: A deep translation (GAN) based change detection network for optical and SAR remote sensing images. ISPRS J. Photogramm. Remote Sens. **179**, 14–34 (2021)
23. Li, X., He, M., Li, H., Shen, H.: A combined loss-based multiscale fully convolutional network for high-resolution remote sensing image change detection. IEEE Geosci. Remote Sens. Lett. **19**, 1–5 (2022)
24. Shao, L., Wu, D., Li, X.: Learning deep and wide: a spectral method for learning deep networks. IEEE Trans. Neural Netw. Learn. Syst. **25**(12), 2303–2308 (2014)
25. Liu, Q., Sun, Y., Hang, R., Song, H.: Spatial–spectral locality-constrained low-rank representation with semi-supervised hypergraph learning for hyperspectral image classification. IEEE J. Sel. Top. Appl. Earth Obs. Remote Sens. **10**(9), 4171–4182
26. Yang, M., Jiao, L., Liu, F., Hou, B., Yang, S.: Transferred deep learning-based change detection in remote sensing images. IEEE Trans. Geosci. Remote Sens. **57**(9), 6960–6973 (2019)
27. Zhang, W., Lu, X., Li, X.: A coarse-to-fine semi-supervised change detection for multispectral images. IEEE Trans. Geosci. Remote Sens. **56**(6), 3587–3599 (2018)
28. Hou, B., Wang, Y., Liu, Q.: A saliency guided semi-supervised building change detection method for high resolution remote sensing images. Sensors **16**(9), 1377–1398 (2016)
29. Peng, D., Bruzzone, L., Zhang, Y., Guan, H., Ding, H., Huang, X.: SemiCDNet: a semisupervised convolutional neural network for change detection in high resolution remote-sensing images. IEEE Trans. Geosci. Remote Sens. **59**(7), 5891–5906 (2021)
30. Dai, Z., Yang, Z., Yang, F., Cohen, W.W., Salakhutdinov, R.R.: Good semi-supervised learning thatequires a bad GAN. In: Advances in Neural Information Processing Systems, vol. 30, pp. 6510–6520 (2017)
31. Ren, S., Zhou, F.: Semi-supervised classification for PolSAR data with multi-scale evolving weighted graph convolutional network. IEEE J. Sel. Top. Appl. Earth Obs. Remote Sens. **14**, 2911–2927 (2021)
32. Razavi-Far, R., Hallaji, E., Farajzadeh-Zanjani, M., Saif, M.: A semi-supervised diagnostic framework based on the surface estimation of faulty distributions. IEEE Trans. Ind. Inform. **15**(3), 1277–1286 (2019)
33. Rasmus, A., Valpola, H., Honkala, M., Berglund, M., Raiko, T.: Semi-supervised learning with ladder networks. In: Proceedings of the 28th International Conference on Neural Information Processing Systems, vol. 2, pp. 3546–3554 (2015)
34. Valpola, H.: From neural PCA to deep unsupervised learning. In: Bingham, E., Kaski, S., Laaksonen, J., Lampinen, J. (eds.), Advances in Independent Component Analysis and Learning Machines, pp. 143–171. Academic (2015)
35. Chen, Y., Bruzzone, L.: Self-supervised change detection by fusing SAR and optical multitemporal images. In: 2021 IEEE International Geoscience and Remote Sensing Symposium (IGARSS), pp. 3101–3104 (2021)
36. Sun, Y., Xue, B., Zhang, M., Yen, G.G.: Evolving deep convolutional neural networks for image classification. IEEE Trans. Evol. Comput. **24**(2), 394–407 (2020)
37. Shi, J., Liu, X., Lei, Y.: SAR images change detection based on self-adaptive network architecture. IEEE Geosci. Remote Sens. Lett. **18**(7), 1204–1208 (2021)
38. Hinton, G.E.: Autoencoders, minimum description length and Helmholtz free energy. In: Advances in Neural Information Processing Systems, vol. 6, pp. 1–8 (1994)
39. Shi, C., Pun, C.-M.: Multiscale superpixel-based hyperspectral image classification using recurrent neural networks with stacked autoencoders. IEEE Trans. Multimedia **22**(2), 487–501 (2020)

40. Geng, J., Fan, J., Wang, H., Ma, X., Li, B., Chen, F.: High-resolution SAR image classification via deep convolutional autoencoders. IEEE Geosci. Remote Sens. Lett. **12**(11), 2351–2355 (2015)
41. Wang, R., Wang, Y.: Classification of PolSAR image using neural nonlocal stacked sparse autoencoders with virtual adversarial regularization. Remote Sens. **11**, 1038–1058 (2019)
42. He, K., Zhang, X., Ren, S., Sun, J.: Deep residual learning for image recognition. In: 2016 IEEE Conference on Computer Vision and Pattern Recognition (CVPR), pp. 770–778 (2016)
43. Han, W., Feng, R., Wang, L., Cheng, Y.: A semi-supervised generative framework with deep learning features for high-resolution remote sensing image scene classification. ISPRS J. Photogramm. Remote Sens. **145**, 23–43 (2018)
44. Jiang, F., Gong, M., Zhan, T., Fan, X.: A semisupervised GAN-based multiple change detection framework in multi-spectral images. IEEE Geosci. Remote Sens. Lett. **17**(7), 1223–1227 (2020)
45. Liu, J., Gong, M., Qin, K., Zhang, P.: A deep convolutional coupling network for change detection based on heterogeneous optical and radar images. IEEE Trans. Neural Netw. Learn. Syst. **29**(3), 545–559 (2018)
46. Lei, L., Sun, Y., Kuang, G.: Adaptive local structure consistency-based heterogeneous remote sensing change detection. IEEE Geosci. Remote Sens. Lett. **19**, 1–5 (2022)
47. Sun, Y., Lei, L., Li, X., Tan, X., Kuang, G.: Patch similarity graph matrix-based unsupervised remote sensing change detection with homogeneous and heterogeneous sensors. IEEE Trans. Geosci. Remote Sens. **59**(6), 4841–4861 (2020)
48. Saha, S., Bovolo, F., Bruzzone, L.: Unsupervised deep change vector analysis for multiple-change detection in VHR images. IEEE Trans. Geosci. Remote Sens. **57**(6), 3677–3693 (2019)
49. Gong, M., Zhao, J., Liu, J., Miao, Q., Jiao, L.: Change detection in synthetic aperture radar images based on deep neural networks. IEEE Trans. Neural Netw. Learn. Syst. **27**(1), 125–138 (2016)
50. Zhan, T., Gong, M., Jiang, X., Zhang, M.: Unsupervised scale-driven change detection with deep spatial–spectral features for VHR images. IEEE Trans. Geosci. Remote Sens. **58**(8), 5653–5665 (2020)
51. Nielsen, A.A.: The regularized iteratively reweighted MAD method for change detection in multi- and hyperspectral data. IEEE Trans. Image Process. **16**(2), 463–478 (2007)
52. Tang, J., Deng, C., Huang, G.-B., Zhao, B.: Compressed-domain ship detection on spaceborne optical image using deep neural network and extreme learning machine. IEEE Trans. Geosci. Remote Sens. **53**(3), 1174–1185 (2015)
53. Gong, M., Yang, Y., Zhan, T., Niu, X., Li, S.: A generative discriminatory classified network for change detection in multispectral imagery. IEEE J. Sel. Top. Appl. Earth Obs. Remote Sens. **12**(1), 321–333 (2019)
54. Achanta, R., Shaji, A., Smith, K., Lucchi, A., Fua, P., Süsstrunk, S.: SLIC superpixels compared to state-of-the-art superpixel methods. IEEE Trans. Pattern Anal. Mach. Intell. **34**(11), 2274–2282 (2012)
55. Gong, M., Liang, Y., Shi, J., Ma, W., Ma, J.: Fuzzy C-means clustering with local information and kernel metric for image segmentation. IEEE Trans. Image Process. **22**(2), 573–584 (2013)
56. Liu, J., Gong, M., Qin, A.K., Tan, K.C.: Bipartite differential neural network for unsupervised image change detection. IEEE Trans. Neural Netw. Learn. Syst. **31**(3), 876–890 (2020)

Chapter 6
Concluding Remarks

Abstract This book covers fundamental topics in remote sensing image change detection and computational intelligence. In previous chapters, we have reviewed core concepts of change detection and presented deep learning solutions for both homogeneous and heterogeneous scenarios. We have also explored emerging computational intelligence techniques such as neural architecture search to further improve change detection performance and enhance model autonomy. Despite these advances, many challenges remain unresolved. In this chapter, we outline promising future research directions from five perspectives, aiming to bridge the gap between current capabilities and real-world demands in complex, evolving, and resource-constrained environments.

Keywords Change detection · Remote sensing · Time series analysis · Human-in-the-loop · Edge computing

6.1 Future Directions and Challenges

While significant progress has been made in remote sensing change detection, several gaps remain between current methodologies and the practical demands of real-world applications. The following subsections discuss five key challenges that deserve further attention to support the development of more robust and intelligent change detection systems.

(1) Over-Reliance on High-Precision Preprocessing Weakens Algorithmic Robustness

Most methods treat preprocessing as a separate step, assuming inputs are perfectly registered and radiometrically consistent. In practice, multi-temporal images often suffer from radiometric inconsistencies due to differences in acquisition time, sensors, atmosphere, or phenology. Misaligned image pairs further disrupt feature alignment and degrade detection performance. Future work should develop representation learning mechanisms with intrinsic tolerance to geometric and radiometric distortions. These mechanisms need to explicitly handle registration errors and

J. Shi et al., *Computational Intelligence for Remote Sensing Image Change Detection*, SpringerBriefs in Computer Science,
https://doi.org/10.1007/978-981-92-1404-4_6

noise, reduce dependence on high-precision preprocessing, thus improving stability in real-world scenarios.

(2) Limited Coverage of Existing Methods Across Diverse Remote Sensing Data
With the diversification of remote sensing platforms, an increasing variety of data types has become available for change analysis. For instance, hyperspectral image captures subtle spectral changes in vegetation, water, or minerals through dozens to hundreds of spectral bands. Very high-resolution UAV or satellite images reveal fine-scale evolution of buildings and roads. Moreover, global high-resolution products enable large-area monitoring. However, dedicated algorithms for these emerging data types remain scarce, and public, realistic, multi-temporal benchmark datasets are still extremely limited. This gap between data availability and methodological progress hinders applications in precision agriculture, smart cities, and disaster response. Future efforts must broaden the coverage of change detection across diverse remote sensing modalities, develop data-specific detection methods, and build high-quality, well-annotated, multi-temporal public datasets.

(3) Static Bi-temporal Paradigms Cannot Support Dynamic Change Understanding
Real-world land changes are continuous, non-stationary, and spatiotemporally evolving. Most current change detection methods focus on comparing bi-temporal image pairs, failing to model long-term dependencies, change onset, or evolution rates. In recent years, constellations like Planet now provide near-daily high-resolution time series, and platforms including SkySat and Jilin-1 even capture satellite video. This shifts the goal from "finding differences" to "tracking motion". However, satellite videos suffer from low frame rates, small targets, and complex backgrounds, rendering standard video analysis ineffective. Future research should develop temporal architectures that support incremental learning, memory retention, and event modeling. These architectures can reconstruct continuous change trajectories and enable semantic-level temporal understanding, facilitating a transition from detection to cognition.

(4) Closed-Loop Inference Limits Human-AI Collaboration and Practical Usability
Current methods follow a one-way input-output pipeline with no user interaction. Experts cannot provide feedback to refine results, limiting accuracy and generalization in complex scenes. Outputs also lack explainability and editability, making them hard for users to trust or act upon, thus reducing real-world applicability. Future work can combine active learning from human feedback, reinforcement learning, and LLM-based agents to build change detection systems that support natural language queries, intent understanding, and result correction. These capabilities enhance model robustness and user trust, promoting a shift from expert-only tools toward accessible, understandable, and controllable decision assistants.

(5) High Computational Demand Hinders Deployment in Edge and Resource-Constrained Settings

With the increase in model parameters, deploying change detection models on resource-constrained platforms such as online services or mobile terminals incurs significant memory and computational overhead. While lightweight architectures discovered through neural architecture search offer partial relief, they remain insufficient for global-scale or real-time video stream processing. Future work should combine lightweight strategies, such as dynamic sparse activation, knowledge distillation, and quantization-aware training, to develop change detection models that balance capacity and scalability under limited annotations and computing resources. This will enable wide-area, rapid-response monitoring on satellites, drones, and emergency field systems, promoting the deployment of high-performance change detection in real-world resource-constrained scenarios.

Finally, this book is suitable for students as a study book or for researchers who have just entered this field as a reference book. Meanwhile, this book cannot avoid defects like typos, technical drawbacks, etc. It is thus highly expected that readers can help us to find out and correct the errors if any.

GPSR Compliance

The European Union's (EU) General Product Safety Regulation (GPSR) is a set of rules that requires consumer products to be safe and our obligations to ensure this.

If you have any concerns about our products, you can contact us on ProductSafety@springernature.com

In case Publisher is established outside the EU, the EU authorized representative is:

Springer Nature Customer Service Center GmbH
Europaplatz 3
69115 Heidelberg, Germany

Batch number: 10437383

Printed by Printforce, the Netherlands